Eatherly, Claude 92

Huie, William Bradford
The Hiroshima pilot

Date Due

 PRINTED IN U.S.A.

THE HIROSHIMA PILOT

BY WILLIAM BRADFORD HUIE

Documentaries

THE EXECUTION OF PRIVATE SLOVIK

THE CRIME OF RUBY MCCOLLUM

WOLF WHISTLE AND OTHER STORIES

THE HERO OF IWO JIMA AND OTHER STORIES

THE HIROSHIMA PILOT

Novels

MUD ON THE STARS

THE REVOLT OF MAMIE STOVER

THE AMERICANIZATION OF EMILY

HOTEL MAMIE STOVER

War Reports

THE FIGHT FOR AIR POWER

CAN DO: THE STORY OF THE SEABEES

FROM OMAHA TO OKINAWA

THE CASE AGAINST THE ADMIRALS

FILMS FROM MR. HUIE'S STORIES

Wild River, produced by Elia Kazan from Mud on the Stars

The Outsider, produced by Sy Bartlett from The Hero of Iwo Jima

The Revolt of Mamie Stover, produced by Buddy Adler from the novel

The Americanization of Emily, produced by Martin Ransohoff from the novel

The Execution of Private Slovik is to be produced by George Stevens Jr. from the documentary

THE HIROSHIMA PILOT

William Bradford Huie

G. P. PUTNAM'S SONS

NEW YORK

© *1964 BY WILLIAM BRADFORD HUIE*

Library of Congress Catalog
Card Number: 63-7742

MANUFACTURED IN THE UNITED STATES OF AMERICA

THE HIROSHIMA PILOT

One

I CAN'T recall exactly when I became conscious of the name Claude Robert Eatherly.

Because I have written several true, offbeat stories about Americans who served in the Second World War, and because these stories have been translated into other languages, I receive suggestions for stories from readers throughout the free world. These suggestions are often accompanied by clippings, sometimes by books. About 1958 some of these letters began mentioning a former Air Force pilot who was said to have been "at Hiroshima" and to have subsequently become mentally ill.

Since these letters seemed to be filled with misinformation, I paid little attention to them. But they continued to arrive, and by late 1961 I had accumulated a file of clippings, most of them from British, German and French publications. Moreover, the letters had become steadily more urgent. Why didn't I *help* Major Eatherly? Didn't I know that Major Eatherly had become "the American Dreyfus"? Didn't I know that the pilot who "led the Hiroshima raid" was "imprisoned in a military mental hospital in Waco, Texas, because he repented the crime of Hiroshima"? Didn't I know that Major Eatherly had "turned to ordinary crime seeking punishment for the greater crime of Hiroshima"?

A publisher then informed me that the "Eatherly Case" had set off a "storm of controversy" in Europe and Japan; and the publisher suggested that I investigate the case and present the truth in a book. Later I was sent this clipping from London: from *The Spectator* of February 16, 1962:

7

It seems a pity that the official American information services have offered us no guidance in the Eatherly Case. Surely the case has been enough of a propaganda football in the past three years, in Europe and Asia, that the State Department might have been expected to circulate some official version of the story. That no such version has been offered encourages the charges of injustice.

From all this I concluded that Major Eatherly must indeed be, to some degree, a victim of some sort of injustice. And since I am plagued with an innate suspicion of power, particularly of military power, I decided to see if the major needed my help. I began by studying my entire Eatherly file.

What interested me was, first, the false information conveyed in the published stories, and secondly, the missing information. I had never met Major Eatherly but I knew that he had not "led the Hiroshima raid." I had met Brigadier General Paul W. Tibbets who as a lieutenant colonel piloted and commanded the B-29 *Enola Gay*, who led the Hiroshima raid, and who commanded the 509th Composite Group which dropped the atomic bombs on both Hiroshima and Nagasaki. A motion picture was based on Colonel Tibbets' experience.

Moreover, I knew that no Major Eatherly is mentioned in the official Air Force history of the atomic attacks on Hiroshima and Nagasaki. After the war a careful, scholarly, five-volume history of all Air Force operations was prepared under the editorship of Wesley Frank Craven, of Princeton University, and James Lea Cate, of the University of Chicago. This history is in my library. All the pilots who witnessed the explosions and destruction at Hiroshima and Nagasaki are listed, and Eatherly's name is not among them.

So how had a Major Eatherly, of Texas, become the leader of the Hiroshima raid, and how had he become the American Dreyfus?

I found a clue in the first international publicity given to Eatherly. On April 1, 1957, *Newsweek* Magazine published this account:

HERO IN HANDCUFFS
In the palm-shaded tents and huts around the long airstrip at Tinian, there lived in the summer of 1945 a handful of the most

8

highly trained and highly skilled pilots in all the world. They were members of the U. S. Air Force's 509th Composite Group, and they had been carefully chosen to make the B-29 raids on Japan. From this select group, the five best were picked for a historic mission. Each had to have an outstanding service record and each had to pass a rigid security test, for they were the men who would fly the first A-bomb mission.

One of these super-pilots was a tall, sunburned Texan (6 feet and 180 pounds), with wavy brown hair and piercing green eyes. He was Maj. Claude R. Eatherly, captain of the B-29 named "Straight Flush." The youngest of six children in a pioneer family that ran a farm in Grayson County (where the family enjoyed one of the most respected of reputations), Eatherly had gone to North Texas State College. There he had played end on the football team, and after college he had volunteered for the Air Force. He had showed great skill during his flight training, and had risen to command one of the Air Force's biggest and best ships of the day.

To the crew of the "Straight Flush" and to most of his fellow officers, Major Eatherly was something of a hero. He was a carefree and convivial companion on the ground, always calm and stable in the air—the kind of pilot they knew would not only get where he was going, but would also be sure of getting back.

Early on the morning of August 6, 1945, the "Straight Flush" and three other planes were high over Japan reconnoitering potential target cities for the "Enola Gay" which carried the A-bomb that would be used. Major Eatherly's mission was to scout Hiroshima. When he found bombing conditions suitable he flew to a rendezvous point, accompanied the "Enola Gay" back to Hiroshima and circled over the city after the explosion to take scientific measurements and report on damage. A few days later Major Eatherly carried out a similar mission for the drop on Nagasaki.

For his wartime services Major Eatherly was awarded the Distinguished Flying Cross and other honors. He stayed on in the Air Force for a time, seven years in all, then returned to Texas for his discharge.

To his family, Eatherly somehow seemed changed. His wife said he used to wake up at night shouting: "Bail out! Bail out!" When he came to, he would say that he dreamed he was in a burning plane that had been shot down over Tokyo. In 1950 he voluntarily entered the Veterans Administration Hospital at Waco for treatment of extreme nervousness.

In time his family heard reports that were even more disturbing: Eatherly was in trouble with the police. Between his stays in the hospital, he was arrested in New Orleans, Beaumont, and Houston. Divorce broke up his marriage. He served a year for forgery in New Orleans in 1954–55. Last fall he and a companion were questioned about four armed robberies, but not indicted. Both were then out of the hospital for a 90-day trial period. "I don't know why we did it," Eatherly said. "We didn't need money." He draws a $237 monthly pension for mental disability.

Last week Major Eatherly was arrested again, accused this time of breaking into post offices in West Texas, and ordered to be brought from the hospital at Waco to Forth Worth to face the charges.

From that account I concluded that Eatherly *must* have been one of the 509th's pilots; that he had scouted Hiroshima in advance of the raid; and that his scouting expedition, along with much other reconnaissance, had not been reported in the Air Force history. But I suspected that *Newsweek* had allowed some writer to invent the rest of Eatherly's exploits at Hiroshima and Nagasaki. I doubted that Eatherly had "accompanied the 'Enola Gay' back to Hiroshima" and "circled over the city after the explosion." Such an exploit would hardly have gone unreported by Professors Craven and Cate.

What, for me, further discredited the *Newsweek* story was their report that Eatherly received the Distinguished Flying Cross. That was the Air Force's highest decoration. Relatively few men received it, and they are listed alphabetically in the Air Force history—which, I assume, is in *Newsweek*'s library. No Eatherly is on that list. So I concluded that the *Newsweek* story was written hurriedly, with no research, by an inexperienced writer.

Why would a magazine like *Newsweek*, which has a wide overseas circulation, allow an inexperienced man to write about a subject as important as Hiroshima?

The next item in my file was a book, *Formula for Death*, which was published in France and Britain in 1958. Its author was Fernand Gigon, a French journalist. Mr. Gigon wrote of Eatherly:

Major Claude R. Eatherly was a powerfully built man with pale eyes, twenty-three years old when he went to Tinian. He had been an extremely successful pilot, with thirty-three air victories already to his credit. At twenty-one he had become one of the youngest majors in the service.

He came from Grayson, Texas, where his father was a rich and successful farmer. He had been studying at North Texas College at the time of Pearl Harbor and he immediately volunteered for the Air Force. His extreme calmness of manner had won him the nickname of Poker Face. After risking his life in the skies, he would return to the base and risk his pay at cards or dice . . . and he always won. He himself had named the B-29 which he flew to Hiroshima "Straight Flush."

"Straight Flush" reached the burning town fifteen minutes after the "Enola Gay" had dropped the bomb. Major Eatherly wrote his report and was delighted by the success of the mission against this "ideal target." Three days later he carried out the same job over Nagasaki. In his bearing, however, there was no trace of any particular delight. He remained poker-faced until after peace had been signed.

Then he returned to Texas, a much decorated hero to be greeted with processions, bands, flags, pretty girls, speeches by the Mayor. Eatherly did not wait for the ceremonies to be over, but suddenly in apparent displeasure fled from the festivities. He was found hiding in the barn, in tears. His friends did their best for him, speaking of nervous depression, the reaction which affected so many soldiers who had been heroes yesterday and today were simply men again.

His friends assumed that family life with his young and pretty wife, whom he had married while on leave during the war, would restore his nerves to normal. Then one day Mrs. Eatherly sued for divorce. The small town was amazed. She told the Judge: "I cannot live with Claude any longer. Not that I do not love him; quite the contrary. But he frightens me. He often jumps up in the middle of the night and screams out in an inhuman voice which makes me feel ill: 'Release it! Release it!' Then after a moment or two, during which my husband seems to be in hell, he shouts: 'Not now, not now! Think of the children! The children are burning!' When I look at Claude's face at such times I am terrified. His features are distorted and show terrible fear. He trembles all over. After these nightmares he awakes in a fever. If I speak to him he does not hear me. With his eyes wide open he asks me to help him pack, since the Pentagon is sending him to Hiroshima to see what happened to the children there. When he sees a policeman, or even the postman, he runs away. My husband is going mad."

11

The divorce was granted and Eatherly continued to live a life of flotsam, drifting with the current. He left Grayson and worked as a laborer on a farm in Texas. He often spoke of "those people who wanted to force me to return to Japan to estimate the damage done to Hiroshima and Nagasaki." He vacillated between long periods of sanity and brief moments of madness. The doctors who examined him at Waco Military Hospital diagnosed extreme nervous depression and he was returned to public life with a pension of $237 a month.

He regards this pension as a premium for murder, as a blood payment for what he did to the Japanese cities. He has never touched this money.

That book was reviewed in London, in *The Observer*, in August, 1958. One of Britain's "angry young men," John Wain, read the review. He then wrote a long, moving poem titled "A Song about Major Eatherly." The poem appeared in these periodicals: *Audience, Bulletin of the Atomic Scientists, Colorado Quarterly, Encounter, The Listener, The London Magazine, Poetry* (Chicago), *The Spectator*, and the *Texas Quarterly*. The poem was then included in a volume titled *Weep Before God* and published by Macmillan and Company Limited in London, Bombay, Calcutta, Madras and Melbourne. It was published in Canada and the United States by St. Martin's Press. In this book the poem is prefaced by this note:

The book [Fernand Gigon's *Formula for Death*] also describes how Major Claude R. Eatherly, pilot of the aircraft which carried the second bomb to Nagasaki, later started having nightmares. His wife is quoted as saying: "He often jumps up in the middle of the night and screams out in an inhuman voice which makes me feel ill: "Release it, release it!"

Major Eatherly began to suffer brief periods of madness, says Gigon. The doctors diagnosed extreme nervous depression, and Eatherly was awarded a pension of $237 a month.

This he appears to have regarded "as a premium for murder, as a payment for what I had done to the two Japanese cities." He never touched the money, and took to petty thievery, for which he was committed to Forth Worth prison.

Report in *The Observer*, August, 1958.

After that note, the poem begins in this manner:

> Good news. It seems he loved them after all.
> His orders were to fry their bones to ash.
> He carried up the bomb and let it fall.
> And then his orders were to take the cash,
>
> A hero's pension. But he let it lie.
> It was in vain to ask him for the cause.
> Simply that if he touched it he would die.
> He fought his own, and not his country's wars.

For thirty-one moving verses the poem continues, and it ends with this verse:

> O, give his pension to the storekeeper.
> Tell him it is the price of all our souls.
> But do not trouble to unlock the door
> And bring the Major out into the sun.
> Leave him: it is all one: perhaps his nightmares
> Grow cooler in the twilight of the prison.
> Leave him; if he is sleeping, come away.
> But lay a folded paper by his head,
> Nothing official or embossed, a page
> Torn from your notebook, and the words in pencil.
> Say nothing of love, or thanks, or penitence:
> Say only "Eatherly, we have your message."

In addition to being published throughout the world, Mr. Wain's poem was given a dramatic reading, in its entirety, over the network of the British Broadcasting Corporation.

On January 20, 1961, *The New Statesman* in London published a poem by George Barker. Here is a portion:

> He keeps bawling in movies
>   And burgling things from shops
> So he can prove his crime is
>   A little thing for the cops.
> And in and out of the nuthouse
>   That dupe and scapegoat's led
> With a mushroom as big as America

Growing out of his head.
Dupe Eatherly, Dupe Eatherly
Why on earth be so human?
Forget the whole thing. Hold a
Press Conference
Just like Harry Truman.

In 1959 many newspapers in Europe and Asia published an unverified report that Bob Hope had offered Eatherly $250,000 for his life story. Eatherly was said to be deciding whether Audie Murphy or Robert Ryan should portray him.

On May 25, 1959, *Newsweek* published a second story which it headed "PSYCHIATRY, The Curse of Hiroshima." This story quoted an unidentified "Waco doctor" as describing Eatherly's case as a "classic guilt complex." The *Newsweek* story explained that "the flier has tried to punish himself for the self-imagined wrong of Hiroshima—he has twice attempted suicide—and failing suicide, Eatherly has sought the punishment of society by acts (forgery, robbery, breaking and entering) which would bring down its wrath."

That *Newsweek* story led several European and Japanese newspapers to report that "it has now been established that Major Eatherly is suffering from a classic guilt complex, and he is committing ordinary crimes seeking punishment for the extraordinary crime of Hiroshima."

After reading the *Newsweek* story, two German writers turned their attention to Eatherly. A Viennese philosopher, Gunther Anders, began corresponding with Eatherly; and from that correspondence came a book first published in Germany under the title *Off Limits für das Gewissen* (*Off Limits to Conscience*) and later published in Britain and the United States as *Burning Conscience*. A portion of this book is Eatherly's brief letters, as edited by Mr. Anders; but the major portion is Mr. Anders' explanations to Eatherly of the nature of his "Hiroshima guilt" and the nature of America's guilt.

All three editions of the Anders-Eatherly book have introductions by a journalist named Von Robert Jungk. He has published two Hiroshima books: *Children of the Ashes* and *Brighter Than a Thousand Suns*. He has also written a series about Eatherly in the French newspaper *France-Soir*. He has written several versions of his Introduction, but here are portions of the version in the proof-copy distributed by the British publishers, Weidenfeld & Nicolson:

The Strange Case of Claude Eatherly, Who Commanded the Hiroshima Raid, told in his Letters to Gunther Anders.

Had Eatherly never visited Nagasaki, had he never gazed, shortly after the war, on that atomic desert which he had helped to create in the green and flourishing countryside of Japan, he would probably have remained as unmoved as were his brother pilots of the 509th Composite Group which he commanded. For them the operations against the target areas of Hiroshima and Nagasaki, places they had only seen from a great height, were no more than two important, decisive missions in the vast pattern of war in the air. But they remained far away from the stark realities of aerial bombardment. Eatherly, on the other hand, had gazed into the faces of his victims; he had seen their eyes fixed on him, had observed the expression of misery, of that lack of any desire to live after they had witnessed the end of the world.

. . . After this shattering experience Major Eatherly spoke to no one for days on end. On the island base of Tinian, however, where he and his bomber group, which had acquired such worldwide but doubtful notoriety, were awaiting demobilization, nobody took his silence very seriously. "Battle fatigue," they said. It was a common enough complaint, and in 1943 Eatherly himself, after thirteen long and unbroken months of duty in the South Pacific, had been a victim of it. On that occasion, after a fortnight's treatment in a New York clinic, he had completely recovered.

. . . When Eatherly had his first glimpse of his homeland on landing at a military airfield near San Francisco, he received the news that his mother had died while under an operation for cancer. Then there burst from him something which had been torturing him for many weeks, and to the waiting reporters he said something quite out of keeping with their picture of this hero of the atomic bomb. "It's a punishment!" he cried. "We shall all be further punished! We shall all have to make atonement!"

. . . Even when Eatherly, the much-decorated hero, refused to be feted by his home town of Van Alstyne . . .

. . . After his demobilization, Eatherly first tried to find a solution by emigration. Disgusted with political developments in his own country, he left the United States and enlisted as a pilot in the

15

Israeli Armed Forces, which was then defending their new state against the Arabs. Then he returned home and, like all the others around him, he tried to forget, to devote himself to earning money. He became an employee of a petroleum company in Houston, went to his office every day, attended evening classes to study law and finally rose to the position of sales manager.

. . . But at night faces and nightmares still tormented the ex-pilot. At first things were not too bad. A few drinks sufficed to cure his depression and a few pills to banish his insomnia. Very soon, however, these simple remedies proved to be inadequate. In his dreams Eatherly saw the agonized faces of those burning in the hell fires of Hiroshima. He threshed about violently in his bed. "The children!" he cried. "Save the children!" and he roared orders to his bomber crew to bail out.

. . . It was about this time that he started to cram bank notes into envelopes and send them to Hiroshima, to write letters to Japan, in which he alternately condemned and gave excuses for what he had done. But this "medicine," too, was of no avail. So in 1950 . . . the year in which President Truman, without having previously consulted public opinion, announced that America was now to manufacture a far more powerful atomic weapon, the hydrogen bomb—Eatherly tried in a hotel room in New Orleans to end his life with an overdose of sleeping pills.

. . . He was still alive when he was discovered. Then a peculiar plan began to take shape in his mind. He would, he decided, fight against this jingoistic tendency in America which had just elected a Second World War general to be its President. He would fight it by knocking that national paragon, the virtuous war hero, from his newly elected pedestal. He would compromise and expose him; and the victim of this act of unmasking would be himself, the Hero of Hiroshima, Major Claude Robert Eatherly.

. . . Early in 1953, among a host of other petty offenders, a man was brought before a court who had forged a cheque for a quite insignificant amount. Rapidly the magistrate jotted down a few personal details, asked a question or two, and passed sentence: "Nine months, next case. . . ." Eatherly barely had a chance to open his mouth. He had no chance to tell the court that he had paid the money into a fund for the assistance of the children of Hiroshima. . . .

. . . After he attempted a hold-up, the authorities reached the conclusion that Eatherly was suffering from a mental disability attributable to war service and he was discharged with a small pension of $132 a month. This sum was doubled later—the authorities

16

would neither brand him as a criminal, as he had hoped, nor grant him that boon of punishment through which he hoped to find relief from the great burden of guilt that oppressed him.

. . . His wife divorced him. Her plea that her husband should not be allowed to visit the children was granted, and she formally waived any financial claim on him for their maintenance. The first of these conditions Eatherly respected, but he continued voluntarily to make a monetary contribution toward the education of his children.

. . . The morally more healthy Eatherly could not come to terms with the sick society into which he was continually being let loose, because he had failed to develop that protective thick skin which enabled his normal contemporaries to accept complacently the crimes of Auschwitz and Hiroshima.

With that introduction, the book *Burning Conscience* was published in London in January, 1962. Here is part of the publisher's statement on the jacket:

Eatherly has certainly been punished. His sense of guilt was intensified by a visit to the survivors in Hiroshima. He tried to escape his conscience by enlisting in a foreign Air Force and by attempting suicide more than once. Later, back in the United States, he sent bank notes to Hiroshima and talked continually of his sense of guilt. In 1953 he was sent by the embarrassed authorities to the Waco Mental Home. A morally healthy man, he could not come to terms with a sick society.

On the same book jacket, Britain's ninety-year-old Nobel Prize winner, Bertrand Russell, made this comment:

The case of Claude Eatherly is not only one of appalling and prolonged injustice to an individual, but it is also symbolic of the suicidal madness of our time. No unbiased person, after reading Eatherly's letters, can honestly doubt his sanity, and I find it very difficult to believe that the doctors who pronounced him insane were persuaded of the accuracy of their own testimony. He has been punished solely because he repented of his comparatively innocent participation in a wanton act of mass murder. The steps he took to awaken men's consciences to our present insanity were, perhaps, not always the wisest that could have been taken, but they were actuated by motives which deserve the admiration of all who are capable of feelings of humanity. The world was prepared to honor him for his part in the massacre, but, when he repented, it turned against him, seeing in his act of repentance its own condemnation. I most earnestly hope that as a result of publicity the Authorities may be persuaded to adopt more just views of his case and do what lies in their power to redress the wrong that he has suffered.

Burning Conscience, in Britain, was reviewed widely by reputable reviewers. Here are excerpts:

THE MANCHESTER GUARDIAN:—The patriotic press in America thought Eatherly was a war hero who had had a prolonged nervous breakdown. The Air Force provided for him and tried to keep him out of harm's way and also out of sight. . . . [By committing felonies] Eatherly was trying to force society to punish him for his guilt. Eatherly wanted to be punished for the crime of Hiroshima, but society did not think Hiroshima was a crime and refused Eatherly punishment. So Eatherly had to do something (like a forgery or a hold-up) society would think wrong.

THE OXFORD MAIL—Eatherly. Major Claude Eatherly. Remember the name? We should remember, for he was the man chosen by the Allies to drop the bomb on Hiroshima. From then on his life has been a hell from which there is no escape. He only did his job, but the weight of his guilt has proven more than he could bear. His president, who gave the orders, could regard it strictly in the line of duty and, we are told, has felt no pangs of conscience. Perhaps Major Eatherly was of slighter stuff; or perhaps the difference was that he dropped the thing. He saw it happen.

THE CATHOLIC HERALD—When he tried to draw punishment on himself, he was put in a mental hospital, though the evidence for any sort of madness seems to have been very thin.

COLIN WELCH IN THE SUNDAY TELEGRAPH—Of all the grim reminders of Hiroshima, there is none more pathetic than Major Claude Eatherly. His contrition has struggled ceaselessly for adequate expression. It is impossible not to feel a profound sympathy for this apparently brave, sensitive and honorable man. This sympathy can only be deepened by suspicions that he has been treated by the American authorities without due consideration or understanding, if not with actual injustice.

HOWARD CULPIN IN THE REYNOLDS NEWS—He has been forgiven; but he cannot forget. He devotes all his income to maintaining 19 children in foreign lands as their foster father. He has been certified as insane by embarrassed American authorities because he cannot come to terms with a sick society. One can only question the sanity of a world that locks up its penitents and feeds them tranquilisers lest their remorse infect others.

RONALD DRYDEN IN THE SPECTATOR—Early in December, 1961, a Canadian magazine reported that Eatherly is once more at large. Apart from a comment on this Canadian report in the New York *Post,* no American paper has reported the escape, nor has there been any denial of it. It cannot help looking as if the Kennedy Government has decided to shed an embarrassment inherited from its more military-minded predecessor, lest a new hue and cry should lend ammunition to those who claim Eatherly as a political martyr. But their silence can only lend ammunition to charges that an injustice has been done and has still to be publicly righted.

THE LONDON TIMES LITERARY SUPPLEMENT—The case of the Hiroshima pilot, Claude Eatherly, has received worldwide publicity, and he himself has become for our time a legend, a symbol, and a scapegoat. And yet it has been extremely difficult to find out the true facts about him. . . . In one of his letters he states: "I wish to tell you that I made a dedication on that day of August 6, 1945, that I would dedicate my life to destroy the causes of war and the banishment of all nuclear weapons. I said this to myself in a prayer on the trip back to my home base." . . . How Major Eatherly carried out this vow we know in considerable detail. On the one hand he actively helped pacifist organizations, sent money to Hiroshima, visited it in person, and corresponded with well-wishers. On the other hand he engaged in anti-social activities, robbing, forging, making scenes in public and so on, determined to destroy the image of himself as "the hero of Hiroshima."

Then, of course, there was this judgment:

THE LONDON DAILY WORKER (Communist)—Major Eatherly has been framed by the U. S. military because of his insistence on making public his remorse at having taken part in the Hiroshima raid on August 6, 1945.

After reviewing my Eatherly file, I reflected at length. I noted first that everything I had read about Eatherly had been written by men who had never seen him. More surprising, all the writing had been done by men who had not bothered to examine any record, either military, medical or criminal.

Here was an international *cause célèbre* which had attracted poets and philosophers as well as journalists—yet no writer had traveled to Texas to meet the subject!

Why had twelve years elapsed after Hiroshima before anyone reported that Major Eatherly was suffering from a classic guilt complex?

Had Major Eatherly really declined his compensation, as poet John Wain insisted? I happen to know that after an American serviceman is discharged, he can receive disability compensation only by filing a claim for it and by ultimately having his claim approved. Had Eatherly *claimed* mental disability compensation, then *rejected* it as "blood money"? To me this seemed unlikely.

And what about injustice? Was Eatherly being mistreated? Was he the American Dreyfus? Was it possible that some Air Force authority was stupid enough to try to muzzle him? Or that some misguided patriot in the Veterans Administration was trying to imprison him because his opinions were unpopular?

Did Major Eatherly need help?

I didn't know the answers, so I decided to seek them.

Two

BEFORE traveling to Texas to see Claude Eatherly, I decided to learn exactly what he had done at Hiroshima and Nagasaki. War veterans, even those who have not been treated for mental disorder, tend to fabricate as the years pass. The shadows of the Civil War extended into my own childhood in the 1920's. At Gettysburg in 1863 there were 15,000 Southerners in Pickett's Charge. But by 1883 at least 100,000 Southern males were insisting that they had been in Pickett's Charge; and by 1923 most every surviving Confederate veteran had "been with Pickett." So, as Eatherly's fellow Southerner, I thought I had better look at his atomic record before confronting him.

Looking at the record was easy because the Historical Division of the Air Force is in my state: at the Air University, Maxwell Air Force Base, Alabama. Since 1945 there has been no official secrecy about the role of any American who participated in the atomic bombings of Hiroshima and Nagasaki. All flight orders, even individual flight records, are available to the public at the Air University. The following account of Major Eatherly's role is from the records.

On June 15, 1945, Major Eatherly arrived on Tinian with the 509th Composite Group, the 1800-man atom bomb group. This was a self-sufficient unit, with its own housekeeping, police, transport, communications and ground crew personnel. In this group thirteen B-29 crews . . . 65 officers and 52 sergeants . . . had been trained to perform this assignment:

> To take a B-29 off the ground carrying one 10,000-pound
> bomb and sufficient fuel (about 7,400 gallons) to fly 3000

miles in about thirteen hours. To fly the bomb 1500 miles, lifting it en route to an altitude of 32,000 feet. To drop the bomb, *aiming visually in daylight,* and miss the Aiming Point no more than 500 feet. To return 1500 miles to take-off point.

Major Eatherly commanded one of these thirteen crews. He piloted and commanded a B-29 called the *Straight Flush.* He and his crew were qualified to drop atomic bombs. In ten months of training they had made scores of simulated A-bomb flights: over land from Wendover, Utah, and over water from Batista Field, Cuba. After reaching Tinian they continued to make training flights—to Truk and Marcus Islands—and on July 20, 24, 26 and 29, 1945, the *Straight Flush* made simulated A-bomb drops on the Japanese cities of Tokyo, Otsu, Tsugawa and Maizuru.

Of these thirteen crews which had been trained to drop A-bombs, seven were assigned roles in Special Bombing Mission No. 13 (Hiroshima). The chief role went to the *Enola Gay,* piloted and commanded by Lieutenant Colonel Paul Warfield Tibbets, commander of the mission, commander of the 509th, and the man personally selected by Air Force General Henry H. Arnold to drop the first atomic bomb.

Two B-29s were assigned to fly alongside the *Enola Gay:* the *Great Artiste,* piloted and commanded by Major Charles W. Sweeney; and *No. 91,* piloted and commanded by Major George Marquardt. The *Great Artiste* would carry blast gauges; *No. 91* would carry cameras.

Three B-29s were assigned to serve as weather scouts—one B-29 to each of three possible target cities which, in order of priority, were Hiroshima, Kokura and Nagasaki. These scouts were needed because of the terrible insistence on accuracy: the bombardier had to be able to see, with natural vision, the Aiming Point throughout the bomb run. The three B-29s assigned to these roles were: for Hiroshima, the *Straight Flush,* piloted and commanded by Major Eatherly; for Kokura, the *Jabbit III,* piloted and commanded by Major John Wilson; and for Nagasaki, the *Full House,* piloted and commanded by Major Ralph Taylor.

The seventh B-29, the *Top Secret*, piloted and commanded by Captain Charles F. McKnight, was assigned to fly to Iwo Jima and park off the runway near a specially constructed pit. If the *Enola Gay* developed mechanical trouble, it would land at Iwo and the bomb would be transferred to the *Top Secret*.

At 1:37 A.M.,* August 6, 1945, by the clock and calendar on Tinian, the *Straight Flush* took off and headed for Hiroshima on the exact course which would be flown later by the *Enola Gay*. At the same moment, from other runways, the *Jabbit III* and the *Full House* took off for Kokura and Nagasaki.

At 1:51 A.M. the *Top Secret* took off for its standby role at Iwo Jima. At 2:45 A.M. the *Enola Gay*, carrying the bomb, took off, accompanied by the *Great Artiste* and *No. 91*. All of the seven "mission crews" in Special Bombing Mission No. 13 were airborne.

At sunrise Major Eatherly, in the *Straight Flush*, was nearing Japan at an altitude of 32,000 feet. About 300 miles behind him, on the same course and climbing to that altitude, came the *Enola Gay* with the *Great Artiste* and *No. 91*. The *Jabbit III* was approaching Kokura; the *Full House* was approaching Nagasaki; and the *Top Secret* was sitting on the hardstand at Iwo.

At 7:09 A.M. the *Straight Flush* reached the Initial Point near Hiroshima—a point seventeen miles from the Aiming Point which was a river bridge in Hiroshima. A "bombing run" is begun at an Initial Point, and the "run" is toward the Aiming Point. On the exact course which would be followed by the *Enola Gay*, the *Straight Flush* made a simulated bomb run toward the Aiming Point, with all hands observing visibility and drift.

At 7:25 A.M. Major Eatherly sent this radio message to Colonel Tibbets and to the headquarters at Tinian:

CLOUD COVER LESS THAN 3/10THS AT ALL ALTITUDES. ADVICE:
BOMB PRIMARY.

* There has long been some confusion timewise about the bombing of Hiroshima. Its source is the one-hour difference in Japanese time and Tinian time. In John Hersey's book Hiroshima was bombed at 9:17, because he uses Hiroshima time. In Air Force records Hiroshima was bombed at 8:17 because the Air Force used Tinian time.

Primary meant the primary target city, Hiroshima. After delivering that message, the *Straight Flush* headed back toward Tinian.

At 8:15 A.M. the *Straight Flush* was about 225 statute miles from Hiroshima. Major Eatherly and each member of his crew heard the beginning of a continuous radio tone signal which had been switched on by the bombardier of the *Enola Gay*. The signal meant that the *Enola Gay* was "running on Hiroshima" and that within fifteen seconds the bomb would drop. The men in the *Straight Flush,* as did all the other mission crews including the one on the ground at Iwo Jima, listened intently; and at 8:15 plus seventeen seconds the tone stopped. The signal had been broken by the *Enola Gay*'s bomb-bay doors springing open as the bomb fell.

The tail gunner on the *Straight Flush,* along with other crew members, searched the skies toward Hiroshima with glasses, but they could not see the flash or the bomb cloud: they were too far away. The only "weather crew" which reported being able to see the bomb cloud were the men on the *Jabbitt III,* which was about 200 miles from the blast.

At 2:07 P.M. Major Eatherly landed the *Straight Flush* back at Tinian. He and his crew were cheered and congratulated, after which they joined hundreds of airmen, reporters, photographers and generals who were waiting for the *Enola Gay*. At 2:58 P.M. the *Enola Gay* landed to applause and cheers, and General Carl Spaatz awarded Colonel Tibbets the Distinguished Service Cross.

From the records, here is further clarification of Major Eatherly's role at Hiroshima:

He did not, as some accounts insist, "select the target." Hiroshima had been selected as the primary atomic target in Washington by the Combined Chiefs of Staff, and the selection had been approved at Potsdam by Truman, Churchill and Attlee. (Russia was not then at war with Japan.)

When the *Enola Gay* reached a specified point near landfall on the Japanese islands, Colonel Tibbets, as planned, received reports from all three weather planes. Visibility was favorable not only at Hiroshima but also at Kokura and Nagasaki. From these reports Colonel Tibbets, fifty minutes from Hiroshima, made the decision to proceed to Hiroshima as he had been ordered to do if visibility was favorable.

Except over his own crew Major Eatherly exercised no command authority. He neither *selected* nor *decided*. His role was to provide his commanding officer with an accurate weather report. In performing this role Major Eatherly was a party to the bombing of Hiroshima. He saw the city before the bomb fell; and, finding the weather suitable, he "advised" his commanding officer to bomb Hiroshima as ordered. So it can be said, with some truth, that his report helped "seal the doom of Hiroshima."

He was not awarded the Distinguished Flying Cross. He was awarded the Air Medal "for participation in combat missions against the Japanese Empire 20 July–8 August, 1945." This decoration was awarded to every officer and enlisted man in the 509th who made similar flights to Japan.

The date "8 August" is significant in Major Eatherly's citation. On that date he piloted the *Straight Flush* on another training flight—a simulated A-bomb drop on the Japanese city of Yokkaichi—and that was his last wartime flight.

The mission on which the second A-bomb was dropped on Nagasaki was flown on August 9, 1945. In that mission Major Eatherly and the *Straight Flush* had no role of any sort.

The war ended August 14, 1945.

The Historical Division of the Air Force also identified for me the men who flew with Major Eatherly in the *Straight Flush* to Hiroshima. They were:

The Co-Pilot: Lieutenant Ira Weatherly, Memphis, Tennessee. (So the *Straight Flush* is remembered as being piloted by "Eatherly and Weatherly.")

The Navigator: Captain Francis D. (Felix) Thornhill, Poplarville, Mississippi—now living at Ukiah, California.

The Bombardier: Lieutenant Frank Kenneth Wey, Chattanooga, Tennessee—now living at Gadsden, Alabama.

The Engineer: Lieutenant Thomas Grennan, Mercer Island, Washington.

The Radio Operator: Sergeant Patrick L. Bowen, North Walpole, New Hampshire.

The Gunner: Sergeant Gillon T. Niceley, Elizabethon, Kentucky. (He was the tail gunner; the tail guns were the only guns on the 509th's B-29s.)

The Radar Operator: Sergeant Albert Barsumian, Winnetka, Illinois.

The Assistant Engineer: Sergeant Jack Bivans, La Grange Park, Illinois.

In 1945 Eatherly was twenty-seven; Thornhill was twenty-five; Wey, Weatherly and Grennan were twenty-three; and the sergeants were "kids" of nineteen and twenty.

I wrote to each of these men. I explained my interest in Major Eatherly; I enclosed copies of the *Newsweek* articles, of the John Wain poem, and of some of the British book reviews; and I asked them for pertinent recollections. The first to reply was the radio operator:

DEAR MR. HUIE:

It pleases me to learn that you are considering publishing the truth about Claude Eatherly.

I was radio operator on the *Straight Flush.* I'm Patrick L. Bowen, 22 East Street, North Walpole, New Hampshire. I am an insurance broker and own my own agency. My wife's name is Jacqueline. We have three children, all girls. Bonnie, the youngest, Jill in the middle, and Pamela the oldest. We live in a lovely home overlooking the village and facing the Green Mountains of Vermont, which, by the way, I am looking at through my office window now.

Claude Eatherly and I were close in 1944-45. I have never met another man like him; I consider him one of the finest men I have ever met. I first met him at Wendover, Utah, when I was first assigned to his crew. I'm not the bravest man in the world, but after flying with Claude for many months, I can truthfully say I felt at ease in the air. He had everything it took to be a good pilot: always cool and calm, never upset. When it was time to play, he played hard; and when it was time to work, he worked hard.

Like the other crew members, I owe my life to Claude Eatherly. We picked up the *Straight Flush* at the factory, at Omaha, Nebraska;

and I believe it was the first B-29 with the new reversible pitch props. We flew from Omaha to Wendover, and as we approached for our landing, one of the activating switches apparently went into reverse. This left us with three engines pulling and one pushing. The plane rolled until it was standing straight on a wing tip. I didn't think we had a prayer. But Claude Eatherly, cool and calm as ever, righted that plane for a perfect landing. I don't believe any other pilot at Wendover could have done that.

I make this flat statement: Claude Eatherly was the finest pilot in the 509th. He never met a situation in which he was not in full control. He had nerves like iron. He was quiet and capable . . . never boastful . . . and Colonel Tibbets used him to check out most of the other pilots. And I think we were the best crew in the 509th: the closest, the friendliest, and the most expert. We are the only crew in the 509th which has held a Crew Reunion.

Moreover, Claude Eatherly had a talent for making us feel that rank meant nothing; all that counted was skill, and the ability to pull together. I never heard him scold or complain at a single member of the crew. And I remember more than once when he sneaked me through the back door of the Officers Club to feed me some of their better food.

It's true that our role at Hiroshima was relatively small. We don't deserve much credit. The flight wasn't difficult. There was no opposition. It was like flying over one of our own cities on a beautiful sunny day. We reached the target shortly after 7 A.M., and we flew over it, then back over it for perhaps 15 minutes, making sure that the entire target and the Aiming Point were clearly visible. As the radio operator, I reported this condition to headquarters at Tinian and to the *Enola Gay.*

When we got back to Tinian, we were ordered to go to our quarters and not hold any conversations with anybody. By that time the island was swarming with reporters, photographers, and generals, and since we had not been there when the bomb dropped, I didn't expect us to get much attention. But I must admit that I was surprised, and a little disappointed, when we got absolutely *no* mention and *no* attention. Colonel Tibbets apparently didn't tell anybody that the *Straight Flush* had any role at all.

I believe I have read all the major publicity about Hiroshima. I saw the movie, *Above and Beyond.* And I don't believe that the Air Force, or Colonel Tibbetts, has ever once mentioned Claude Eatherly and the *Straight Flush.* I know that in my community 99.9 percent of the people are unaware that I was at Hiroshima. I haven't hidden the fact, but neither have I ever made any public mention of it. I'm sure that this was Claude Eatherly's experience in his own home town.

I believe that Claude Eatherly was deeply hurt by the manner in which Colonel Tibbets overlooked him in all the publicity. And I think that much of Claude's personal tragedy stems from this. Being overlooked didn't hurt the rest of us: all the other crew members apparently are doing well. But Claude Eatherly was the sort who needed some recognition; he deserved it; and he was hurt deeply when he didn't get it.

Claude didn't show this hurt immediately after the war. We flew back to our base at Roswell, New Mexico. Because he loved to fly, Claude expected to spend his life in the Air Force, and repeatedly he sat with me and begged me to stay in the Air Force with him.

I didn't see him again until we met at the airport in Louisville for our reunion in 1958. We spent four days together: he looked just as neat and sharp as ever, and he talked just as sane, with exactly the same manner, as when he had been Major Eatherly, commander of the *Straight Flush*. He was still in charge; he was still the Skipper as far as we were concerned.

In Louisville we all waited for him to tell us something about his more serious troubles: his being in jail, in the mental hospital, etc. But he never mentioned them. He told us that newspaper and magazine writers were always coming to see him, wanting to write about him. He told us about someone from Hollywood coming to see him and wanting to make a movie about his life. But he said he had turned the movies down because there might be some things in a movie that might not be good for his three children. He said his wife was a TV star in Houston, Texas, and he said she had divorced him. This disturbed all of us, because we had all met her at Wendover, and also at Roswell, and they seemed to get along so well then.

How do I feel about Hiroshima? I feel very, very sorry for all the atomic victims . . . just as I feel sorry for the many more victims of napalm and torpex. But I'm not sorry the United States dropped the atomic bomb. I think that bomb saved lives. It would have been dropped on us if the Japanese had had it. We were fighting a war: the bomb ended that war, and everybody, both Japanese and American, went home to his family.

Has Claude Eatherly ever been insane? All I can say is I can't believe it. In 1944–45 and again in 1958 I found him to be a fine, friendly, alert and capable man; and to me he still stands 12 feet tall.

Even if he wasn't mentioned in the publicity about Hiroshima,

I can tell you he was there. He did well what he was assigned to do. And he still has the respect of every man who flew with him.

Sincerely,
PATRICK L. BOWEN

That letter answered another question which had occurred to me. Why hadn't I heard of Eatherly in 1945? As a correspondent I was twice on Tinian. If Eatherly was a "hero of Hiroshima," why hadn't I heard of him? The answer was that he had not been called a hero in 1945. Not until 1957 had he been called a hero; and Mr. Bowen believed that neglect—his *not* being called a hero—had caused Major Eatherly's personal tragedy.

What about repentance? Where was the conscience-stricken Major Eatherly? The pilot who returned from Hiroshima and didn't speak to anyone for days? The returning hero who fled from his welcoming parade to hide in the barn in tears? Mr. Bowen remembered no remorse or repentance. Mr. Bowen remembered Eatherly as the capable pilot who loved to fly, and who returned from the Pacific begging his crew members to stay in the Air Force.

What about the crew reunion in 1958? Mr. Bowen said Eatherly looked and acted like he always did. Not a word about guilt did he speak, and he told his crew members that he had been bothered by writers wanting to write about him. Obviously, much of what had been written about Eatherly was inaccurate, but the central questions remained. Had he repented his role at Hiroshima? Had Hiroshima contributed to his mental disorder? And had he been punished for repenting?

A letter from the navigator of the *Straight Flush* gave me a fellow officer's recollections of Major Eatherly:

DEAR MR. HUIE:
It has been almost seventeen years since I have seen Claude Eatherly. He and I were close friends as well as members of the same Flight Crew. My wife and his wife were good friends. We both had one child about the same age. Our wives and kids visited a lot while we were flying.

I guess I was with Claude every day for almost a year and a half. Knowing him as well as I do, it is hard for me to believe that he

29

has developed any "guilt complex" over our activities against the Japanese.

Claude was a real happy-go-lucky type of person. He believed in having fun and enjoying life. I don't know anyone who seemed to enjoy himself and the things he did every day, any more than Claude. He loved to fly. He never bitched about the missions we were scheduled for. Colonel Tibbets had him in his office for a couple of times, but it was for off-post activities.

One instance, to give you some idea of what Claude was like. In Utah in order to buy liquor you had to have a state Liquor Permit. It cost $1 for servicemen. Each permit entitled you to buy one bottle of liquor a week. You could buy a permit at any state liquor store, but you were only supposed to have one permit. The State of Utah finally caught up with Claude: He had fifteen liquor permits in his possession. The Colonel chewed him out about this. The Colonel also called Claude in his office for having too many speeding tickets. I don't think Claude was scared of anything or anybody.

We were in the Chi Chi Club one night in Salt Lake City and Claude and I started to leave. The hat check girl wouldn't give Claude his flight cap. He got in an argument with her when up walks an infantry major. (Claude was a captain at this time.) The major told Eatherly and me to leave, that the girl didn't have his cap. Claude got sore and knocked the major flat. The MPs came running, but Claude and I ran out the back and didn't get caught.

Claude drank moderately. Like the rest of us, sometimes he would overdo it. But he didn't drink every day.

Claude's greatest weakness was he liked to gamble. He was a good poker player. He won lots of money in Utah and on Tinian. He liked to shoot dice at the State Line Hotel in Wendover. I have seen him shoot dice by the hour at $100 a throw, constantly bitching because $100 was the house limit.

He would do anything to please other people. He was well liked by all of our crew, and I never knew anyone in the 509th Group who didn't like him. He was always friendly and smiling. If people didn't like what he did or said, it didn't bother him in the least. He was married to a real good-looking girl. She was a nice person. She was really fond of Claude. My wife and I hated to hear of their divorce. I know about practically all the things he has done. I tried very hard to find him in 1947 as I went through Texas, but I never did find him.

As for myself, I'm a native Mississippian. I joined the Air Force in November 1940. Washed out of pilot training and went to the navigation school at Pan American Air Lines in Miami, Fla. I graduated in the top part of the class and was selected to be a navigator instructor.

I taught the first class of navigators at Mather Field, Sacramento, California. I met my wife, who is from Ukiah, California, where we now live.

We now run a liquor and sporting goods store. I have two girls, one 18 and one 12. The oldest is a freshman in college. About three years ago we adopted two boys from France. We have lived in Ukiah since 1946 when I got out of the service. We have a nice home, swimming pool, patio, etc. Things have been real good for me so far. We live in the redwood tree country. I like to fish and hunt, and there is lots of it here. The town is about 10,000 population and is a 115-mile drive north from San Francisco.

As far as my attitude toward Hiroshima, well I think dropping the bomb was the thing to do. It has not affected me in any way that I know. I do feel sorry and low when I hear about Claude's trouble.

I think the bomb saved thousands of American lives and probably killed a lot less Japanese than would have been killed if we would have had to invade Japan.

I didn't go to the crew reunion at Louisville, Kentucky, in 1958. I would like to go to Chicago in August of this year as the 509th Group is having a three-day reunion.

My nickname is and was Felix. So if you speak to Claude or any of the other crew members, they'll know me by that name.

Sincerely yours,
Francis D. (Felix) Thornhill

Those letters, plus my trip to Maxwell Air Force Base, had given me some understanding of Eatherly as he was in 1944–45. In addition, I had had the revealing glimpse of him at the crew reunion in 1958. But the principal questions remained, and before I sought more answers, I needed to see him.

I learned by telephone that Eatherly was now (March, 1962) in Galveston, Texas, on one of his numerous "trial visits" away from the Waco hospital. His medical diagnosis was "schizophrenic reaction, chronic and undifferentiated"; and this illness was said to be in remission. Since in 1961 he had been held by a court to be "competent to manage his own affairs," he had no guardian. He was living in a Galveston hotel and being treated privately by a psychiatrist.

I flew to the Houston airport, rented a Hertz Oldsmobile, drove fifty miles to Galveston, and at midnight I checked into the Jack Tar Hotel. My room looked out onto the Gulf of Mexico. Next morning I telephoned, not Eatherly, but his psychiatrist Dr. Wiebke Thomsen, a German woman from Hamburg, educated in Germany and spending her third year in the United States. Dr. Thomsen is on the staff of the John Sealy Hospital, which is part of the University of Texas School of Medicine. Eatherly was not a hospital patient, but a private patient of Dr. Thomsen's.

I met Dr. Thomsen and talked with her at length. She told me she had learned about Eatherly in letters from Europe, after which she had visited the Veterans Administration hospital in Waco where Eatherly was a patient. She had discussed him with VA psychiatrists who had offered to allow her to talk with Eatherly. She declined this offer and did not see Eatherly in Waco. However, Eatherly learned of her inquiry, and when he ran away from the Waco hospital on August 10, 1961, he came to Galveston and called Dr. Thomsen. He said he wished to become her patient. She agreed. And the Waco hospital authorities, on being advised of his whereabouts and that he wished to become her patient, had agreed for him to remain in Galveston.

"One of his difficulties," Dr. Thomsen said, "is that he feels so alone. After eleven years in and out of a mental hospital, he feels that his brothers and sisters no longer want him to visit them. His mother is dead. His father is very old. His wife divorced him nine years ago, remarried, and he no longer visits his three children. So he feels that most everyone has 'given up on him.' He lives here in a small hotel, and he comes to see me at the hospital in the late afternoon."

"How does he pay his bills?" I asked.

"Well, he has his government compensation, which I believe is $264 a month. Then I believe he has received some money from publication of the book *Burning Conscience*. He has to live modestly, but he seems to have enough."

"How does he occupy himself? What does he do when he isn't talking with you?"

"He wants to write, or to collaborate on some writing project, and all sorts of writing people come to see him. He receives many letters about world peace from persons both in the United States and abroad. Pacifist organizations seem interested in him. He also gets excited about motion pictures, and persons who say they are going to make pictures write to him and come to see him."

"Does he drink?"

"He drinks some, but he is not an alcoholic. Sometimes he goes away and drinks. He has been away for the last week, and he returned to Galveston today."

I asked Dr. Thomsen if she was aware that in Europe the impression had been created that Eatherly was a "prisoner" in the Waco hospital—a prisoner of either the Air Force or the Veterans Administration.

"Yes, I've read that," she replied. "Over the eleven years he has been admitted and released many times at the Waco hospital. I don't have his complete record, so I'm not prepared to say whether or not he was held at some time when he might have been released. Certainly he is no *prisoner* now."

I told Dr. Thomsen that I had come to her before approaching Eatherly because, before he talked with me, I wanted him to understand what my purpose was, and I wanted him to have time to reflect and seek advice. Moreover, I wanted to talk with him only with his physician's approval, and only if she advised me that my questioning would not harm him in any way.

"Dr. Thomsen," I said, "I will appreciate your explaining to Eatherly that I am, first of all, an investigator. I'm not here either as his friend or his foe. I'm not here to promote the cause of world peace or to oppose it; or to defend or attack any policy of the United States. I'm here only to seek the facts of Eatherly's experience. So my mission is much less exciting than that of the other writers who visit him or write to him. I'm not here to collaborate with him; he already has collaborators. Nor am I here to promote a motion picture or a television show. If he is being mistreated in any way, if he is the victim of any injustice because of what he advocates or believes, I'll try to help him.

33

But I'm interested only in facts. I'll appreciate your telling him that I'll want to look at his Air Force record, his medical record, and his criminal record. And I want him to talk with me only when and if, after information and reflection, he chooses to do so."

Dr. Thomsen then said: "You have caught him at a very bad time. Like many people in his condition, he has good weeks and bad weeks. I have told you that he has been away, that he returned only this morning. I could not advise him to talk with you this week, or you with him."

"I understand," I said. "Talking with him tomorrow would save me the expense of returning here, but I'll follow your advice. Meanwhile, here are two of my stories: *The Execution of Private Slovik* and *The Hero of Iwo Jima*. Both have been published in several languages. One has been filmed, the other is in preparation for filming. Both are offbeat stories about Americans who served in the Second World War with tragic consequences. Both are as factual as I could make them. If I write anything about Claude Eatherly, I'll write in the same manner as I wrote about Eddie Slovik and Ira Hayes. These stories, plus whatever advice he can get, should enable him to decide whether or not he wants to talk with me."

Dr. Thomsen said she would deliver the books along with my explanation; and if Eatherly wished to talk with me he could communicate with me later. Next morning I drove back to the Houston airport and flew to Alabama.

Three

TWO days later I received a telephone call from Claude Eatherly. Dr. Thomsen had given him my books and my message, and he was disappointed that I hadn't come to see him while I was in Galveston.

"The reason I didn't visit you," I said, "was that Dr. Thomsen told me you weren't feeling well."

"I was all right."

"Are you feeling better now?"

"Sure. I'm okay. I'm busy with my correspondence. We're working on my autobiography. We're going to make a short Ban-the-Bomb film in Mexico City. And we're finally getting the big motion picture rolling. I've just signed a good deal. It's for a really big picture to be made in Hollywood."

"You do sound busy," I said. "Have you reflected on what Dr. Thomsen told you about me? Are you sure you want to talk with me?"

"Sure I want to talk with you," he insisted. "A lot of guys who really can't do anything come to see me. That's why I want to see you. You can do something. Aren't you going to write anything?"

"That's the point," I said. "If I write anything, what I write may be quite different from what already has been written. Do you understand that?"

"Sure I do."

"Have you read all that has been written?"

"Well, I've read a lot of what's in English. I saw *The Big Story* TV show on NBC. I've read the script for the big motion

35

picture. Some of the stories in German and French have been read to me. I don't have anybody who can read Japanese."

"Do you approve of what you have read?"

"Sure. The writers are famous men. They are good men crusading for peace."

"Perhaps that is even more to the point," I said. "You see, I'm not famous. And I'm not a 'good man crusading for peace.' I'm only a reporter. The only thing about you which interests me is the truth. If I come back to Texas and talk with you, and if I then decide to examine your records and your whole experience, I'll write nothing except what I believe to be true. You want to help me do that?"

"Sure," he said. "You can write what you want to. I don't have anything to hide. Just come to see me and we'll talk. Or maybe I can meet you somewhere?"

I paused a moment. Then I said: "If we understand one another, Mr. Eatherly, I'll come to see you. But I want you to understand the difference between a poet, or a philosopher, or an essayist, or a TV writer, or a motion picture writer, and a reporter. Poets and philosophers and essayists are often men with big purposes: they have ideas to sell and cases to make. TV writers and motion picture writers must sell soap and cigarettes and tickets. So when they write about a man, they select and sometimes exaggerate those things about him which seem to serve their purposes. A reporter only wants to tell the truth and let the true story serve what purpose it can. That's the sort of writer I am. Do we understand one another?"

"I think we do."

"All right. I can't come immediately because I have other work to do. But within about two weeks I'll call you. And I'll fly to Houston and drive down for a talk."

That seemed to satisfy him, and the conversation ended.

A week later I was in Chicago on other business, so I located a third member of the *Straight Flush*'s crew: former Sergeant Jack Bivans. He is now an account executive for the Columbia Broadcasting System. We talked at the O'Hare Inn near the airport.

Despite his youthfulness in 1945, Jack Bivans was the "famous" member of that crew. A wisecracking, nice-looking, talented young actor, he had earned $500 a week as a "child star" in radio soap operas which once emanated by the dozen from Chicago. He had been Chuck Ramsay in *Captain Midnight*, Butch Brent in *Road of Life,* and Junior in *Ma Perkins.* On the Hiroshima flight, as on many a long, boring training flight, he told me his job was to keep Major Eatherly and the crew laughing as he joked and mimicked on the intercom.

"Tell me, Mr. Bivans," I said, "after the bomb drop—after you had listened on the radio to the drop, and after you had learned of the death toll—do you remember noticing anything unusual about Eatherly's behavior? Did he appear to be depressed? Did he seem to want to avoid conversation? What is your recollection as to how he acted during the few hours or few days immediately following Hiroshima?"

Mr. Bivans answered: "I can't remember noticing any change in the Skipper. Except he was disappointed."

"Disappointed? In what way?"

"The Skipper had wanted to drop the first bomb. We had a good crew. . . . I think we were the best in the 509th. So the Skipper was disappointed when we drew only a weather-scout role for Hiroshima. He was more disappointed when we were left out entirely at Nagaskai. When he realized the war was ending and we weren't going to get to drop an A-bomb, well, he felt let down and left out. He had watched Tibbets get the Distinguished Service Cross; and over the radio he had heard about all the Hiroshima publicity, and he felt that he and his crew were being overlooked."

"How do you know he felt that way?"

"He told me he did. About a week after Hiroshima he came to me and said, 'Jack, we were at Hiroshima, too, and we're not getting credit for it. So I want you to write something. You know how to do it. You're in that business. Books will be written about Hiroshima. Movies will be made. And nobody is ever going to know we were there unless we tell them. I want you to write something and send it to your mother in Chicago and she can give it to the newspapers. You're famous in Chicago, and the papers will run it. Tell everybody that the *Straight Flush* was at Hiroshima.' "

I asked: "Was he serious when he said that to you? Or joking?"

"He wasn't joking," Mr. Bivans replied. "He was dead serious. But I pointed out one handicap to him. 'You're forgetting one thing, Skipper,' I said. 'Censorship. I can't mail anything like that to my mother.' "

" 'Sure you can,' he said. 'You're forgetting something. Any officer can censor an enlisted man's mail. You write your mother and I'll put the censor's stamp on it.' "

"Did you write the letter?"

"Yes. I found a typewriter and I wrote about the *Straight Flush*—how we led the way, how we got to Hiroshima first. When I showed it to the Skipper I thought he might think I was laying it on too thick. But he liked it. We mailed it to my mother and she gave it to the Chicago *Tribune*. You can read it in the files. It was a good Chicago story: Local Youth, Former Child Star on *Captain Midnight*, Leads Attack on Hiroshima. It was good for me: maybe it helped me get my role back on *Captain Midnight* when I got home. And of course the only other name featured was Al Barsumian, the other crew member from the Chicago area. We were just two kid sergeants who had been 'at Hiroshima,' but we got publicity. The Skipper got very little; and for the next twelve years—until he began getting publicity for his crimes and his guilt complex—I suppose the only people who knew he was 'at Hiroshima' were those he told about it."

I asked Mr. Bivans: "When he came to you on Tinian and suggested you write that letter, did it occur to you that his desire for publicity perhaps exceeded normal desire?"

"Oh, no," Mr. Bivans replied. "Remember I've come up through show business. Hunger for publicity seems normal to me. And remember, in 1945 I was nineteen. The Skipper was twenty-seven and my commanding officer. I spent a year with him. I idolized him. I still think he was a great guy. He knew how to get you there and get you back. And he must have been the best poker player in the Air Force. He always had a fistful of dough, and he loaned us money anytime we wanted it. We thought he was rich—off a big ranch in Texas. He told us he had been flying since he was seventeen, and that he had flown

38

many combat missions in the South Pacific. He was a swell guy to drink with and chase girls with. He always carried the book with plenty of girls in it. From Wendover, Utah, we used to race in two cars over that hundred miles to Salt Lake City. The Skipper and I would pass the whiskey bottle back and forth, from one car to the other, at eighty miles an hour. Certainly it didn't occur to me that there was anything abnormal about the Skipper. I just thought he was hungry for somebody to pin a medal on him and put his picture in the paper. I meet a good many people who are hungry like that."

"What about his guilt feelings?" I asked. "A lot has been written about his guilt complex. Do you believe guilt may have made him sick?"

"I'd have to answer No," Mr. Bivans replied. "But you see, I can't believe he has ever really been sick. I served with him for more than a year. I regarded him as an intelligent, friendly, highly capable, carefree man. I met his wife at Wendover. She was beautiful, capable, and seemed devoted to him. When I left the Air Force in 1945 he was begging me to stay in. That was three months after Hiroshima, and he had never mentioned regret, guilt or remorse to me. Then I didn't see him for thirteen years. In May, 1958, we held a crew reunion in Louisville, Kentucky, during Derby Week. Gil Niceley, our tail gunner, who lives near Louisville, entertained us. Six of us, including the Skipper, spent four days and nights together—in a motel and going to the Derby. All of us had heard about the Skipper's troubles. We knew he had been in and out of a VA mental hospital. We knew he had been in jail. We knew that his wife had left him, taking the three children. So all of us went to the reunion expecting . . . well, maybe not even to recognize the Skipper. But he was exactly the same! That same curling-lip grin, like a kid who has been caught in the cookie jar. All of us noticed how much he looked like Donald O'Connor, the dancer. Sure he was older. He was about forty. He had put on a little weight. His face looked fleshier. But he was as carefree as ever. He wanted to drink, play poker, and chase girls. And in the poker game he was in there pushing all the time, winning, complaining when we wouldn't agree to raise the limit, and complaining if anybody wanted to quit and get some sleep. Ken

Wey, our bombardier, slept in the room with him, and Ken told us the Skipper could still fall asleep the minute he hit the sack and sleep like a baby. The Skipper never told us about any guilt feelings, or hallucinations, or nightmares. He was the same old Skipper to all of us, and none of us can believe he has ever been crazy."

"Well," I said, "it seems to be a fact that the VA is paying him maximum mental disability compensation. Doesn't that indicate to you that, at some point during those thirteen years when you didn't see him, something went wrong? Something must have made him mentally sick to some degree; and somebody in the VA must have thought it was 'service-connected'? What made him sick?"

Mr. Bivans reflected, then answered: "If he has really been sick, my guess is that he was or is sick of something like show business hunger. The Skipper had two small contacts with show business. In 1943 he married this pretty, ambitious, Italian-American girl he had met at Pasadena Playhouse. She wanted to be an actress. She was called a 'movie starlet.' I think she had had a bit part on Broadway. I'll bet she suffered some hell before she gave up all her dreams. Maybe she gave him some hell. And maybe the Skipper caught a little show business hunger from her. Then he met me, and I guess he was impressed by what I had earned as a kid. He liked to spend his liberties with me and the other sergeants instead of with his fellow officers. By the time he got to Tinian maybe he needed attention more than any of us suspected. When he got no attention out of Hiroshima, maybe he felt hurt; and when life got tough down the line, he went back to trying to get attention out of Hiroshima."

Mr. Bivans paused, then continued: "Maybe the Skipper can't live without attention any more than you can live without water. So why don't we just let him confess to what he calls the crime of Hiroshima, and keep confessing, and why should anybody take him seriously? He's harmless, isn't he? And once he was a fine pilot . . . a great guy to have fun with . . . a good friend to every member of his crew. People ought to just leave him alone."

Then Jack Bivans added: "I guess that's the trouble. People

can't leave the Skipper alone and still give him the attention he needs."

Flying back to Alabama from Chicago, I reflected on what Jack Bivans had said. Like the radio operator and the navigator, Bivans was convinced that Eatherly had never been insane. Bertrand Russell had written that "no unbiased person" can honestly doubt Eatherly's sanity. The Viennese philosopher Gunther Anders, in *Burning Conscience,* had argued that Eatherly was not insane. So the crew members and the writers were in agreement on sanity. Temporarily, at some period, they believed, Eatherly may have been mentally ill, but never insane.

On another point the writers and the crew members disagreed. The writers insisted that Eatherly suffered remorse after Hiroshima. The crew members insisted that he suffered only disappointment at not being assigned to drop an atomic bomb. He regretted, perhaps resented, being overlooked in the publicity; and, with Bivans, he had violated security in trying to publicize the role of the *Straight Flush* at Hiroshima.

The writers insisted that the "American people" had made Eatherly "the Hiroshima hero" after the war; had feted him and set him on the pedestal of the virtuous hero. The crew members made clear the truth: that the American people had not known that Eatherly had been at Hiroshima. So Eatherly could hardly have revolted against being called a hero! He had never been called a hero.

Two days after I returned to Alabama from Chicago I received another telephone call from Claude Eatherly.

"I'm sorry to bother you, Mr. Huie," he said, "but . . . when are you coming?"

"I have been delayed," I answered. "It may be another week."

"I just can't wait that long. I need some money. I need five hundred dollars and I need it right now."

"Are you in trouble?"

"No, no trouble," he said. "But something has come up. If I'm going to make it on the outside, I've got to have something to do . . . some interest besides my writing that will keep me busy an hour or so a day. Dr. Thomsen says I must find something. Well, I've met this woman. . . . She's a real nice woman. She works in a beauty shop, and she wants to buy a shop. We like to be with each other. She has two children and I like them and they like me. I want to help her buy a shop, then I'll keep the books and help her look after things."

"Are you going to become a hairdresser?" I asked.

"Oh, no," he said. "I'll just help manage things."

When I said nothing, he continued: "Well, I've got this big movie deal . . . with big, famous men. They have paid me five hundred dollars and they owe me another thousand now. They'll owe me six thousand dollars more in a year. And I have a big percentage of the picture. And I'm expecting to get a five-hundred-dollar advance from the publishers of my autobiography in Washington; and our foreign publishers—the ones who are publishing my letters—they are supposed to deposit another thousand dollars for me in Switzerland. So I've got plenty of money coming. But I need five hundred dollars today. Can't you wire it to me?"

"No, I can't do that," I told him.

"But you are going to write something, aren't you? Maybe a book? And you can pay me something? Or you can just lend me this five hundred dollars and I'll pay it back when I get my movie money from Mexico City."

"Mr. Eatherly," I said, "I haven't made my position clear. I haven't yet decided to write anything about you. And if I do I don't plan to pay you anything since what I might write is not likely to be profitable."

That halted him. Then he assumed I was lying.

"You're kidding," he laughed. "Your books sell millions. I see them in paperback on the newsstands."

"Some of my books sell well," I said. "Others don't. They don't have a mass appeal. They are the truth, so they are too sad. They don't have sympathetic heroes or happy endings."

"A book about me by you," he said, "is bound to make money. We're already doing all right with books. The book with my letters in it is now selling in ten languages, and money is coming in every day. Writers have been after me for years to help me with my autobiography, and big, famous writers are working on the big movie."

42

"Then why hasn't your autobiography been written, or a film been made?"

"You know why," he said. "The Air Force is against me. The State Department is against me. And these things take time. You have to find the right people. Isn't that right?"

"Perhaps."

"Mr. Huie," he said, "you and I can make a deal. I know we can. And I need money today. I need money in a bundle, so I can invest it and not spend it. Won't you wire me five hundred today? I really need it . . . and I need it now."

"No, Claude," I said, "I won't wire you the money. I won't promise to pay it to you, or give it to you, or lend it to you. But I will fly out there and talk with you. I'll come tomorrow morning."

"I'll be glad to meet you in my car at the Houston airport."

I wondered how he had obtained a driver's license with maximum mental disability.

"No, thanks," I said. "That's too much trouble. Airplanes are sometimes late. You telephone me at the Jack Tar Hotel about two P.M. I should be there by then. You can join me. You tell Dr. Thomsen that you have called me and that I'm coming. I'll want to see her tomorrow evening. You and I will talk, then I'll decide if there is any way I can let you have the money."

When Claude Eatherly came to my room I was sitting in shorts and terry cloth jacket, on the porch overlooking the Gulf, trying to relax. It was a sunny Sunday afternoon in late March, the temperature was 78°, and many persons were walking along the beach. On arrival I had telephoned Dr. Thomsen and told why I had returned. I asked her about Eatherly's condition. She said he was better, but asked me not to let him talk more than an hour.

His appearance was no surprise. I've visited too many jails and mental hospitals not to know that the "disordered" man today often looks "just like everybody else," and in many cases he seems to act "just like everybody else." Eatherly is six feet tall and smokes cigars. His jaws have fleshened, to make his face round; and his forehead slopes backward to curly, reddish,

43

receding hair. He had arrived in an old-model car, and his dress was ordinary. He doesn't appear alert, but I sensed calculation in his manner. He seemed distrustful, watchful, each word is a maneuver; and he still has that tendency, reported by his crew members, to curl his lip and grin.

"You must be an asset to this hotel," I remarked.

"Why?"

"You attract guests. This is twice I've been here because of you. I'm sure there have been others like me."

He grinned. "Yeah, there have been quite a few."

Looking at him closely, I said: "I must have met you on Tinian. I remember the 509th. Riding out here this morning I have been trying to recall individual faces."

I picked up a copy of the Pictorial Album of the 509th Composite Group—which notes on its title page that it was "written and published by and for the members of the 509th Composite Group, Tinian, 1945." He recognized the book and, for all his poker face, he evidenced disturbance.

What makes this book disturbing to him is that it doesn't mention his name in connection with Hiroshima. He is pictured with his ground and air crews and the *Straight Flush*—along with the twelve other crews—but you can read every line and look at every picture and never learn that Claude Eatherly was "at Hiroshima." This is not an oversight. Nor is it due to somebody's not liking Major Eatherly. It is the nature of war reporting.

Every one of the 1800 men in the 509th thought he had some role in the *support* of Hiroshima—the ground crews who serviced the bombers, the communications men, even the cooks and the security police. These are proud Americans: they are proud because they think they "ended the war." And "Hiroshima" to these men means, not a city, but the *attack* on Hiroshima. Eatherly's weather flight was not part of the attack, it was only part of the support. So Eatherly is not mentioned, and all the book's pages which are devoted to "Hiroshima" are filled with eyewitness accounts of the men who were in the *attack*—who made the decisions, took the risks, dropped the bomb, saw the explosion, measured the blast, assessed the damage.

44

So this album, so cherished by every other member of the 509th, has been avoided for seventeen years by Claude Eatherly. He dropped his eyes when he saw it in my hands.

I next handed him the letters from his navigator and his radio operator. He read them, alternately frowning and smiling. Then I handed him a marked clipping from *The London Spectator:*

Eatherly's letters are innocent. It may be an unreal, artificial innocence, a sign of unnatural withdrawal in a man of forty-two, but it angers me to see this innocence exploited. . . . I find this book, said to be based on Eatherly's letters, extremely distasteful. I find the idea of exploiting this unhappy, middle-aged man revoltingly cruel.

He was shaken. He opened his mouth twice to speak, but only sighed. Then he said: "They say here I'm being used. Well, I want to be used."

"I can understand that," I said. "There is nothing wrong in your wanting to be used."

"I'm a pacifist now. There are many pacifists in the world. Important people. Famous people. They are interested in writing about me. I want to be useful to them."

"Nothing wrong in being a pacifist. I'm friendly to pacifists."

"But you are not a pacifist?"

"No," I answered. "I couldn't qualify. I believed in the Second World War. I advocated war against Hitler as early as 1937 and was called a warmonger."

"Are you still a warmonger?"

"I don't think so. I'm for peace—coexistence if possible. But I'm not for peace-at-any-price. I believe there are evils worse than war—worse than death—worse than the death of a city or a nation."

"But I know what atom bombs can do."

"So do I. I know what any bomb can do. I have seen bomb victims. The first time I saw a child blinded by flying glass in London I wept as much as I could have wept for all the children of Hiroshima."

The conversation lagged a moment, then I said slowly:

45

"Claude, remember our understanding on the telephone? I'm not here to debate nuclear policy. I generally support the nuclear policies of Presidents Roosevelt, Truman, Eisenhower and Kennedy. But I'm not a political essayist or philosopher. I'm only a reporter. You live in a comparatively free country. You have the right to be a pacifist. You have the right to repent whatever you did at Hiroshima, or whatever was done at Hiroshima. You have the right to join every Ban-the-Bomb group on earth. You have the right to advocate anything you like, including the overthrow of the government of the United States. If anybody attempts to abridge that right, you telephone me collect and I'll rush out here and try to help reestablish it. Whether I agree with you is irrelevant."

"Then you want to help me?" he asked.

"Well, I'm here," I said. "You want five hundred dollars from me. You want me to write something about you. I'm here to see what, if anything, I can write. You told me you had signed a contract for a motion picture?"

He dug into his pocket and handed me a two-page instrument he had signed in Galveston before a notary about a month earlier. To a man named William Rowland it conveyed Claude Eatherly's portrayal rights for a film to be titled *Medal in the Dust*. The consideration was $500 paid on signing, another $1000 to be paid in thirty days, and a final $6000 to be paid within a year if the picture was made. Then there was a percentage clause, promising Claude Eatherly a percentage of profits.

"You signed this?"

He nodded.

"Did you read a script before signing?"

"Yeah."

"You like it?"

"Yeah, it's all right."

"Who wrote it?"

"Paul Wellman and A. B. Guthrie Jr."

"Is that the Mr. Guthrie who won the Pulitzer Prize for the novel *The Big Sky*? And is that the Mr. Wellman who wrote books like *Jubal Troop* and *The Commancheros,* and some of whose books have been selected by the Literary Guild?"

"I guess so. They are both famous. They know what they are doing, don't they?"

"I assume they do," I said. "I don't know either of them personally, but they both have substantial reputations."

"They think my story can do good," he said. "They think it can contribute to peace and to abolishing nuclear warfare."

"Well, those are worthy purposes," I said. "But if I'm to write anything, I need to begin understanding just what your story is. Let me ask you a few questions. Did you ever tell anybody you saw the blast at Hiroshima and then flew through the bomb cloud?"

"Yeah."

"And you knew it was a lie when you told it?"

"Sure."

"Did you ever tell anybody you were at Nagasaki?"

"I don't think so."

"Did you ever tell anybody you visited Japan and 'looked into the faces of your victims'?"

He looked at me, then dropped his eyes. "They made that up," he said. "Like me being struck dumb."

I said: "Did it ever occur to you to write to *Newsweek* and tell them that their reports were incorrect: that you were two hundred and twenty-five miles from Hiroshima when the bomb fell, that you were not at Nagasaki at all, that you didn't win the Distinguished Flying Cross, and that nobody ever called you a hero because nobody except your associates knew you were *at* Hiroshima?"

He shook his head.

"This poem about how you refused your compensation— it was published right here in Texas, someone must have sent it to you—did it occur to you to write to the poet and tell him he had been misinformed?"

He shook his head.

"All right," I said. "You were in the 509th . . . you piloted the *Straight Flush* . . . you did have a modest role at Hiroshima . . . you left the Air Force . . . you began to suffer from nervousness and anxiety . . . and you attempted suicide. *Newsweek* and the writers overseas say you twice attempted

47

suicide. Once in a New Orleans hotel room. One version says you slit your wrists. How about that?"

He held out his scar-free wrists to me.

"I never touched my wrists," he said. "I never attempted suicide in New Orleans."

"Did you ever attempt suicide anywhere, anytime?"

"I took some pills. In Houston."

"Is there a police report on it?"

"I don't know."

"What hospital did they take you to?"

"I don't remember."

"Was your wife with you when you took the pills?"

"Yes."

"After you took the pills, did you tell her you had taken them?"

"I think I did."

"Then you went to the VA hospital, you began receiving treatment, you were awarded service-connected compensation which you sought and accepted, and at some point the psychiatrists decided you were suffering from a guilt complex over your involvement at Hiroshima? Is that the story?"

"That's it," he said.

"And because you felt guilty, you began seeking punishment? You committed strange crimes, hoping to be jailed or punished in some fashion, but what you wanted to be punished for was what you did at Hiroshima? Is that correct?"

"That's it," he said.

"And all this became known in 1957?"

"Well, that's when the publicity started," he answered. "Just when I began feeling guilty, I don't know. Maybe I started feeling guilty when I was flying back from Hiroshima."

"And after your publicity started in 1957, in *Newsweek* and elsewhere, your story was televised? Then Mr. Rowland, Mr. Wellman and Mr. Guthrie began trying to make a motion picture? And your story began attracting attention in Europe and Japan?"

He nodded.

"Then here is the most important question I have for you,

48

Claude," I said. "When you started getting all this publicity, did anybody attempt to hurt you?"

He hesitated, then he answered: "All I know is what the doctors told me. Until the publicity started, I had never been held in the 'closed ward' at Waco. They put me in the 'closed ward' and Dr. Frank told me it was because I was a 'political prisoner.' Dr. Constantine told me that General Twining, of the Air Force, was trying to transfer me to Walter Reed Hospital in Washington so that the Air Force could keep me where I couldn't talk to anybody or write to anybody."

"The doctors told you that? And those are Veterans Administration doctors?"

"They sure are, and that's what they told me."

I paused and reflected. I looked at my watch, remembering my promise to Dr. Thomsen. We had been talking for an hour.

"Then I'll ask only one more question," I said. "Are you willing for me to look at your Air Force service record? At your FBI criminal record? At your VA medical record?"

He hesitated again, then replied: "Sure."

"Are you willing to sign letters asking each of these organizations to make your records available to me?"

"Sure."

"You understand what you are saying?"

"Sure."

"You have no objections to my publishing whatever is true about you?"

"No. Just so you be sure it's true . . . and not just what somebody tells you. I have my own records."

"Well, here's what I'll do," I said. "I told Dr. Thomsen I wouldn't talk with you more than an hour. The hour is up. This evening I'll talk with her. I'll think over our conversation. You come back here at nine A.M. tomorrow. I think I may decide to look at all your records, to examine your whole life experience. I may write a book. And I think I'll pay you five hundred dollars to help me find the truth."

Late that evening, after I had gone to bed, my telephone rang and it was Claude Eatherly. He sounded forlorn. He wanted to know if I had been talking to people about him and I told him yes. He said he was looking at television and began to describe some program, and as he talked I sensed his loneliness.

"That's one of his problems," Dr. Thomsen had said. "After eleven years in and out of a mental hospital he feels that his brothers and sisters no longer want him to visit them. His mother is dead. His father is very old. His wife divorced him several years ago, remarried, and he no longer visits his children. So he feels that most everyone has given up on him. That's one reason why he welcomes the letters about world peace from many different countries. That's why he likes to talk about writing books and making motion pictures."

The guilt publicity had given Eatherly new reason for being. It had given him letters to read and write, callers to receive, great enterprise to contemplate. Why should he have corrected poets and reporters, dramatists and philosophers? They had made him feel valuable and useful and less lonely.

Next morning, promptly at nine, Claude Eatherly rapped on my door. He had come to collect his $500. I had already written his check, and I had also written four letters for him to sign. The letters:

Major James Sunderman,
Chief,
Magazine & Book Branch,
Office of Public Information,
U. S. Air Force,
The Pentagon,
Washington, D. C.

Dear Major Sunderman:
It is my desire that Mr. William Bradford Huie be allowed to consult every record bearing on and pertaining to my service in the USAF. I hereby request you to go over these records with Mr. Huie, and I hereby authorize you to do so.

Respectfully,
Claude R. Eatherly
0423234

THE DIRECTOR,
Veterans Administration Hospital,
Waco, Texas.

DEAR MR. McMAHAN:

It is my desire that Mr. William Bradford Huie be allowed to consult every record bearing on and pertaining to my treatment for mental disorder in the Waco VA hospital. I hereby request you, sir, to go over these records with Mr. Huie; I hereby authorize you to do so; and I urge you to allow and instruct all the doctors who have treated me to discuss my case freely with Mr. Huie. I also request you, sir, to allow all the aides and attendants at the hospital who have known me to talk freely with Mr. Huie.

Respectfully,
CLAUDE R. EATHERLY

THE CHIEF LEGAL OFFICER,
Veterans Administration,
Vermont Avenue at H Street,
Washington, D. C.

DEAR SIR:

It is my desire that Mr. William Bradford Huie be allowed to consult every record bearing on and pertaining to my treatment for mental disorder in the Waco VA hospital. It is my further desire that Mr. Huie be allowed to discuss my case freely with all the VA doctors who have treated me. I therefore urge you, sir, to assist Mr. Huie in obtaining these records and in arranging these interviews. For Mr. Huie's purposes alone, I hereby waive all rights of privacy legally guaranteed to VA patients; and I request you, sir, to assist Mr. Huie and me in the manner I here indicate.

Respectfully,
CLAUDE R. EATHERLY

HON. JOHN EDGAR HOOVER,
Chief,
Federal Bureau of Investigation,
Pennsylvania Avenue at Ninth Street, NW,
Washington, D. C.

DEAR MR. HOOVER:

It is my desire that Mr. William Bradford Huie be allowed to consult every record bearing on and pertaining to my criminal activities within the legal jurisdiction of the United States. I hereby request you, sir, to take the necessary steps to enable Mr. Huie to examine these records.

Respectfully,
CLAUDE R. EATHERLY

He sat down at the desk, read the letters hurriedly, signed them without question, and I handed him the $500 check.

"Now that this transaction is completed, Claude," I said, "I'm curious about one point. Do you believe your signature is valid? Do you believe you are legally and medically sane and competent?"

"Sure I'm sane and competent," he answered. "No court has ever appointed a guardian for me. Nobody has ever suggested that I need a guardian. I have always handled my own affairs. Whatever I sign is legal."

He then asked me: "You don't think I'm incompetent, do you?"

"How could I?" I answered. "Your crew members are convinced you've never been insane or incompetent. And Lord Bertrand Russell is said to be one of the world's most intelligent men. He says that no unbiased person can doubt your sanity. So how can I doubt your sanity or competence?"

He smiled and pocketed my check. "I suppose I'll be seeing you again," he said.

"You can count on it," I said. "But let me emphasize one other development you can count on. About six months from now you can sit down in this room, and in plain English you can read all that is true about your life and your behavior which I could find. Do you think you'll enjoy reading my book?"

His defensive half-grin came to his face. I had the feeling that he didn't believe me. That he had talked to so many men about so many books which had never been written, and about so many films which had never been made, that he assumed this would be the case again. He no more thought that I'd write a book than he thought that the producer who had paid him $500 would make a film.

"We'll see," he said. "We'll see what happens."

He carried my bag down to the car, and I headed for the Houston airport and Alabama.

Four

THE military service records of about eighteen million living Americans are stored in a Records Center near St. Louis, Missouri. Two weeks are generally required for a record to be found at these warehouses and delivered to Washington. To obtain Claude Eatherly's service record I sent my request, along with his letter, to the Magazine & Book Branch, Office of Public Information, United States Air Force, the Pentagon, Washington, D. C. I later went to Washington and examined the record in the presence of Lieutenant Colonel Gene Gurney, representing the Secretary of the Air Force. After copying each date and entry in the record, I then went back to Texas to try to gain an understanding of Claude Eatherly's experience from his birth until he left the Air Force.

In extreme northeast Texas, on the Oklahoma line, is agricultural Grayson County. You reach it by driving forty miles north from Dallas, through McKinney. The county seat of Grayson County is Sherman, a city of 17,000. The community of Van Alstyne, population 1,605, is between McKinney and Sherman. The land is flat and black, and this is not where rich people live in Texas: the people are poor and "of moderate means." Once much cotton was grown in Grayson County, but as cotton moved westward, cattle-growing replaced it, and much of the land is now uncultivated, assigned to the government Soil Bank. Many of the people who once worked the farms have gone to the cities.

Six miles from Van Alstyne, on a farm-to-market road, is a

425-acre farm which has been owned for sixty years by James E. Eatherly. He is now eighty-seven. . . . He lives there, with only his eighty-five-year-old brother; the two old men do their own cooking. The two-story farmhouse is ramshackle, unpainted, and there is no telephone. The farm is no longer worked; a few cattle are "run" on it.

Here on October 2, 1918, Claude Robert Eatherly was born, the youngest of six children. Three boys; three girls. One of the girls died in her teens; and today the other two girls are married . . . "doing well" . . . living in middle-sized Texas cities with their husbands, children and grandchildren. The other two sons, James and Joe Eatherly, are connected with Humble Oil Company. James Eatherly, with his wife and family, lives in Midland, Texas, where he is directly employed by Humble; and Joe Eatherly, with his wife and two children, lives in Van Alstyne where he is the Humble distributor. He has the fuel pumps and the galvanized tin shed on the north side of Van Alstyne and his wife keeps the books. It is the sort of modest fuel wholesaling seen on the outskirts of every community in America.

Joe Eatherly and his wife still "look after" his father. They go out to the "home place" once a week, clean up, and see if anything is needed.

All these five children, boys and girls, went to school in Van Alstyne, graduated from Van Alstyne High School. The family belonged to the Van Alstyne Baptist Church. They all attended the nearby college—North Texas Teachers College, Denton, Texas. The only one to graduate was James Eatherly; he got a master's degree and taught school for a while before going with Humble.

The only one to go into the service was Claude Robert. He enlisted in the Air Force in Dallas on December 30, 1940. He was six feet tall, weighed 155 pounds, and he had attended the college during the school years 1936–37, 1937–38, 1938–40. He had completed 76 semester hours out of 128 needed to graduate. About half his grades were D's, most of the balance were C's. He had three B's: two in chemistry, one in physical education. The Air Force record says he "had never been employed except to help his father on the farm."

In Van Alstyne I asked people if they had any particular recollections of Claude Eatherly. One elderly farmer remembered him as "Claudie." Others told me he was "about like everybody else." He "liked fun and didn't study much"; he liked "all kinds'a games"; maybe he "liked the girls a little more'n average." "He wasn't particularly handsome" but he had "a sort of little-boy grin that seemed to attract the girls." He didn't talk a lot; he was "a nice guy to be around." He "just never seemed very serious about anything."

The woman who was married to Claude Eatherly from 1943 to 1955 wrote to me:

His parents were a farm couple, of moderate means, and they worked very hard. They so much wanted their children to have an education. His mother was a good, religious, hard-working woman. I think she babied Claude.

When she died in 1946 she thought he had never touched a drop of liquor, and I'm glad that she didn't live to see the mess that Claude made of his life. It would have killed her. It always seemed such a shame that, with his parents sacrificing so much to help him, Claude squandered his years in college, making such sorry grades. Even in college he felt compelled to act the "big shot." I have heard him brag about his extensive social life in college and how expensive his clothes were.

Three citizens of Van Alstyne signed letters recommending him to the Air Force: A. F. Thompson, H. L. Hartley, and City Clerk Roscoe Garver. They said, ". . . his mother and father are outstanding members of the community" . . . "good, dependable citizens."

Claude Eatherly received his primary training (three months) at Cal-Aero, Ontario, California; his basic training (two months) at Goodfellow Field, San Angelo, Texas; and his advanced pilot training (two months) at Barksdale Field, Louisana. It was at Barksdale on August 16, 1941—near his twenty-third birthday —that he was pronounced capable of flying two-engined aircraft, commissioned a second lieutenant, and assigned to the Ferrying Command, Long Beach, California.

At Long Beach Lieutenant Eatherly accumulated 107 flying hours in four months of ferrying duty: chiefly flying Lockheed

Hudsons to Canada. On December 2, 1941, he went to the 2nd Bomb Group, Langley Field, Virginia. He was there on December 7th—Pearl Harbor day—flying B-18s on patrol. On February 2, 1942, he joined the 34th Bomb Group at Pendleton, Oregon, where he accumulated 103 hours flying LB-30s.

On April 5, 1942, he was transferred to the 3rd Bomb Squadron, Panama, and from March 12, 1943, to April 7, 1943, he was with the 25th Bomb Squadron on the Galapagos Islands, near Panama. This gave him about twelve months of antisubmarine patrol in the Canal area.

On April 26, 1943, he was assigned to the 39th Bomb Group at Davis-Monthan Field, Tucson, Arizona. He was at Tucson for eight months, and it was during this period that he married. In 1941, while he was a cadet at Cal-Aero, through mutual friends he met the Texas girl who was to become his wife. She was working at Pasadena Playhouse, trying to become an actress. She was pretty, Catholic, and Italian-American, and they were married at the base at Tucson on June 3, 1943.

In this book I shall not mention her name. She bore three children by Claude Eatherly; the first in 1944, the third in 1953. In 1957 she divorced him, and subsequently made a successful second marriage. Reluctantly, she gave me some assistance, and she read this book in manuscript. But at her request I shall not use her name, nor the names of the children, nor shall I disclose their place of residence.

On December 12, 1943, Captain Eatherly moved to the 359th Headquarters Squadron, Alamogordo, New Mexico. For two months he was at Clovis, New Mexico. Then, on June 1, 1944, he was assigned to the 393rd Bomb Squadron, Fairmount Field, Geneva, Nebraska.

It was this squadron—the 393rd—which was picked to become the nucleus of the specially organized atomic group, the 509th Composite Group. And with this squadron, on August 1, 1944, a full year before Hiroshima, Eatherly moved to Wendover Field, Utah, to begin his atomic training.

It is untrue, however, to say that "each pilot" in the 509th was a "picked super-pilot." The pilots were not picked: the 509th took the entire 393rd Squadron as it was composed on August 1, 1944.

In 1962 at the Pentagon I discussed this point with Brigadier General Paul Tibbets.

"No, I didn't *pick* Eatherly," General Tibbets explained. "I inherited him along with the rest of the 393rd. After their assignment to me, all personnel of the 393rd were given special checks, including security, but that was the extent of the picking."

"This is not to say," the General continued, "that I would *not* have picked Eatherly. He was capable. What we called the Typical Texas Pilot, with his boots and flamboyance and a little something extra added to his dress. He was reckless in his off-duty life, and I remember calling him on the carpet for too much speeding, drinking and gambling. But he knew how to fly. I trusted him as a pilot. He had a splendid crew, with excellent morale. Had the war continued, and had we been ordered to drop more atomic bombs, without hesitation I would have entrusted one of those bombs to Major Eatherly. There was, however, never any chance that he'd be selected to drop the first bomb. That was my responsibility: I had been ordered to drop it. And Eatherly had had no combat experience. Nor was there ever any chance that he'd drop the second bomb. That bomb was assigned to Eatherly's superior officer, the commander of the 393rd Squadron, Major [now Brigadier General] Charles W. Sweeney, who had flown alongside me with the gauges at Hiroshima.

"Eatherly was a fine pilot," General Tibbets concluded, "but by no means the finest. He was one among many fine pilots."

From August 1, 1944, to June 9, 1945, Eatherly trained for the atomic mission: at Wendover; at Inyokern, California; and at Batista Field, Cuba (twelve miles south of Havana). On June 10, 1945, he "departed for the Pacific Theater," to quote the record, with the 509th. He flew the *Straight Flush* by way of Hawaii and Kwajalein. By mistake he landed on Guam instead of Tinian, and this landing is remembered because the *Straight Flush* was the first B-29 with reversible propellers to be seen at that B-29 base. Eatherly attracted a crowd of vetern B-29 crewmen, watching him "back up" several times before he took off for North Field, Tinian.

In my efforts to learn more about Eatherly from the time he arrived on Tinian until he left the Air Force, I was lucky to find that two people who knew him were my neighbors. Kenneth Wey's father is in the laundry business at Chattanooga. Ken's wife, Kay, is from Monterey, Tennessee, on the Cumberland Plateau; and Ken and Kay have three daughters.

In 1957 Ken and Kay Wey bought a laundry business in Gadsden, Alabama, and when I found them they had both been working for four years without a vacation, trying to establish their business. They came to my home for a weekend, and Ken brought his personal records and photographs to supplement the official Air Force records.

"I suppose I knew Claude Eatherly as well as anyone who served with him," Ken said. "I served with him longest. I was his bombardier from the time we were organized at Wendover; I made all the flights from Tinian; I was his bombardier during all the training for Bikini, I was with him at Bikini, all the way down to the fall of '46 when I left the Air Force. From the records you have shown me, I suppose I aimed every bomb that was dropped from an airplane flown by Claude Eatherly."

In each of the A-bomb training flights made by Eatherly and his crew, a 10,000-pound practice bomb was dropped. These simulated atomic bombs were called "punkins" (pumpkins) because of their shape. In the training flights made from the United States and Cuba, the punkins had been filled with concrete. But on July 20, 1945, when the *Straight Flush* made its first training flight to Japan, the punkin was filled with an explosive mixture known as torpex.

"Well," Ken Wey explained, "that was the first combat flight that the *Straight Flush* had made. Eatherly had told us that he had flown combat flights before, in the South Pacific. Now you show me from the record that he had never flown in combat before, so July 20th was the first time that any of us had ever flown over enemy-held territory. We flew from Tinian up to Japan, and we were at 30,000 feet, and we had on our flak suits, but we didn't see anything that looked like an enemy. In fact we didn't see anything at all, since all of Japan was obscured by heavy cloud cover. Our assigned target was obscured, and we were considering what to do with our torpex punkin when Jack Bivans made a suggestion. Jack was always coming up with something funny to make us laugh.

" 'Let's drop it on the Emperor,' Bivans said on the intercom. 'Why shouldn't we end the war today? Just plant it right on Hirohito's head.'

"Eatherly liked the idea. 'Give me a heading on the palace,' he said to Felix Thornhill.

"When we found Tokyo socked in, Eatherly ordered me to make a radar drop from thirty thousand feet. I did my best. . . . I aimed at the palace, . . . but from what we heard later I only managed to plant that punkin in the moat surrounding the palace grounds. Maybe I drenched a bunch of Japanese.

"That evening Tokyo Rose reported on that drop, and what she said was printed in the 509th's daily news sheet. Here it is."

The tactics of the raiding enemy planes have become so complicated that they cannot be anticipated from experience or common sense. The single B-29 which passed over the capital this morning was apparently using a new sneak tactic aimed at confusing the minds of the people.

Ken Wey showed me his personal flight record for the other five "combat flights" made to Japan by the *Straight Flush:* the flights to Otsu on July 24th, to Tsugawa on July 26th, to Maizuru on July 29th, to Hiroshima on August 6th, and to Yokkaichi on August 8th. On each of these flights, except the Hiroshima flight, a torpex-filled punkin was dropped. No one can say with certainty whether anyone was killed by these five punkins dropped by the *Straight Flush* on Japan. If so, they were the only human beings killed by an aircraft piloted by, or commanded by, Claude Eatherly.

The Air Force record says that during his entire war service Eatherly flew "180 patrol missions, 6 combat missions." These "combat missions," as described here, totaled "74 hours, 20 minutes" in the air, and they were "unopposed by any form of enemy action."

"No," Ken Wey said, "we never saw any flak on any of those six trips to Japan. We were above thirty thousand feet every minute we were over Japan, and the Japs had nothing to bother you at that altitude by July, 1945. Also, the Japs were so short of fuel that they could no longer send fighter planes up to thirty thousand feet to challenge a lone B-29. We didn't expect any opposition; we carried no guns except a couple of tail guns."

This means that Claude Eatherly has an unusual Air Force service record. He was commissioned before Pearl Harbor, yet throughout the entire war he never heard an enemy bomb fall or an enemy shot fired. He never "met the enemy" in any form. He never saw a man die, and he never flew over enemy territory until he flew to Japan in the last weeks of the war when the Japanese had no means of threatening a B-29 at 30,000 feet. And his flights from Tinian to Japan were made long after we had established the emergency base at Iwo Jima and after our air-sea rescue units had begun operating within sight of the Japanese coast.

So no one can escape this conclusion from the record: the fates gave Claude Eatherly one of the safest experiences of any man commissioned by the Air Force during the war.

"Tell me," I asked Ken Wey, "what happened to Eatherly after August 14, 1945—after the war ended?"

"Nothing much," Ken replied. "We stayed on Tinian for a couple of months, just standing by, killing time, drinking, playing poker."

"Was Eatherly depressed? Remorseful? Conscience-stricken?"

"Of course not. He wasn't reflective or complex. He was mechanically minded. He has one talent: machines. In his crew were men much more complex and better educated than he was. But they had washed out of pilot training. He hadn't. He could look at an airplane and spot a loose rivet. He could listen to an engine, like a musician listening to a symphony, and spot a sour note. Other than that you can't imagine a simpler man. He wanted to fly airplanes then take a drink and deal the cards or chase a girl. He wanted a good time."

"Do you think he was disappointed at being left out of the Hiroshima publicity?"

"Well, not seriously," Ken Wey replied. "He wanted publicity, sure. But I don't think he took it very seriously. He felt a little let down . . . all of us did . . . the war ended so quickly. You see, we were in a strange position. For a whole year we had believed that we were something Very Special. We didn't know exactly how we were going to do it, but we knew this: we were going to *end the war*. We were going to take off with *something* weighing ten thousand pounds and shaped like a pumpkin. We were going up to thirty thousand feet and drop that punkin no farther than five hundred feet from an Aiming Point. And we were going to be the heroes who ended the war. Then we got to Tinian. One bomb was dropped . . . then two . . . and *bam!* the war was over. Only two crews got to drop a bomb. That left eleven other crews feeling that we had trained for a whole year for nothing. I know this sounds terrible, but we were just human. Nobody likes to work for a whole year, learning to drop a special kind of bomb, and then not be needed. So we all felt sort of suddenly let down in the weeks after the war ended. We weren't Special any longer. We had just been part of the war's waste."

"And during those weeks Eatherly never mentioned Hiroshima to you?"

"Of course not. The war was over. He played poker, and he must have won three or four thousand dollars. Then we finally took off for home. We had some passengers in the airplane, including Colonel Blanchard. And we were lucky again. We were supposed to refuel at the base near San Francisco then proceed directly to Roswell, New Mexico. But an engine malfunctioned so we officers went into San Francisco for a two-day celebration at the Mark Hopkins Hotel. Then we flew on to the base at Roswell where our wives and children were to join us."

"How did you live when you got back to Roswell?"

"Well, Kay joined me and his wife joined him. We both had children about eighteen months old. We both lived off the base. We both like to play golf. So we flew some . . . and played a lot of golf . . . and once in a while we got together in the evening."

I turned to Kay Wey. "What did you think of Eatherly?"

"I liked his wife," Kay replied. "She was at Wendover for several weeks. She was sweet, pretty, devoted to him—worked

61

hard. At Roswell I saw her considerably more than at Wendover. She was trying hard. I can't say that I ever really liked Claude Eatherly. I didn't dislike him. I didn't think he was handsome. He had a sort of little-boy charm—if you like men with little-boy charm. I don't. He didn't talk much. He gave me the impression of a man who is uncomfortable in any domestic situation. He seemed proud of his wife because she was pretty; but I never saw him display any affection or even concern for her. He didn't seem particularly fond of his child. I think he was the sort of man who is comfortable when he is with men, or when he's chasing a woman. But he is not comfortable sitting down with wives and husbands for a friendly evening."

"Are you surprised at what happened to him?"

"Well, I wouldn't have predicted that he'd wind up in a mental hospital," she said. "But I guess I would have predicted trouble— Especially if I had known that he was going to leave the Air Force. When I knew them there was never any thought that he'd leave the Air Force. He was going to stay in and he was trying to persuade everybody else to stay in. I certainly would have predicted trouble the day that Claude Eatherly had to get out and hit it and try to make a living for a family."

Kenneth Wey said that early in 1946 he and Claude Eatherly were back "dropping the punkin again." All the other members of the "old crew" had become civilians, and their places in the *Straight Flush* had been taken by others. But Eatherly and Wey were still together . . . and still "dropping the punkin."

"We were dropping the punkin," Ken Wey explained, "because five of the crews which had been trained to drop atomic bombs were assigned to duty in OPERATION CROSSROADS . . . Bikini . . . the first atomic test series after the war. At Bikini there was to be one aerial bomb drop—only *one*—before all the brass and photographers and reporters and diplomats. And the five crews were to compete for the honor of making that drop. We were to make a series of competitive drops, and the winner was to be the crew with the best CE."

CE means Circular Error. The scientists in charge at Bikini also wanted accuracy. They wanted the bomb dropped "within 500 feet of the Aiming Point," with a CE "not to exceed 500 feet." So for several weeks the five crews trained and made their competitive drops.

"Well," Ken Wey continued, "Claude Eatherly wanted to make that drop at Bikini. I mean he really wanted to make it. He had his heart set on it. He was a fierce competitor; he liked to win; he wanted to be first. So over that New Mexico desert we really sweated with that punkin. We were dropping on that range between Albuquerque and Alamogordo—just bare, hot, red desert. And you see, you are six miles up, trying to drop the punkin in what we call 'the pickle barrel.' A football field is three hundred feet long. So we were six miles up, with this big, old, five-ton, concrete-filled punkin, trying to drop it on a football field. You couldn't even see the Aiming Point with natural vision. And there is a lot of luck in dropping over that desert. Because in that six miles of free fall that punkin can hit all sorts of crosswinds and updrafts and downdrafts which you can't know are there and which you can't allow for. We worked and sweated and cussed, but we just couldn't get that punkin to drop true. It would sail on us in spite of all we could do. We made some good drops but we also made some bad ones. We had one really bad drop—a big miss—and that ruined our score. Our CE was something like nine hundred feet. We didn't win . . . we didn't come second . . . we finished fifth and last. It was a bitter disappointment to Claude. It was tough on me, too, because since I was the bombardier I was more to blame than he was. And he chewed me out unmercifully!"

(Eatherly's former wife later told me: "The most important thing in his life was that he get to drop the Bikini bomb. I have never seen anyone so intense about anything as Eatherly was during that contest. And Kenny Wey is right about his being 'unmercifully chewed out' the day he made that bad drop. Claude was so furious I thought he was going to attack Kenny. I would say that not being selected to drop the Bikini bomb was the biggest disappointment of Claude's life.")

Despite this poor showing, Eatherly and Wey went to the Pacific with the other four B-29 crews. The record says Major Eatherly, on April 26, 1946, "departed for Kwajalein Atoll for OPERATION CROSSROADS."

The other members of Eatherly's crew for CROSSROADS were:

The Co-Pilot: Lieutenant Robert L. Gungle, Maywood, Illinois.

The Navigator: Captain Jack P. Richardson, Fort Worth, Texas.

The Radar Officer: Captain Darwin E. Rasmussen, Muskegon, Michigan.

The Flight Engineer: Lieutenant Robert E. Dove, Fairsbury, Nebraska.

The Radio Operator: Sergeant Morton Bimstein, Glendale, California.

Scanners: Sergeant Andrew J. Steinman, Riverside, Pennsylvania; and Private Merle E. Brown Jr., Hollywood, California.

Eatherly received one bit of newspaper publicity during OP-ERATION CROSSROADS. Here is the United Press dispatch. The year is 1946:

Kwajalein, July 2. Two B-29 superfortresses stood on Kwajalein airstrip today under heavy guard . . . the "hottest" aircraft in the Pacific.

The two planes were placed out of bounds as the result of a midnight flight through the atomic cloud with full crews aboard.

Both aircraft were so radioactive when they landed after their dangerous flight that it was thought at first it might be necessary to destroy them. But now the 20th Air Force feels certain they can be "washed down."

The airplanes left Kwajalein at 8:30 o'clock last night on a dramatic assignment to find the atomic storm cloud in the mid-Pacific darkness. They were to fly through it to collect samples in precipitrons carried by each plane.

One B-29 was commanded by Major Claude R. Eatherly, 27, Van Alstyne, Texas. The second plane was commanded by Major Allan B. Rowlett, 31, Chula, Virginia.

The precipitrons are newly contrived devices for taking in samples of air in flight and retaining by precipitation all radioactive particles.

The hunt for the black cloud 200 miles away on a moonless night necessarily depended on flying by instruments.

Eatherly's plane found the cloud quickly at 25,000 feet 13 hours after it was formed by detonation over Bikini Atoll. Rapidly ticking Geiger counters told two especially trained monitors aboard that the plane had entered the atomic storm. Eatherly then radioed his position to Rowlett who also went in for his samples.

Eatherly was based on Kwajalein for six weeks and made seven B-29 flights from Kwajalein to Bikini during the atomic test. He carried scientist-observers and blast gauges, and there for the first time he witnessed an atomic explosion. But again he was only in support: the crew which made the aerial drop got most of the attention and publicity. Eatherly received the peacetime "Army Commendation Medal for Commanding BLAST GAUGE AIRCRAFT during OPERATION CROSSROADS January–July 46."

I asked Ken Wey: "What did you do on all those days and nights on Kwajalein? Did you notice any changes in Eatherly?"

"No, he seemed the same," Wey replied. "Of course there isn't much to do on an atoll. You can swim or play volley ball or go to a movie or get drunk or play poker. Claude played poker—sometimes for two or three days and nights at a stretch. And he had his most famous winning streak. He and Roger Ramey* (later a lieutenant general) played head-and-head for a long session. Ramey had just been paid $3000 by *The Saturday Evening Post* for some article. At the end of that session the whole Officers' Club witnessed Ramey endorsing his *Post* check over to Eatherly. So while Eatherly didn't make the bomb drop at Bikini, he sure as hell dropped a punkin on old Roger Ramey."

On August 3, 1946, Eatherly returned to Roswell, and Ken Wey left Roswell and the Air Force shortly thereafter. So again I asked Wey: "In your last days at Roswell, after you had returned from Kwajalein, did you notice any change in Eatherly?"

"Well," he answered, "I didn't see him very much after we came back from CROSSROADS. He had to rush home because of his mother's death, and I was getting ready to leave the Air Force in September. But now that I think of it, I do remember that

* Lieutenant General Roger M. Ramey, who led one of the fire bomb raids on Japan, died March 4, 1963. He was a native of Denton County, Texas, which adjoins Grayson County; and like Claude Eatherly, he attended what is now North Texas State University.

he seemed to be growing a little more belligerent. He had never been much of a fighter: he got along with most everybody. But at Kwajalein he beat up a guy in a poker game. He accused this guy of cheating, grabbed him by the collar, jumped on him, and beat him up pretty bad. So maybe he was becoming more belligerent."

After CROSSROADS Eatherly himself was manhandled by the fates. While he and General Ramey were playing head-to-head poker at Kwajalein, an exploratory operation was performed on his mother at a hospital in Sherman, Texas. The surgeons found hopeless cancer, and she lay waiting for the end. This news was conveyed to Eatherly by the Red Cross when he landed in California on August 2, 1946, en route to Roswell.

Von Robert Jungk and others who have written about Eatherly have exploited this dramatic situation—"the Hiroshima pilot landing on the soil of the United States and being informed that his mother is dying of cancer."

In these stories he learns of his mother's impending death as he returns from Hiroshima, not Bikini. He gets the death message shortly after he has been "struck dumb" . . . and after he has visited Japan to "look into the faces of his victims." So he "cries out in anguish" in 1945, not 1946.

What actually happened was, after receiving news of his mother's condition upon his return from Bikini, he flew on to Roswell, was granted a 30-day leave, and he and his wife went to the old farm home to await his mother's death. For three weeks the entire family was gathered there, visiting his mother at the hospital at Sherman and waiting. If Claude Eatherly ever associated his mother's death with Hiroshima, neither he, nor any of his crewmen, nor his wife, nor Joe Eatherly, remembers it.

Two disasters, however, hit him within a week. On August 21, 1946, he learned by telephone that his application for a regular commission in the Air Force had been turned down. This application had been supported by Brigadier General W. H. "Butch" Blanchard,* who wrote that "despite certain deficien-

* In 1963 Lieutenant General W. H. Blanchard was Inspector General of the Air Force.

cies" he believed Major Eatherly could be valuable to the peace-time Air Force. Eatherly's failure to get his regular commission jeopardized his chances of being able to stay in the Air Force. His former wife remembers that he was "terribly upset" by this news. Then, on August 26, 1946, his mother died. He and his wife returned to Roswell after the funeral, and she remembers that he was "very concerned" about his future in the Air Force.

On November 1, 1946, remaining in the Air Force on his reserve commission, Major Eatherly transferred to the Meteorology School, Keesler Field, Biloxi, Mississippi. The record says he "assumed duty as a student."

When I noted this in his record in 1962, I was puzzled. Why would a man who liked to fly choose to leave a glamorous flying outfit like the 509th to become a student of meteorology? Even though he had been denied a regular commission, couldn't he have remained in the Air Force on his reserve commission? Why didn't he remain at Roswell? He had always been a poor student; why did he choose to study meteorology?

Seeking this answer, I wrote to Colonel Walter Y. Lucas, who had been Eatherly's squadron commander at Roswell in 1946. Colonel Lucas in 1962 was Wing Commander, 9th Strategic Aerospace Wing, Mountain Home Air Force Base, Idaho. He replied:

I have contacted two or three officers who were in the squadron at the time Major Eatherly was a member of the unit and discussed with them the questions you raised.

Unfortunately, none of us were close friends of Eatherly's and do not really know details. We are of the opinion that his decision to go to Meteorological School at Keesler was brought about by a feeling he had for wanting to get into some other type work to further his career. He was doing an average job in the squadron and had not "fouled up" or "goofed off," so to speak. In other words, he had no reasons for leaving the outfit other than a desire to try something else.

We are certain that his not receiving a Regular Commission was an influencing factor in his desire to transfer and that the selection of the Meteorological School was primarily based on a request from higher headquarters for volunteers at this particular time. The possibility that Keesler was closer to certain gun-running activities is not to be discounted. He had discussed somewhat in a joking fashion this gun-running business while still at Roswell. However, none of us had the feeling that he intended to engage in these activities while a member of the Air Force.

I am sorry that I cannot be of more assistance, but he was actually in my squadron a very short period of time and I hardly knew him. A couple of the officers I contacted flew with him during the CROSS-ROADS tests and they state at this time that he was "happy-go-lucky" and did his job about like anyone else. We all had the feeling that his not receiving the Regular Commission had considerable impact on his personality. In other words, he was very upset.

I realize most of this information is rather nebulous, but it is about all I can dig up at the present time. If you have any further questions, feel free to write me and I will see what I can do about getting you some answers.

This left me still puzzled. But Eatherly's former wife was able to give me the answer. She wrote:

I can explain his application to Meteorology School at Keesler Field. As you say, he was pretty upset after his application for a regular commission was turned down. About this time the Air Force began "releasing personnel from active duty," and you will recall that thousands were released. Eatherly actually received an order releasing him from active duty. But General Blanchard interceded for him and somehow managed to get him in the Meteorology School. This was positively the only way Eatherly could stay in the Air Force. His going to that school was his desperate, last resort, arranged by General Blanchard. I went with him to Biloxi with misgivings. He had never been a student and, at that point in his life, I did not believe he was capable of studying.

On December 3, 1946, Major Eatherly's Air Force record becomes uncomfortably formal. He is "relieved of duty as a student." Through channels his commanding officer informs the Adjutant General:

. . . this officer is to be separated from the service not as a result of any physical disability.

. . . a decision to reclassify this officer has been reached for the following reason: undesirable habits or traits of character as evidenced by: CHEATING ON WRITTEN CLASS EXAMINATION.

... it is recommended that this officer's resignation be accepted and that he be discharged without specification as to the character thereof. Officer has been informed that such separation is because he has exhibited undesirable habits or traits of character, which do not properly allow recommendation for an honorable discharge, and that he is not entitled to a Certificate of Service or mustering-out pay and will not be granted accrued leave.

The Air Force regarded then—and still regards—an officer's cheating on a written examination as grounds for dismissal. When other men's live can depend on a man's knowledge, that man has no right to cheat and thereby claim he has knowledge which he doesn't have. To his commanding officer Eatherly admitted he cheated; he admitted it to me after I found it in his record. He told me he "wasn't even present at the examination" because he had arranged for another man to take it for him. He had intended to stay in the Air Force until he qualified for a retirement pension. He lost this opportunity.

However, the stern recommendations of his commanding officer were modified in Eatherly's favor. To make him eligible for veteran's benefits and so as not to handicap him in seeking private employment, the Air Force, on January 23, 1947, gave Eatherly a Certificate of Service and an honorable discharge.

Furthermore, under a law which granted officers going on active duty before Pearl Harbor a bonus of $500 a year on leaving active duty, Eatherly received a windfall of about $3000.

Five

ON a third trip to Galveston I questioned Claude Eartherly about the stories that he had emigrated after he left the Air Force and that he had flown for Israel. He insisted he had never told anyone he did this, that the stories were inventions of writers; and he said the stories may have been distortions of an experience he had with Lieutenant Colonel William I. (Wild Bill) Marsalis, USAF, Retired.

Eatherly then told me an amazing story. He said that in January, 1947, while he was waiting to be processed out of the Air Force, he met Colonel Marsalis in the Officers' Club at Keesler Field, Biloxi, Mississippi, and that he accepted a job from Marsalis for which he was to be paid $100,000!

As a result of this first civilian "job," Eatherly delayed any effort to establish a home with his wife. She left Biloxi and returned to her parents' home, and for the next three months Eatherly lived with Colonel Marsalis in hotels in Gulfport, Mississippi, and in New Orleans and Havana.

Colonel Marsalis was born in Mississippi in 1904. After attending Mississippi State University, he joined the old Army Air Corps, trained at Kelly Field, Texas, and from 1925 to 1935 he was one of the wild ones who tried to make America air-conscious by stunts, flying acts, air carnivals and air races. Much of his talk is of days when he and "Chennault" were stunt-flying together, or when he and "Doolittle" dominated some air race. During the Sceond World War part of his service was in the Middle East with General Lewis Brereton, and he is said to have flown 119 combat missions and to have slain every enemy who

70

came within reach of what he calls "mah big Irish hands." In 1962 the Air Force informed me that he was living in Chapala, Mexico, and drawing a $401-a-month Air Force retirement pension.

I wrote to Wild Bill, asking him about his association with Eatherly, and I received this reply on the stationery of the Heidelberg Hotel, Baton Rouge, Lousiana:

22 June 62

DEAR MR. HUIE:

I was unable to answer your letter from Mexico. I'm doing some gold-mining down there, and I had a little cave-in which busted a couple of my ribs, and I came to the Air Force hospital in Tucson for two weeks and then over here to Baton Rouge to try to collect some money before my return to Chapala.

I stopped in Waco but could not locate Claude Eatherly. I first met Claude in 1947 at the Officers' Club at Keesler Field where I had gone to recruit pilots for my invasion of Cuba. He was a thoroughly fine man and an excellent pilot. He in turn helped me get other pilots. The only fear I ever heard Claude mention was that he had had too much radioactivity. (His wife had miscarried twice because of him being radioactive.) You see at that time our plans were to make Cuba the 49th state. I was with Claude constantly for four or five months and he had a lot of remarkable qualities and showed no fear at all.

I am here at the hotel for a few days and will be glad to talk with you.

From conversations with Marsalis and Eatherly, and from court records and newspaper files, I tried to establish the facts about Eatherly's role in this planned Cuban coup. I was assisted by a New Orleans private detective, William H. Gurvich.

In 1946 the Marsalis Construction Company was incorporated in Louisiana with Marsalis as president, Anthony R. St. Philip, of New Orleans, as vice-president, and George W. Rappleyea, of New Orleans, as treasurer. Rappleyea had been vice-president of Higgins Industries, the boat-building firm which became famous during the war for the "Higgins boats" used by the Marines at Tarawa and elsewhere in the Pacific. Marsalis's last Air Force assignment before he retired had been base commander at an Air Force base at Baton Rouge. The Marsalis company opened a hole-in-the-wall office on the New Orleans waterfront at 3410 Magazine Street. Rappleyea later declared that the firm was in "the mahogany business in British Honduras," and that was the story which Eatherly told his wife. But both Marsalis and Eatherly assured me that from the beginning, the firm's sole purpose had been to support a coup in Cuba.

Marsalis told me his operation was "big." He said that in 1946 he flew by way of Pan American Airways to Argentina where he picked up $1,000,000 from "Perón." He said he flew to New York, stopped at the New Yorker Hotel, and "arranged" to change the thousand-dollar bills into smaller bills. He returned to New Orleans and stored the money in a deposit box in the Whitney National Bank. He said he deposited $100,000 of the money in the Gulf National Bank in Gulfport, Mississippi.

Marsalis said he used vacant houses and warehouses in Gulfport as his base. That for months he accumulated guns, ammunition, tanks and landing craft. That he bought tanks from which guns had been cut with blowtorches, then bought the guns and welded them back on the tanks.

"I built my own arsenal there at Gulfport," he said. "I was making my own grenades and bombs, and there was no doubt that we could make Cuba the 49th state if everything went according to plan."

Both Eatherly and Marsalis mentioned prominent Americans they said were involved with them. I can't report these names because I don't know that they were involved and I couldn't prove it if they were.

Eatherly described for me a three-week trip he and Marsalis took to Havana in February, 1947. He said they stayed at the El Presidente Hotel, and when he wasn't renewing wartime acquaintances, they conferred with "revolutionaries." One Cuban they saw seems to have been named Eugenio DeSosa: Eatherly said he was rich and they conferred with him several times at a newspaper office. They also looked over the Havana Yacht Club where Marsalis planned to "bring in the landing craft."

Marsalis told me that, working from a taxicab, he "disarmed half the guns guarding Havana." He said taking Havana would have been easy, he could have done it almost single-handed "with mah big Irish hands and with old Claude and a couple of P-38s over me."

Eatherly told me that when he flew back to New Orleans from Cuba he brought $85,000 in cash. He said he sneaked it through customs in a false-bottom trunk. When I asked Marsalis if Eatherly had done this, he replied: "Well, all that happened, except Eatherly didn't do it."

When Marsalis recruited Eatherly he asked him if he could fly a P-38. Eatherly said he could, and Marsalis explained that Eatherly would command a squadron of P-38s and bomb Havana in advance of the landing, then cover Marsalis and the landing party.

Most Americans will remember the P-38 for its twin fuselages. Costing about $300,000, it was a long-range fighter-bomber suitable for supporting surface attacks. Marsalis said he purchased five P-38s—two in Tulsa, Oklahoma, and three in Downey, California—for $1500 each. These were new planes, just as they had come off the assembly line. Marsalis and Eatherly flew to California on a commercial flight and flew two P-38s back to New Orleans. They stopped at El Paso en route and got drunk in Juarez, Mexico. The third P-38 purchased in California was flown to Louisiana by another pilot, but he was forced to bail out in the swampy region near Shreveport and that plane was lost. The two P-38s purchased at Tulsa were flown to Venice, Florida, and parked near an Air Force strip. The plan was for Eatherly and three other pilots to take off from Venice in darkness, cover the invasion, then return to Venice if Marsalis was delayed in securing a Cuban strip.

With the success of the coup, Eatherly, after being paid $100,-000, was to remain in Cuba with Marsalis. The other pilots, whom Eatherly recruited, were to be paid $50,000 each.

The story reached the newspapers on March 2, 1947 (New Orleans *Times-Picayune*):

Federal agents have uncovered a cache of atomic weapons and deadly ammunition in Gulfport, Mississippi, and charged four men with conspiracy to violate the Firearms Act. Arrested were Major C. R. Eatherly who said he piloted an escort plane in the atomic

bombing of Hiroshima . . . and Marsalis, St. Philip and Rappleyea.
. . . Arms confiscated including Reising Machine guns, aerial bomb
cases, and 6 cases of high explosive powder.

Also seized in Gulfport were two LCTs (landing craft tank) which
were ready to sail. Names of these vessels are the *Libertad* and the
Pepin Rivero. On these LCTs were two 30-ton tanks. Also ordered
seized were four P-38 airplanes.

Rappleyea, former vice-president of Higgins Industries, said the
aircraft were to be used for "the aerial mapping of rivers in Central
America where Marsalis Construction Company has mahogany
operations." He said the two LCTs were bound for British Honduras, and that the arms were to be used for "hunting in South
America."

Also seized were five half-tracks and five three-ton trucks.

The men arrested furnished $5000 bonds and were freed.

Marsalis said: "Somebody is going to get in trouble about this."

March 5, 1947 (*Times-Picayune*):

Two railroad flat cars arrived in Gulfport, Mississippi, today with
four more former armored gun carriers consigned to Marsalis Construction Company. Point of origin was an Army installation in
Texarkana.

Two P-38 airplanes, property of Marsalis Construction Company,
were seized today by customs agents at an airfield in Venice, Florida.
Seizure was made to prevent "an attempt to export military equipment without a license."

March 13, 1947 (*Times-Picayune*):

Federal District Judge Wayne G. Borah today signed an order giving
customs agents indefinite custody of two airplanes, property of
Marsalis Construction Company, at a New Orleans airport. It was
claimed these aircraft were to be exported in violation of Federal
law. The planes were seized because they are designed, adapted and
intended for aerial combat.

March 31, 1948—a year later (AP, *Times-Picayune*):

Three defendants . . . Marsalis, St. Philip and Rappleyea . . .
pleaded guilty in Federal Court in Biloxi, Mississippi, today to

74

"conspiracy to ship arms and ammunition illegally to British Honduras." Each was sentenced to a year and a day. Each was given a five-year suspended sentence on charges of possessing unregistered firearms.

April 24, 1948 (AP, *Times-Picayune*):

Marsalis, St. Philip and Rappleyea arrived at the Federal Correctional Institution at Texarkana, Texas, to start serving sentences. They arrived in the custody of a U. S. deputy marshal.

For two months after the arrest, Eatherly and Marsalis were together in New Orleans. Eatherly escaped prosecution by not having been an officer of the corporation which owned the arms. And since there was no trial and therefore no public record, many of the facts of this conspiracy remain obscured or "not publishable." Who really put up the money? Exactly what was planned? Who arranged for Marsalis to buy new P-38s at $1500 each?

At Biloxi on March 31, 1948, the federal court trial of Marsalis, St. Philip and Rappleyea was in progress and the jury was being impaneled when the plea of guilty was made and accepted. This plea of guilty prevented others from being identified.

That the conspiracy was directed against Cuba was not publicly revealed until September 8, 1948, and how it was revealed is shown in these news dispatches (*Times-Picayune*):

An American aviator was asked to bomb Havana, Cuba, during 1947 according to a deposition made public in Federal District Court in New Orleans today. The statement of Lester R. Zollars, former pilot for Marsalis Construction Company, was taken in Houston, Texas. . . . The flier said, "Major Claude Eatherly propositioned Mr. Flowers (another pilot) and myself, to see if we would like to make money on the side, and when we argued with him, he took us outside the office and said although he wasn't supposed to tell us yet, that they intended to drop bombs on Havana, Cuba."

September 9, 1948:

Federal District Judge Wayne Borah signed an order of forfeiture of aircraft in New Orleans today. During course of hearing on the forfeiture, William Flowers, who had been hired as a pilot by Rappleyea, said that a Major Claude Eatherly, Chief Pilot for Marsalis Construction Company, asked him and another pilot how they "felt" about bombing Havana, Cuba. . . . Eatherly explained to the pilots that the planes were to take off from Venice, Florida, during the night, bomb the Cuban capital, and return at night.

Both Zollars and Flowers professed to have been shocked by the "cold-blooded" manner in which Eatherly explained to them how, under his command, they were to bomb "the peaceful city of Havana."

After learning all I could about this Cuban affair, I had a final conversation with Colonel Marsalis.

"Just remember this," the colonel said. "In anything you write about Claude Eatherly remember that he was one of the finest guys I ever met. A real, regular guy. Nothing bothered him. The only time I ever saw him scared was one night I had a batch of grenades in the back of the car and he thought I was driving too fast over a bumpy road."

"He wanted you to slow down, did he?"

"Yeah, he sure did." The colonel laughed. "I laughed like hell at him and it sort of got his goat. And he was loyal to me. It was Eatherly who found out that Rappleyea was going to have me shot in Cuba 'accidentally' after the coup. So I fixed it up to dispose of Rappleyea when he reached Cuba."

"Colonel," I said, "I notice that the newspapers identified Eatherly as having been at Hiroshima. One imaginative reporter decided that because of Eatherly you must have had 'atomic' weapons in your cache. Did Eatherly ever talk to you about his experience at Hiroshima?"

"No, he never talked about it," Colonel Marsalis answered. "Except he told me he was there. He was the advance scout, and after the drop he flew back through the mushroom surveying results. He did the same job at Nagasaki."

"And that's how he had become radioactive—from flying through those bomb clouds?"

"Yeah. That's what he said. He said he thought he might have had too much."

As a final question I asked Colonel Marsalis how much Eatherly was paid, either by himself or by Rappleyea.

"I couldn't have paid him anything," the colonel replied. "The Federals tied up all my money. I got out with forty thousand dollars which the Federals didn't find on me because I was carrying it in a paper sack I picked up at a grocery store. I had some potatoes on top of the money and the Feds forgot to look under the potatoes. But I used all that in the legal fight. Claude would have been fixed for life if we had ever got to Cuba. But he got nothing—except what I spent on him, and that was a lot, taking him with me to Cuba and around, and some little expense money was doled out to him by Rappleyea."

When I was concluding my conversation with Eatherly about this adventure with Marsalis, I questioned him as to how much he was paid.

"Tell me, Claude," I said, "carefully and exactly, how much money you got out of Marsalis and Rappleyea?"

"I got a thousand dollars a month," he said, "and I got out with twenty-seven thousand dollars in cash."

"Did you pay tax on the twenty-seven thousand? Will I find it on your return?"

"No. I paid tax on the thousand a month. But not on the twenty-seven thousand."

"What did you do with the twenty-seven thousand dollars?"

"We used it, me and my wife, in living. We bought a house in Houston . . . in Bellaire . . . at 4601 Holt Street."

"How much did you pay for the house?"

"Twelve thousand."

I changed the subject, and a few minutes later I asked him quickly: "Did you buy that house with a GI loan?"

He nodded.

"A hundred-per-cent loan? You paid only the closing costs? Less than two hundred dollars?"

He nodded again.

"All right, Claude," I said. "Let's look at what you are telling me. You tell me that you want to be used by your pacifist friends. What makes you useful to those friends is the statement that you *repented the crime* of Hiroshima. Now did you really repent? Almost two years after Hiroshima you were capable of planning to bomb the peaceful people of Havana for no more than the dream of having a hundred thousand dollars in your hand. That's correct, isn't it?"

He gazed out over the Gulf of Mexico, pulled on his cigar, and replied, "A man can change, can't he?"

"Sure," I said, "a man can change. Saul of Tarsus changed. People have written that you began changing within hours after Hiroshima. The London *Times* quotes you as saying: 'I made a dedication that day of August 6, 1945, that I would dedicate my life to destroy the causes of war and the banishment of all nuclear weapons.' Your Cuban experience indicates that you may not have changed that early. What I'm looking for is evidence that you changed later—when and why you changed."

"Well, I changed," he insisted.

"Did you?" I asked. "Look at your behavior now. You have this moment told me you got twenty-seven thousand dollars out of the Cuba adventure. You told your crew members that in Louisville in 1958. It isn't true. How can a man repent what he regards as one crime and still keep insisting falsely that he got paid twenty-seven thousand dollars for a later crime?"

He didn't answer, and I waited for what may have been two or three minutes for him to admit he was lying about the $27,-000. He had admitted other lies; why was he unable to admit this one? He didn't insist it was true, but he seemingly could not bring himself to admit it wasn't true.

I tried to make retraction easier for him by remarking, "Many men exaggerate war experiences, Claude. Many men in your position would have begun telling people that they saw the blast at Hiroshima, or that they assessed the damage. Normally you could have lived your life making your role at Hiroshima more important each year and nobody would have cared. But Hiroshima was something different: it wasn't another air battle like Schweinfurt or Ploesti. It was a deliberate demonstration of terror. The men who ordered it were well-intentioned men who thought they were acting in the name of humanity. They thought they were saving lives by ending a war. Other men now call Hiroshima a crime, a crime to be equated with Auschwitz. And your pacifist friends have set you up as a man of superior morality. You say you have repented and that you are trying to help good people build a better world. So lies

78

about getting money for promising to kill people in 1947 are a luxury you can't afford. So tell me again, did you or did you not receive twenty-seven thousand dollars for promising to bomb Havana, Cuba, in 1947?"

He opened his mouth two or three times, trying to answer, then he said slowly, "I changed. I repented. You can't prove I didn't."

"Why do you assume I want to prove you didn't?" I said. "I had rather prove you did. I'm not here to make a case against you. You invited me here, remember? You asked me to investigate you and write about you. You agreed to cooperate with me in finding the truth. Now I'm asking you how you can repent Hiroshima and still keep insisting falsely that, long after Hiroshima, you were paid twenty-seven thousand dollars for agreeing to bomb Havana."

He couldn't bring himself to say anything more than "I changed. I repented."

From this Cuban incident I concluded that two years after Hiroshima, Eatherly had neither voiced nor evidenced any atomic guilt feelings. On his arrest by federal agents he told newspapermen the approximate truth about his role at Hiroshima. But to Marsalis he had added that he had "flown back through the bomb cloud"—an error which was to be repeated by *Newsweek* ten years later.

In 1947 Eatherly was in no position to accuse the United States of having committed a crime at Hiroshima. The United States had just arrested him for complicity in a conspiracy against the people of Cuba.

I couldn't understand then why Eatherly kept insisting that he was paid $27,000 by Marsalis. Later I found out why.

Six

FOR Eatherly's further experiences as a civilan employee, my sources are Eatherly; his wife at the time; his brother, Joe Eatherly; some of his employers; and various records which I will specify.

Claude Eatherly was employed in Houston—with high hopes —on July 28, 1947, by Texaco. Starting salary: $70 a week. Promotion possibilities: unlimited. Substantial pension guaranteed at sixty-five.

Texaco hired Eatherly to be a "salesman of petroleum products." He had to "train" for one year, but then he could win his first promotion. He could be given a company car and, dressed in a business suit, could be a "salesman supervising a number of filling stations." He could then become a county manager, district manager—his sky was limited only by his resourcefulness and perseverance. To improve his "executive and administrative possibilities," he could go to school under the GI bill. His government would pay him while he improved himself. So he enrolled for night courses in the Southwest School of Law in Houston.

The rub was that one year of "training." During that period with Texaco, Major Eatherly had to make the classic comedown in America—the one the jokes are all about. He had to come down from the glamorous Air Force major to the "filling station attendant." The man in the coveralls at the big company station who is learning to punch a clock, to meet the public, to clean windshields and check tires, to sell petroleum products "from the ground up."

He survived the training period. In fact, that may have been the best period of his life. He worked long hours—hard, dirty work. He had some minor troubles: he got drunk a few times and didn't punch the clock. But he made it. The people he worked with liked him just as his crew members had liked him. He knew how to get along. At the end of the period he won his promotion—his white collar and his company car. He was on his way.

His wife had tried to help him. Though they had been married four years, they had never lived together for any length of time. Their longest period together had been at Roswell, with shorter periods at Tucson, Wendover and Biloxi. She had lived with her parents. When he went to work for Texaco, she happily brought their child and moved in with him. Not into an apartment. After Eatherly's adventure with Marsalis they couldn't afford an apartment. At her insistence they moved into a single room because she wanted to live within his income.

Eatherly had told his wife that he had "quit" the Air Force because he was "sick of it." She didn't know differently until I showed her the record in 1962. He had also told her that the Marsalis Construction Company was in the "mahogany business" and that the government's charges had been false. Despite her doubts, she struggled to help him. His regular hours at the filling station helped her help him. Since she knew when he was supposed to go to work and when he got off, she tried to help him avoid the whiskey and poker games. At the end of his "coverall" year they celebrated his promotion by moving into a modest apartment at 3934 Caldwell Street, Houston.

"I remember clearly," his wife told me, "that about this time he and I read *Hiroshima,* the story about all the suffering the bomb caused. He was very interested. He told me he was sorry for the victims but that the bomb should have been dropped because it saved many more lives, both American and Japanese, than it cost."

I showed his wife the published stories in which she is said to have reported that he suffered from nightmares during this period—that he screamed in the darkness "Bail out!" and "Save the children!" She told me that she had never made any such statement; that not once in her life with Eatherly had she heard him yell "Bail out" or "Save the children"; that not once had he ever expressed to her, or evidenced in any manner in her presence, any emotional reaction, including regret or anxiety, over his experience at Hiroshima.

In addition to his wife's help, Claude Eatherly had the help and loyalty of his brothers and sisters. His older brother, James, lived in Houston at that time. James Eatherly is a friendly, capable, and well-educated man with a master's degree; and everyone I talked with told me "James was right there whenever Claude needed him." Claude's other brother, Joe, living in Van Alstyne, was equally loyal. His two sisters wrote him encouraging letters, inviting him to visit them.

He enjoyed continuing government help. He quickly gave up the law school classes, but while he and his wife were living at the Caldwell Street apartment they selected their new home in Bellaire, Houston—the house at 4601 Holt Street. The house had not been built because the area was only then being cleared, but it was to be a "model veterans community" with 100 percent government-guaranteed, thirty-year financing at 4 percent interest. From the builder's plans Eatherly and his wife selected a corner lot, and they were to pay "nothing down," only a few dollars in "closing costs."

Claude Eatherly had only to persevere to establish himself as a suburban husband, father, and wage-earning citizen.

In 1948 he made his first effort to obtain "service-connected disability compensation."

At the regional office of the Veterans Administration, Houston, Texas, he filed a claim with the Veterans Administration asserting that he had been damaged physically by radiation poison; that his flying through the atomic cloud at Bikini had deformed some of his spermatazoa; that this had resulted in a miscarriage for his wife; and that he may have been rendered incapable of siring normal children.

Regarding this, here is his wife's written statement to me:

In 1947, after my husband, Claude Eatherly, began working for Texaco, I became pregnant. I started having trouble immediately.

82

On December 4, 1947, I began hemorrhaging badly, and my doctor moved me to Herman Hospital. I miscarried, and my doctor told me the fetus was not normal. Since I had read of and been told of my husband's flight through the atomic cloud at Bikini, I asked the doctor if he believed radiation could have had any damaging effects on my husband. The doctor advised a sperm test which revealed that my husband had an unusually large number of abnormal sperm. On the basis of this finding, to my surprise and without my approval or consent, Claude Eatherly filed a claim with the Veterans Administration.

This claim was considered for a year, then denied by the Veterans Administration. In opposing the claim, VA doctors contended that men who had been exposed to radiation at Hiroshima, Nagasaki and Bikini were siring normal children; and that no evidence existed of any physical damage to any American from any atomic explosion. Before the claim was finally denied, Eatherly's wife had borne a normal child, their second; and thereafter she had no more miscarriages, and in 1953 she bore another normal child.

In 1962 the Veterans Administration notified me that Claude Eatherly is unique in having filed claims against the United States for physical or mental disability growing out of "atomic operations." Of all the men involved in all the atomic operations—Hiroshima, Nagasaki, Bikini, and other tests—Eatherly alone has claimed physical or mental damage. No evidence exists that any American has suffered any form of disability as a result of "atomic experience." As for spermatazoa deformity, all evidence is to the contrary. The men involved in atomic operations have sired an unusually large number of healthy children. The man with the most atomic experience, Brigadier General Charles Sweeney, who piloted the blast-gauge plane at Hiroshima and whose B-29 dropped the bomb at Nagasaki, has sired eight robust children since Nagasaki.

Eatherly stands alone in claiming disability as the result of any atomic experience.

In 1949, suddenly, for no apparent reason, Claude Eatherly began drinking immoderately and quarreling with his superiors. He quit his job at Texaco on March 25, 1949.

He told me he quit because he was tired of taking orders. He and another salesman planned to become partners in an oil business. All they needed was for Eatherly's wife to borrow $2000 from her father.

"Well," his wife told me, "that created a difficult situation. My father had accumulated what little he had by thrift and hard work as an Italian-American storekeeper. He and Claude Eatherly were not men who could ever like one another. My father thought Claude was selfish and reckless, and he had never foreseen anything but disaster for us. But I wanted Claude to have his chance to make it on his own. So I asked my father, for my sake, to lend Claude the money. My father was certain the money would be wasted, but he made the loan. And his judgment proved horribly correct. The proposed business partnership collapsed before it started when Claude quarreled with his partner. Claude began drinking steadily, staying out all hours, and playing poker. The money disappeared, and for the first time Claude began subjecting himself and me and his brothers to the nightmare of 'hot' checks."

These were not forged checks. They bore Eatherly's signature and were drawn on nonexistent funds. They didn't result in arrest because his brothers helped him make them good.

Eatherly then obtained a second job—with Ada Oil Company. He began work on August 30, 1949. He was still a "salesman to filling stations." But now he had to furnish his own car, so he bought, not an inexpensive car, but an expensive one. He worked with some success for five months, then alarmed his wife by suddenly appearing one day and announcing that they were moving at once into a more expensive apartment: Apartment No. 1, 6903 Academy Street, Houston.

"This move was folly," his wife told me. "The apartment was much too expensive and not even suited to our needs. But an even stronger reason for our not moving was that our house on Holt Street was under construction, would soon be finished, so we needed to stay where we were and move only once instead of twice. I had this small baby; Claude had been staying out all hours; I never knew where to find him; I often prepared dinner for him and he didn't appear or telephone. But now he had quarreled with our landlord, so without even notifying me he

84

had rented the larger apartment, ordered the moving van, and then came to order me to move at once."

They moved into the new apartment on February 10, 1950.

The suicide attempt, about which much has been written both in the United States and abroad, occurred ten days after Eatherly and his wife moved into the Academy Street apartment.

On the evening of Monday, February 20th, his wife told me that she prepared his dinner but he didn't come home for it. Nor did he telephone. When he reached home a little after 9 P.M., there was a scene between him and his wife.

"I tried to bring him to his senses," she said. "We quarreled about money, discipline, and our responsibility to a small baby and to a six-year-old child just starting to school. During the quarrel he went into the bathroom, and after a while he came out and said he wouldn't be around to bother me any longer since he had taken sleeping pills. I didn't think he was telling the truth, but then he began to get scared and asked me to call the doctor. I called an ambulance and Dr. E. T. Clark."

This case at Herman Hospital, Houston, Texas, is No. 50-3999. The record shows that Claude R. Eatherly was admitted to that hospital at 11:05 P.M., February 20, 1950. He was placed in Room 662-E; and at 10:45 A.M., February 21, 1950, less than twelve hours after he was admitted, he was dismissed.

Years ago, when I was a young police reporter just out of the University of Alabama, I began covering sleeping pill suicide attempts. So I have long been familiar with state laws, hospital practices, police practices, and what to look for. Texas law requires that if in the opinion of the physician suicide has been attempted, the police must be notified and the police must file a report. If there is any police report on Claude Eatherly's alleged suicide attempt, neither I nor an FBI-trained private detective could find it.

So while Eatherly may have attempted suicide, and whatever he did may be evidence of mental illness, until a police report is found there is no legal evidence that he ever attempted suicide.

Back in his apartment, Eatherly talked at length about his

85

troubles and about why he had attempted suicide. He talked with his wife, with his brother James, and with James's wife. He told them something they had not suspected: that he was a Benzedrine addict, and he said all his troubles stemmed from this habit.

His wife told me he said: "I started taking Benzedrine pills when I was overseas. I had to take them to keep awake during those long bomb runs up to Japan."

All he needed, he said, was to be hospitalized for a few days —just a little help to get off Benzedrine—and he would be all right. He'd work; he'd support his family; he'd live within his income; he'd keep regular hours; and he'd write no more bad checks.

That same afternoon James Eatherly and Claude Eatherly's wife went to the regional office of the Veterans Administration at Houston and asked the VA to admit him to the Waco hospital on an emergency basis. The VA agreed—with what seems to have been unusual rapidity. The VA decision to admit him was conveyed to his wife on the morning of February 23, 1950; and that afternoon she, James Eatherly and Claude Eatherly drove the 188 miles to the Waco hospital.

Claude Eatherly entered the Admitting Ward at the Waco hospital at 5:15 P.M., February 23, 1950. James Eatherly and Claude Eatherly's wife returned to Houston that evening.

This sequence of events meant that during February, 1950, Claude Eatherly, more than during any previous period in his life, talked seriously about himself and his "problem." He talked to his wife and brother in his apartment. He talked with them during the ride to Waco.

"Certainly he talked about remorse," his wife told me. "Over and over he said he was sorry for the way he had treated his children, his brothers and me. He said he was ashamed of staying out at night and losing his money and not looking after his family. But he certainly didn't tell us that he felt guilty or remorseful or even disturbed over anything that he had done during the Second World War."

That was four and a half years after the bomb fell.

Seven

WACO, Texas, is a city of eighty-five thousand, lying ninety-four miles southwest of Dallas. Its Veterans Hospital, first opened in 1931, has a total of 88 buildings standing on 340 elevated, terraced and tended acres. Sixteen of these buildings are four-story, red brick "major" buildings, of which twelve are "ward buildings." There are roughly two thousand patients, all former servicemen. There are 1240 employees, including twenty full-time psychiatrists. The hospital is headed by a physician-administrator, Dr. George T. McMahan, who happens also to have been born in Van Alstyne, Texas, and therefore "knows all the Eatherlys."

The United States would have to spend $25,000,000 to replace this hospital, and each year the hospital and its employees spend $8,000,000 in Waco. Most of the employees own their own homes. They belong to clubs, play golf or bowl, and send their children to college. Going to college is easy because Waco's other major institution is Baylor University.

The hospital is well managed, well financed, adequately staffed. It is quiet, not noisy. There is no audible hysteria, no straitjackets, no padded cells. About half the patients are "permanents," the other half "temporaries." There are one thousand new admissions each year and a constant waiting list of at least four hundred. Most of the "temporaries" have been diagnosed as "NPs" (neuropsychiatric). They draw from 10 percent to 100 percent compensation and spend much of their time at home, returning to the hospital periodically. The "permanents" also draw compensation.

About eighteen hundred of these patients are "on open

wards." They are not locked in; they have the privilege of the grounds. Anyone can elope at will. Every patient dresses as he does at home; there are no uniforms. Less then 10 percent of the patients are "on" the hospital's single "closed ward." (No patient is ever "in" a ward in a mental hospital: he is "on" a ward. And no patient ever runs away without permission: he "elopes.") This closed ward is an entire building—Building 10, a spacious, modern building with a gymnasium, an indoor swimming pool, and an outdoor exercise area the size of a football field. This building is always locked; the entrances are tended; the windows are barred; the men shave with locked safety razors; and the outdoor exercise area is surrounded by a chain link fence with barbed wire on top. But even in this closed ward there is no hysteria, no patient is "under restraint," because the men are "on" tranquilizers.

None of the patients who come to this hospital was born with any recognizable physical or mental defect. All of them passed rigid examinations to enter the armed services. (One eighth of all men drafted for service in the United States are rejected "for reasons other than physical.") Most of them served without injury. Most of them left the services claiming "no physical or mental disability whatever." Sometimes after their discharge they "began having difficulty functioning." They began drinking chronically, they forged checks, they stole, they wouldn't work, they "acted foolish," they became "overly anxious or nervous," or they "got in trouble with the law," and they came to a VA regional office claiming that their "trouble" was "service-connected" and they therefore deserved VA hospitalization and compensation. The VA regional office, after some investigation, sent them to an "NP hospital" for diagnosis and possible treatment.

The Waco hospital is one of thirty-nine such "essentially psychiatric" institutions maintained by the VA. In these hospitals are 59,335 "psychiatric beds."

Contrary to the understanding abroad, the "VA" in the United States is not the "military." It is a proud and separate bureaucracy—an immense hive operated by doctors and social workers . . . layer-on-layer of dedicated bureaucrats—and it

88

spends more billions each year than most national governments spend.

Most of the patients in these NP hospitals sought to get in; and their relatives "worked" to get them in. Getting men into these hospitals and "winning" compensation for them by "establishing service-connected mental disability" is big business. Enormous amounts of energy and ingenuity are devoted to it. Every Member of Congress spends much of his time "using political influence" to help constituents "get somebody into a VA NP hospital"; then, to "get a favorable diagnosis," *favorable* meaning one which allows compensation; then, over the years, to help get this compensation steadily increased. Local courts and police assist this "getting in" effort because it is a way to shift a community liability to the federal government.

All of which means that a VA mental hospital is an upside-down institution. You must reverse your thinking to comprehend it.

When a patient goes to a private hospital, he hopes the doctors will find nothing seriously wrong. But when a veteran goes to a VA regional office and claims "service-connected NP difficulty"—and when he is then sent to a VA mental hospital for diagnosis—the complaining veteran hopes the doctors can find at least a neurosis, preferably a psychosis.

In a private hospital the patient hopes to get better: he even hopes to be cured. But for an NP veteran cure can mean loss of compensation; and when the psychiatrists decide that his "disturbance has become more severe," his compensation may be raised from, say 50 percent disability to 80 percent.

Most every veteran who induces a VA regional office to send him to an NP hospital for diagnosis hopes first to "get service-connected." This means he hopes to establish that his disorder began while he was in the service, or manifested itself soon after he left the service. He needs to be able to show that he was treated for something while in service or soon after. There is a maze of laws about his having to claim something within a year, or two years, after he left the service. If he has claimed nothing, he needs to be able to point to some mishap or ordeal while he was in service.

The psychiatrists, if they so desire, can evade almost any law or restriction, because they can decide that military service in itself was traumatic for some particular veteran. So in this immense bureaucracy there is immense opportunity for psychiatrists to do most anything.

The "knockout diagnoses" are "no nervous or mental disease" and "psychopathic personality." If a claimant gets one of these diagnoses, he is entitled neither to hospitalization nor compensation. Moreover, he is culpable, and if he breaks a law he goes to jail.

Once a veteran gets past these knockout diagnoses, he hopes to obtain a profitable diagnosis. Nervousness may get him only 10 percent compensation. Anxiety may get him only 50 percent, and by law can never get him more than 80 percent. (Congress has passed laws restricting the amount of compensation which can be paid for the less serious disorders.) But schizophrenia can give a veteran 100 percent; and with a diagnosis of schizophrenia a veteran may also be allowed to leave the hospital, perhaps return periodically for checkups, and draw maximum compensation for life.

This creates a condition which may in itself be conducive to madness. It gives the psychiatrists the power of the purse over every NP claimant and his dependents. And since the psychiatrists often argue among themselves, and always concede the "inexactness" of their "science," situations sometime become absurd.

Often one psychiatrist, controlling one ward, denies a patient a diagnosis which allows a pension. Then political pressure is applied to move the patient to another ward and another psychiatrist. The second psychiatrist disagrees with the first and gives the patient the favorable diagnosis. By law there are layers and layers of "boards" to consider such disagreements, but the VA insists that "all doubt must be resolved in favor of the veteran."

Dr. Hervey Cleckley, who had years of experience in a VA hospital before becoming Professor of Psychiatry and Neurology at the University of Georgia Medical College, writes in his book *The Mask of Sanity:*

Since those veterans who are diagnosed as psychopaths do not draw compensation, being considered by law responsible for their own maladjustment, the general policy in VA hospitals is not to make a diagnosis of psychopath unless the condition is inescapable. . . . The VA insists that the diagnosis of psychopath be made only when the possibility of other psychiatric conditions for which compensation is paid is thoroughly ruled out.

. . . As everyone who deals with such questions knows, it is often extremely difficult to rule out neurasthenia, hysteria, psychasthenia, and post-traumatic neuroses when these conditions are claimed by patients eager for pension money. . . . And when one takes in consideration that the psychopath is almost invariably just the sort of person who will bend his efforts to get everything possible from the government, or from any other source, and that he is entirely unscrupulous and often very clever in doing so, the difficulty will be still further appreciated.

. . . Many of the patients in VA hospitals who finally "win" diagnoses which qualify them for pensions, are psychopaths and nothing more. They are given the profitable diagnoses because the psychiatrists know that a true diagnosis of psychopath would bring protests and calls for further examination, not to speak of the strong political pressure which is sometimes exerted.

A reporter can only report that in the United States in 1962, compensation-seeking is a determined business among many veterans of military service. Some are worthy of it, others are not.

Before focusing on Eatherly and his experience in the VA mental labyrinth, I must make one further explanation.

In 1962, when Eatherly gave me his letters to Dr. McMahan and the VA general counsel, I went first to the Waco hospital. I urged Dr. McMahan to make full disclosure in the Eatherly Case. I urged him to allow me, as Eatherly's agent, to examine all medical records, to discuss the case with every VA psychiatrist who had examined or treated Eatherly, and to question every nursing assistant who had cared for him. As I anticipated, Dr. McMahan referred me to Washington for decision.

I'm familiar with VA headquarters in Washington. I have been there on other cases, including the Slovik case. The information officer, Frank R. Hood, is a former reporter for the Kansas City *Star*. The chief medical director is Dr. William S. Middleton, former dean of the University of Wisconsin Medical School. The general counsel is Cyril F. Brickfield, an expert on laws applicable to veterans' affairs.*

All three of these men heard me out. The issue was legality: Congress has passed many laws restricting veterans information. I spent an entire afternoon with six VA executives. I told them I suspected that VA representatives had made "mistakes" in this case, and to cover these mistakes would be unwise. I pointed out that when an American citizen is adjudged "legally insane" a guardian usually is appointed for him. No guardian has ever been appointed for Eatherly. I held this to be *prima facie* evidence that Eatherly is not adjudged "legally insane."

"Eatherly is a free man," I said. "You are paying his compensation directly to him. A court in 1961 held him competent to manage his own affairs. The VA has held him competent. Therefore he has the right to examine his medical records; and if so, he has the further right to appoint an agent to examine his records. I claim that right; and if his letter is not sufficient, I'll either have him execute a power of attorney, or I'll bring him here and take him to Waco and let him sit with me while I examine his records and question your psychiatrists and nurses."

Dr. Middleton and Mr. Brickfield maintained that "as far as the VA is concerned, Eatherly *is* incompetent." Therefore, under the law, Eatherly himself has no right to examine his medical record, or to question his psychiatrists. So he has no right to make anyone his agent: his signature on a power of attorney is worthless. In effect this means that *no one* outside the VA can have the legal right to examine Eatherly's long medical record with the VA.

I consider this sort of secrecy dangerous, improper in the United States, and I told them so. But Dr. Middleton and Mr. Brickfield insisted that the law gave them no other course. Dr. Middleton invited me to visit the Waco hospital, to inspect it from basement to attic, and to talk at length with Dr. McMa-

---

* These are the positions held by Dr. Middleton and Mr. Brickfield in 1962.

han. But only with Dr. McMahan, and *not* about the medical record.

After losing this argument in Washington, I returned to Waco. I enlisted the help of a local reporter, Ray Bell, who had covered the Eatherly Case for five years. I obtained the cooperation of the courts and the police. Ray Bell and I obtained transcripts and tape recordings of VA psychiatrists testifying in court proceedings involving Eatherly. We unearthed letters from VA psychiatrists to members of Eatherly's family. I questioned Claude Eatherly as to what psychiatrists had told him, and I used his answers as leads.

Most important, I sought information from persons either formerly or presently employed at the hospital. I had to communicate with these people away from the hospital, either at their homes or elsewhere, and I had to protect them in some manner.

The VA decision did not prevent my obtaining most of the pertinent information about Eatherly. The decision did, however, force me to employ a device which is abhorrent to me. To this point I have named the source of whatever I have reported. But from this point I must resort, in a few cases, to quoting only the "informed source."

Eight

ON his first visit to the Waco hospital Claude Eatherly spent five weeks. He was admitted on February 23, discharged on March 29, 1950. Like all ex-servicemen in his position, he had been sent to the hospital by a VA regional office for the purpose of obtaining answers to questions about him. The psychiatrists, after examination, were supposed to supply the answers. The first questions were: was Claude Eatherly mentally ill? Or was he suffering from "no nervous or mental disease"? A yes to the first question entitled him to hospitalization, treatment, and possible compensation. A no to the first question and a yes to the second would "knock him out," deny him the right to VA hospitalization and to consideration for compensation.

The psychiatrists noted that he had experienced difficulty in functioning in private life, that he had proved partially inadequate, that he was frustrated, that his ego was bruised and weakened, that he was anxious and afraid, that he was unable to consider others because he was preoccupied with his own problems, and that he had tended to withdraw before what seemed to him a difficult life situation. They further noted that he had bewildered, embarrassed and burdened his relatives, that he knew this, and that this knowledge may have caused him to regress further and adopt a less than hopeful attitude.

Was he only partially impaired by anxiety? If so, was he suffering from anxiety neurosis—a relatively simple disorder which might be relieved by psychotherapy, by talking with him, helping restore his self-esteem, helping him gain confidence by gaining insight into his condition? Would he then be able to face his life situation and function at a fairly high level?

Or was he seriously impaired by anxiety? Perhaps to the extent of a psychosis like schizophrenia, which means extreme withdrawal from a life situation, a loss of contact with reality, living in a dream world, having delusions, obsessions or hallucinations?

Along with the questions of mental illness, the psychiatrists had to weigh the related question of psychopathy—conscience . . . whether he cared or not. A *psychopath* is "an unstable, unreliable person, abnormally deficient in the sense of right and wrong, although of normal intelligence and in contact with reality." * Some early psychiatrists called psychopaths "moral imbeciles." Most private psychiatrists will not accept a psychopath as a patient because they don't think they can help him. The VA hospitals are supposed to reject the psychopath for the same reason. But as I have stated, many psychopaths find their way to VA hospitals—one in every four applicants may be a psychopath—and I have cited Dr. Cleckley's report on the problem. Here are further remarks from Dr. Cleckley's book *The Mask of Sanity:*

. . . The psychopath shows a striking inability to follow any sort of life plan consistently.

. . . He does not maintain an effort toward any far goal at all . . . on the contrary he seems to go out of his way to make a failure of life. . . . It seems impossible for any devoted relative to place him in any position where he will not succeed in failing.

. . . The psychopath's sexual activities are consistently limited to literal physical contact and are free of the enormous emotional concomitants that make adult love relations a source of human strength. . . . What the psychopath feels for the casual pick-up, or for his wife, is not anything that can bring out loyalty or influence his activities toward a constructive plan.

. . . Despite his pattern of life-negation, the psychopath will seldom take the final determining step of literal suicide. . . . He may make many bogus attempts, sometimes with remarkable cleverness, premeditation and histrionics.

. . . The psychopath who causes his parents hardship and humiliation by forging checks, and causes his wife anguish by sordid relations with picked-up women, may, in the community, gain a con-

* From *Mental Illness, A Guide for the Family,* by Edith M. Stern. Published by The National Association for Mental Health, Inc.

95

siderable reputation for being considerate, responsive and obliging. He may lend money readily; and he may appear inordinately kind to orphans while neglecting his own children.

Did the VA psychiatrists find Claude Eatherly to be suffering from "no nervous or mental disease?" Did they find him to be a psychopath? They obviously did not, because had they answered yes to either question, he would have been denied the right to hospitalization in a VA mental hospital. He "won" this right to hospitalization, so he was found to be "mentally ill," and his illness was diagnosed as "anxiety reaction." This meant he was not found to be seriously ill; he was not psychotic, which means he was not insane; he was not obsessed, deluded or hallucinated; he was a man said to be "only partially impaired by anxiety neurosis." He was treated with "confinement" which is said to "give a man temporary relief from the responsibilities of his life situation," and with psychotherapy, during which he was said to have been "in good contact" and to have evidenced "excellent insight into the nature of his problem." On release he and his wife were assured: "He has now received all the benefits which this hospital presently can give him." The prognosis: "He should be able to function at a moderately high level."

How did Eatherly behave while he was at the hospital? Under what conditions did he live?

During his entire five weeks he stayed on the Admission Ward, which is the hospital's Building 90, and he enjoyed "grounds privileges with occasional evenings in town with an attendant."

A veteran nursing assistant told me in 1962: "Sure, I remember the first time he came here. I used to do a little boxing in the Navy, and during his first visit here he worked out every day in the gym. He liked to punch the bags, and the doctors like for new admissions to punch the bags: it relieves hostility. I gave him a few tips on how to punch the bags, so we became friends. He liked to go to boxing matches . . . he had the dough to buy tickets for us . . . so I remember taking him with me a time or two to see the matches. I even let him buy us a beer or so. He has never been an alcoholic; he's not a compulsive drinker; he just drinks when he wants to drink. He's good company . . . smart as a briar."

"Do you recall any other characteristics?" I asked. "Any likes or dislikes? Did he act *crazy* in any way?"

The nursing assistant shook his head. "If you want to understand the Major," he said, "remember this. Some men are mentally sick and they act sick. Others may be mentally sick but they don't act sick. If the Major is sick . . . and the doctors say he is . . . he is one of those who never acts sick in confinement. He has been in and out of here for years, but nobody has ever seen him do anything crazy or heard him say anything crazy. As for what he likes: well, he likes his sack time. He likes to sleep till noon. . . . He's the soundest sleeper I ever saw. He learned that lying in the sack in the Air Force. And he has always liked Dutch Masters cigars. He has always paid some attendant to get them for him when he has been here."

What was done about compensation on this first visit? Did Eatherly file a claim in 1950? If so, was it granted?

Eatherly insisted to me in 1962 that a claim for compensation is "automatically filed when you go to the hospital." In this he is partially correct. The VA is not supposed to solicit claims, but persons are available at every hospital to advise veterans how to file claims. Similar advisers are available at all VA regional offices. Moreover, these regional offices have social workers who maintain contact with all "probem" veterans, and these social workers are not noted for discouraging the filing of claims. So it is safe to conclude that few veterans who are accepted as patients at VA mental hospitals fail to file a claim of some sort.

One doctor told me with a smile that Eatherly's first effort at the hospital was to try to reinstate his claim for physical disability suffered at Bikini.

"He was still talking about his spermatozoa," the doctor said. "I gently suggested to him that at an NP hospital he perhaps might fare better if he forgot physical damage to his spermatozoa and began emphasizing his fears and his anxieties perhaps concerning his spermatozoa."

97

At both the Waco hospital and at the Houston VA regional office Eatherly signed claims in 1950 for "service-connected mental disability."

Service-connection for Eatherly's anxiety neurosis was a problem. To try to resolve it, the VA obtained his service and medical records from the Air Force, and these records became part of his file at both the hospital and the regional office. If he was to be compensated for mental disability, the psychiatrists not only had to pronounce him mentally disabled, to some degree, but the VA also had to "connect" this disability to something in his service record.

Had Eatherly somewhere, sometime, during his military service been treated for a "possible NP disorder?" If he saw no hazardous service, was he treated at least once for backache or stomach pains or ulcers or some other complaint which might be of "NP origin"?

Eatherly's service medical record shows no complaints and no treatments. The record notes that he was under brief observation after his flight through the bomb cloud at Bikini. But for that he had already claimed physical disability and lost when the VA ruled that the flight had not been "physically hazardous."

The VA declined to tell me why, but they denied Eatherly's claim in 1950 and awarded him nothing for the next three years. Moreover, the word Hiroshima does not appear on any medical record pertaining to his case. That he had been "at Hiroshima" does not appear in any Air Force record supplied to the VA, and apparently Eatherly did not mention Hiroshima to any psychiatrist on his first three visits to the hospital. So his having been "at Hiroshima" was not a factor in any VA decision regarding him from 1950 until 1957.

"When they said he was ready to leave the hospital," his wife told me, "I drove to Waco alone to get him. They told me they thought the confinement had helped him, but that he needed all the family support he could get and they urged me to stick with him and reassure him of my loyalty at every turn. On our drive back to Houston together he was in his best form. He told me that hospitalization had been exactly what he needed—that it had given him time to think, to realize how foolish and unfair

98

he had been. He said he was a changed man. He was off Benzedrine and whiskey and he was going to stay off."*

"Financially, how were you managing to live?" I asked.

"Well," she said, "the day after I took him to the hospital I gave up the expensive apartment we should never have moved into. I stored the furniture and returned to my parents with the children. I cut expenses in every way possible. Then James Eatherly was kind enough to invite Claude and me to live in his home until our new house was completed."

"Did Claude have a job?"

"Yes, the people at Ada Oil Company were very kind to him. They liked him, and they were trying hard to help him. They said nothing about his mental illness and invited him to return to work immediately. Everybody liked Claude and everybody was trying to help him. I crossed my fingers and hoped."

For the next six months Claude Eatherly behaved in a normal manner. In June, 1950, he and his wife and two children moved into their new home at 4601 Holt Street, Houston. His wife went to work in an office, though she felt she needed to be at home with her children who were then one and six years old.

The next disappointment came in November, 1950. Eatherly had begun drinking again, quarreling with his customers, so Ada Oil Company discharged him. James Eatherly came to Holt Street for another family conference.

"One fact stood out in Claude's experience since 1947," his wife told me. "His best period had been the year in the filling station when he punched a clock and wore coveralls and did hard, long, dirty work. His troubles multiplied when he was promoted to a salesman . . . operating a car . . . being somewhat his own boss . . . maintaining irregular hours . . . and perhaps feeling like he had to take drinks with his customers. His best bet obviously was to go back to hard, dirty work in which he didn't have to entertain customers.

"James Eatherly agreed to ask his own employers, Humble Oil Company, to give his brother a job. But the job was to be as a roustabout . . . hard, dirty, physical labor in the crude

---

* I could find no evidence that Benzedrine addiction was ever considered by any psychiatrist who treated Eatherly. As will be shown, Benzedrine was never mentioned at any trial, either by Eatherly or any psychiatrist.

oil fields. So early in 1951 Claude went to work for Humble. Even that job had a future . . . a good future . . . but not as good a future as the other two jobs had had."

Claude Eatherly's job as a roustabout resulted in "real hope" for more than a year. Then the same old behavior began. He stayed out at night, playing poker, drinking. Catastrophe struck in the evening while his wife was doing the laundry and he was "out." She answered a knock at the door and met a grim-faced James Eatherly and an official of Humble Oil Company.

This time Claude Eatherly had not given a "hot" check of his own which James Eatherly could make good. For the first time he had committed forgery—"forgery by alteration." He had altered a Humble check, made himself the payee, and cashed it. In deference to both James and Joe Eatherly, who were then and are now associated with Humble, the company did not press a charge. But Claude Eatherly's employment was "terminated."

(In 1962 Humble officials, still loyal to James and Joe Eatherly, declined to discuss with me "anything at all about Claude Eatherly.")

But Humble's reluctance to prosecute did not help, for other forgeries followed. On April 2, 1952, Claude Eatherly was arrested and charged with forgery and passing worthless checks. This is Houston, Texas, Case No. 54377. He was released on bond posted by James Eatherly.

(There are three types of illegality in "check passing" in the United States. The simplest is giving a "bad" or "hot" check— one that "bounces." Such checks are drawn on a bank in which you have an account but insufficient funds to pay the checks. For this a man is seldom arrested if he can promptly "make the check good." The second type is passing worthless checks. This is giving a check signed with your own name but drawn on a bank in which you have no account. This is a felony, a form of theft. The most serious type is forgery—signing the check with a real name which is not your own, or with a fictitious name.)

During 1952, while he was on bond awaiting trial for his forgeries, Eatherly worked four months as a commission salesman of sewing machines for the Atlas Sew-Vac Company of Houston.

"He could not have done much work," his wife told me, "since he drank steadily, often staying drunk from the time he rose in the morning until he staggered home and went to bed late at night. He had hit his low point thus far. He was the complete drunk, with whiskey bottles in his car, in the closets, everywhere. When the Atlas Company discharged him, he remained unemployed. He drew some unemployment insurance, and I did office work and tried to keep up the monthly payments on the home."

Incredibly, during 1952 his wife became pregnant again. I found this hard to believe in 1962 after I obtained some understanding of the woman who was his wife. She is a genuinely superior woman, with poise, tact, beauty, intelligence and talent. How could such a woman allow herself to get pregnant again by a husband in Eatherly's condition? A source who knows her well, but whom I cannot identify without revealing her present whereabouts, wrote to me:

You see, she was Catholic and Italian and children were involved. She had ten years invested in that marriage. In a spot like that some Catholic women just can't give up until the last hope has been abandoned . . . then abandoned again . . . and finally abandoned again. Moreover, the social workers and psychiatrists were telling her that she *must* stick to her husband . . . that he must not be made to feel that she was giving up on him.

Then, too, you must understand that she was dealing with one of the most convincing liars who ever lived. I don't believe any human being has ever been more capable at feigning remorse and insight then Claude Eatherly. There has never been a more convincing promiser that he was a "changed man" who could "make everything all right" if only he were given another chance.

Even when she was seven months pregnant, she was working all day in an office, then coming home and cooking and washing, trying desperately to maintain her home and family. She was even trying desperately to "reassure her husband of her loyalty." She quit only when her health began to break . . . and when she was eight months pregnant.

The break come in a cruel scene. Inflation and rising property values had given Mr. and Mrs. Claude Eatherly a windfall.

Under the favorable GI terms they had obtained title to their house for $12,000. By 1953 the house was worth $14,000. This enabled them to sell their equity for $1,872.90. They received the check on February 28, 1953. It was made out to both of them, and to cash it they both had to endorse it.

A banker first told me some of what happened, and when I asked Eatherly's former wife about it, she described the scene.

"Yes," she said, "that was the first time I ever stood up to him and fought him. I never expected to see him again. I had two children to support and I was eight months pregnant with a third. I had once begged my father for two thousand dollars which Claude had quickly gambled and drunk away. Many of the payments on the house had been made with money I earned. But Claude was determined to force me to endorse that check so that he could get the entire amount in his hands. He told me he'd give me half of it, but I knew that if he ever got that money in his hands I'd never see a dime of it. He tried to browbeat me with threats and curses and screams. But this time I never gave an inch. I forced him to go with me to a bank, and there I explained the situation to the cashier. While the cashier held the check we each endorsed it, after which the cashier gave each of us a check for $936.45. I went home to my parents to have my third child."

On a hot afternoon in May, 1962, I visited that house at 4601 Holt Street and spent an hour talking with people in the neighborhood. It's a mature neighborhood now: the trees have grown tall, the grass is lush, and many of the GI families have moved away as more children came and larger homes could be afforded. But at every door where I knocked someone remembered hearing about "all the trouble the people on the corner had." Heads began to shake, tongues began to cluck, when I mentioned the name.

"They had so much trouble . . . she worked so hard . . . she tried so desperately to hold things together . . . she was a pretty little thing and she tried so hard. And he was a pleasant guy . . . everybody liked him . . . but he drank and stayed out all hours . . . you could hear them screaming at each other . . . and she got pregnant again and got sick and had to give up."

On the other side of the coin, I listened to members of Claude Eatherly's family blame his marriage and his wife for what happened.

There was just too much difference in them, I was told. She was Catholic and Italian . . . she even had him taking instruction in the Catholic faith at one time . . . she mixed him up to where he didn't know whether he was coming or going . . . she thought she was so pretty and she was so ambitious and she hitched him to her ambitions, not his . . . he wanted to settle up here between Dallas and Fort Worth when he got out of the Air Force, in a simpler environment . . . he didn't want to be a big shot . . . what she really wanted was to go back to California and get by on her looks . . . she made him settle in a big city like Houston . . . she wanted too much . . . he couldn't satisfy her . . . I'm not saying she wasn't a good woman and I'm not saying anything against her . . . I'm just saying she wasn't right for Claude Eatherly.

Those are the two sides of the argument about Eatherly and the woman he married. I don't know where the whole truth lies. I studied them both, and she is and was obviously his superior in appearance, intellect and ambition. And while many men during the war were sexually disloyal to their wives, Eatherly, according to his crew members, felt no sense of loyalty at all to his wife.

Twenty days after the house was sold, on March 20, 1953, in Houston's Criminal District Court No. 2, Case No. 666-53, Eatherly pleaded guilty to forgery and was sentenced to five years' probation by Judge Langston King.

Why was he favored with probation? Why wasn't he sent to prison? Other men, less fortunate but with similar behavior patterns, are sent to prison. Texas has a modern prison system which emphasizes correction and rehabilitation. Why wasn't Eatherly corrected and rehabilitated by the State of Texas? The VA psychiatrists had found him sane, competent and culpable. The VA had not approved his claim for service-connected mental disability compensation. So why did the State of Texas *not* send him to prison?

It is a common practice in the United States for state officials,

103

before allowing the state to assume the liability of sending a war veteran to prison, to try first to persuade the VA to assume him. I can't prove it: such matters are never admitted for the record. I can't even charge it because I might be arrested for contempt of court on my next visit to Texas. But the facts indicate that before Eatherly was sentenced to five years' probation an understanding had been reached that the VA was to assume him.

If this is not true, why did the VA regional office at Houston choose May 22, 1953, as the date to notify Eatherly that he would "now return to the Waco hospital for further treatment"? And why was that date chosen to notify him that he had won a Partial Disability Award?

In order for the VA to make this award to Eatherly, the VA had had to conclude that his anxiety neurosis was service-connected. How had the VA reached any such conclusion? He had the same service record in 1953 that he had had in 1950. Why did the VA decide in May, 1950, that his disability was *not* service-connected, and then in May, 1953, decide that his disability *was* service-connected? What did the VA know about his military service in 1953 that it didn't know in 1950?

What they knew was that Eatherly "wasn't functioning." He had become "more of a problem." Either the State of Texas or the VA had to assume him. The VA assumed him. In order to assume him, the VA had to give him a service-connected diagnosis. Once they gave him a service-connected diagnosis, by law they had to give him compensation.

Because Eatherly and his wife were living apart on May 22, 1953, the letter advising him of his award was delivered to her in another city. She notified the VA that they were living apart. The VA then divided the compensation and began mailing a monthly check for $54.50 to her for the three children. A check for $57.12 was given to him.

This meant that the VA was now paying "50 percent service-connected mental disability compensation." It meant also that the VA held Eatherly to be "incompetent for compensation purposes." Had the VA held him "competent for compensation purposes," the entire amount would have been delivered to him each month, and his wife and children would have been dependent on what, if anything, he wanted to give them.

This brings me to the first mystery of the Eatherly Case. Who gave Claude Eatherly *service-connected* compensation? And *by what right?* How did Eatherly qualify for service-connected compensation *six years* after he was expelled from the Air Force? I'm not referring to public assistance or welfare payments which are made to American citizens and to their dependents on the basis of need. I'm referring to *service-connected compensation* which is supposed to be awarded, under specific laws, to veterans in payment for some *disability* they *suffered* while in the armed service of the United States.

On what wartime or peacetime military experience was Eatherly's claim based? During the Second War he served "overseas" about 90 days. He flew six "combat missions" which were "unopposed by any form of enemy action." So where was his "traumatic experience" which later was to result in "emotional disorder"?

The VA administration refuses to dispel this mystery. I questioned several knowledgeable men in confidence. Each one shook his head, threw up his hands, and said he couldn't figure it out. The only possible answer seems to be that some VA board in 1953 decided to hold that "military service *in itself* had been traumatic for Claude Eatherly."

When Eatherly received news of his award he was visiting his brother Joe at Van Alstyne. He was supposed to report to the hospital on June 1st. En route to the hospital, on May 30, 1953, he was arrested in Dallas for passing worthless checks, Case No. 48562, and lodged in the county jail. When the county attorney learned that the VA had assumed him, charges were dismissed, and the Dallas County Sheriff's office delivered him to the Waco hospital on June 10, 1953.

Nine

ON his second trip to the Waco hospital Claude Eatherly stayed ten weeks—twice as long as on his first trip. He was admitted June 10th; discharged August 20, 1953.

A month after he entered the hospital both Eatherly and VA social workers began communicating with his wife. Her third child was a few weeks old; and she was working, living with her parents in a small city, trying to care for her children. Her husband begged her for another chance.

The social workers came to see her and assured her that her husband was making a remarkable recovery, that he'd be released soon, but that his return to health depended on her. They insisted that she give him another chance. They said he was a man of considerable insight, but that he needed to be reassured of his wife's loyalty and devotion. Without you, they asked, where can your husband go when he leaves the hospital? They said they were confident that Claude Eatherly could "function" if only his wife would reassure him and take him back.

The social workers implied to Mrs. Eatherly that some of the fault for his condition may have been hers; that through some ignorance of psychology she may have hurt him in some way, or failed him, or "said the wrong things to him," or "neglected to reassure him." They further implied that if she gave up on him, or "deserted" him, even more responsibility would be hers.

Eatherly's wife then wrote to the Waco hospital. She said that if her husband was coming back to her, were there any books she could read which would help her to understand him, which could instruct her in what to say to him, what not to say to him and how to reassure him?

She received this reply:

DEAR MRS. EATHERLY:

In response to your letter of August 8, 1953, I am pleased to report that your husband has shown excellent improvement during hospital treatment and is now scheduled to be discharged from the hospital next Thursday, August 20, 1953. The hospital feels that he will have achieved the maximum benefits from his hospitalization prior to that time.

I have worked closely with your husband in both individual and group psychotherapy. I want to assure you that in these sessions he has worked intensively in an effort to understand and get at the causes of his past difficulty. There is every reason to believe that the insight which he has gained should make it possible for him to make a much more satisfactory adjustment in the future. I am convinced that his efforts are sincere and that he has every desire to succeed in his work and marriage when he leaves the hospital.

You will understand, of course, that the actual adjustment that he can make will depend quite largely upon the extent to which you and he are able to work at the problem cooperatively after he comes home. I fully appreciate your feeling the need of advice in understanding his problems and knowing how you can best help him. In my judgment it is doubtful whether reading books is of very much benefit in this regard. I would certainly urge that when he comes home you and he together seek out some professional help such as a psychiatrist, or some psychotherapist to whom he can go in case problems arise in the future. It is also important that you have access to this same professional person in order that you may further learn to understand him and to find your place in working out a satisfactory adjustment for your future lives. If this can be done, I am sure it would greatly increase the possibility of a satisfactory adjustment upon your husband's return home.

Trusting this information may be of service to you, I am,

Sincerely yours,
DONALD R. GORHAM, PH.D.
Clinical Psychologist

The VA had assumed Eatherly from the State of Texas. He had been delivered to the hospital by the sheriff of Dallas County. Yet after only eight weeks of "individual and group psychotherapy" at the hospital, the VA proposed to send him back to his wife, assuring her that he had made a remarkable recovery, and that she should hire a psychiatrist to learn how to reassure him.

When Eatherly left the hospital he went, not to a big city like Houston or Dallas, but to a small city where his wife was working, trying to care for three small children.

"For the first three or four weeks," his wife told me, "he was meek, remorseful and full of promises. He began looking around for a job, and one employment agency in particular began trying to find a good job for him. Then . . . the same old behavior. He began drinking and going to the lowest dives in town including brothels. Trading on my name, he began passing worthless checks again, the police were knocking on our door again, and now we were back in this smaller place where everybody knows everything and everybody. I had a car which I used to go to work in. . . . I refused to let him have it and kept the key from him. He jerked out the ignition wires, tied them together, and ran off with my car. I had no choice but to ask the police to get the car back, and to call his brother to come and get him. The police were looking for him anyway because he had passed more worthless checks. I had to think of the three children; he was unable to think of anyone but himself."

James Eatherly had been transferred from Houston to Midland, Texas. So Joe Eatherly came and got his brother away from the police and took him to Van Alstyne. On November 21, 1953, Claude Eatherly was arrested in Dallas and charged with "Check Swindle over $50." Again he was lodged in the Dallas County Jail, from which on December 19, 1953, he again was transferred to the Waco hospital.

That was the end of the marriage. Eatherly's wife gave up on him. She sued for divorce. The suit was not contested and the divorce was granted. She subsequently remarried; and, except when she has communicated with the VA on behalf of the children, neither she nor the children have been a part of his story since 1954.

On his third trip to the Waco hospital Eatherly stayed five months. He was admitted December 19, 1953; discharged May

19, 1954. During this third visit the VA reconfirmed his diagnosis as anxiety neurosis and raised his compensation to 80 percent. On March 15, 1954, his wife began receiving a monthly check for the children for $91.40. Eatherly received an equal amount.

In 1962, as I worked at reconstructing Eatherly's experience as a mental patient, I continued to search for evidence that his mental difficulties might have been predicted. I asked myself: If I had met the crew of the *Straight Flush* in 1945—as I met other B-29 crews—would I have guessed that "the Skipper" would be the one who, ten years later, would be in a mental hospital suffering from anxiety neurosis?

Seeking an answer to that question I visited another member of the *Straight Flush*'s crew—Albert Barsumian. In 1945 he was nineteen, a sergeant, and Eatherly's radar operator. I found him, with his family, in a new home in suburban Chicago. He is an amiable, successful Armenian-American in his mid-thirties. He and his brother have expanded their father's rug business.

"When Claude Eatherly was my commanding officer," Albert Barsumian said, "I thought he was the greatest guy on earth. I didn't have much money; he always had plenty, and he loaned me money anytime I wanted it. I don't mean he ever gave me any money; I always paid him back; but he was extremely friendly and generous with me and with every other member of his crew. I think he was the best pilot in the 509th, and I think we had the best crew. Our morale was as high as it could be. When we went on liberty—to Salt Lake or Havana—Eatherly carried a passbook with him; and when my three days were up, if I didn't feel like going back to the base all I had to do was find him and he'd write me another pass. He was a swell guy. But there was one thing about him. If he was hung over, or didn't want to fly for some reason, the President of the United States couldn't get him in the air. He'd figure out some way not to make his flight. On one such occasion he almost got me court-martialed; and I did the only thing I'm ashamed of during my war service. We were in Cuba in February, '45, at Batista Field, and we were taxiing out to the runway to take off on a twelve-hour training flight. The Skipper didn't feel so good. There was nothing really wrong with him except he wanted to go back to Havana and drink some more and lie up with some dame. So he suddenly—just like that!—ordered me to malfunction the radar."

"You mean he ordered you to tear it up?" I asked.

"No, not tear it up completely. Just fix it so it wouldn't work. Well, I wasn't reared to tear things up, and I had heard slogans about Keep-'em-Flying, and I could see some little old lady working the swing shift to make that radar equipment. Not to mention the cost of many thousands of dollars to us taxpayers. So I hesitated. I started to suggest that he report to the medics that he wasn't able to fly that day. But hell, there we were at the end of the runway. We were in communication with the tower; we were supposed to take off any minute. I was nineteen; he was my Skipper and I was in his debt. He didn't give me time to question his decision: I heard him reporting to the tower that the radar wasn't working and we were returning to the line. What else could I do? I malfunctioned it; they scrubbed the flight; and the Skipper headed back to Havana."

"Was that the end of it?"

"Like hell!" Albert Barsumian said. "That was the beginning of it. I was supposed to keep that radar working. So I was jerked up on the carpet and relieved of duty. I thought I was going to prison. I was pulled off the *Straight Flush* crew, and I flew with them several days when I wasn't supposed to be on the airplane. You talk about anxiety: I suffered from it. Eatherly tried to come to my rescue by yelling that somebody was going over his head, that his crew was his responsibility; but he didn't tell anybody the truth, and of course I couldn't tell anybody the truth. So I was in a real sweat. I suppose I should have been court-martialed. I was guilty of malfunctioning expensive and essential equipment in wartime. I had temporarily grounded a weapon (the airplane) that cost millions of dollars. Finally it all died down and I was officially returned to duty on the *Straight Flush*."

"Did he talk with you about it while the heat was on?" I asked.

"No, not much," Albert Barsumian said. "He shrugged it off. He was a great guy, all right—a lot of fun, friendly, and a good pilot. But he'd take chances with you—he could get you hurt.

I'm not trying to shift all the blame for my mistake to him. I should have stood up to him and refused to obey his order. All I can say in my defense is that I was nineteen and a sergeant, and he was my commanding officer. It all happened in a minute, and I didn't have time to think about it. Also, after it happened I was willing to face the music, just as I am now voluntarily telling you about it. But you can see that things being what they were I couldn't very well face the music without being disloyal to him."

"I believe you attended the crew reunion in 1958," I said.

"Yes," he continued, "I went to Louisville in 1958. Eatherly was exactly the same man he was in 1945. I can't believe he has ever been insane or sick. The only difference between him and the rest of us is that he lacks the conscience that most of us have. He wants to have a good time; and he can't understand why anybody ever wants to stop playing poker, or drinking, or chasing girls, to do something dull like fulfilling a responsibility."

If I had been at Batista Field in 1945 and had heard that story, and if I had known that two years later Eatherly would be expelled from the Air Force and compelled to try to support a wife and child, would I have guessed that by 1955 he'd be in a mental hospital suffering from anxiety?

I don't know. I might have guessed it.

In February, 1954, the psychiatrists at the Waco hospital treated Eatherly with shock—insulin shock. Massive doses of insulin. They gave him a total of sixty hours of "insulin coma."

"They really poured the juice to the Major," the nursing assistant told me. "They gave him sixty hours of coma. I've never heard of anybody else being given that much around here. Maybe they have given some other patient as much as sixty hours. If they have, I never heard about it."

Did the treatment help? Did it do him harm? I'm not qualified to say. I have been told that if he was suffering from anxiety neurosis, that amount of shock should have had some therapeutic value. But his behavior didn't change.

When he was discharged from the hospital on May 19, 1954, he went to the home of his brother James at Midland, Texas. A city of ten thousand, Midland is a county seat in West Texas, about three hundred miles west of Waco. There Claude Eatherly followed his usual behavior pattern. He lived quietly for several months, worked a little as an automobile salesman, then he left Midland abruptly and went seeking excitement. He went first to Houston, then to Baton Rouge, Louisiana, then to New Orleans, leaving a trail of swindles.

Because so much has been written abroad about his alleged experiences in New Orleans in 1954-55, I tried to recreate several of his adventures there. Again, I was assisted by the detective, Bill Gurvich. Every criminal has what police and the television dramatists call his "MO"—his "mode of operation"; and Mr. Gurvich and I studied Claude Eatherly's MO.

He reached New Orleans on November 24, 1954. He checked into the St. Charles Hotel. This hotel is a landmark. Eatherly had stayed there in 1947 with Marsalis. In 1954 it belonged to the Dinkler chain; it is now controlled by Sheraton and is called the Sheraton-Charles. Eatherly registered as Paul Chenchar and was assigned room 624 which had a rate of $6 a day. Paul Chenchar is one of Eatherly's aliases in his FBI record. There is also a real Paul Chenchar. Eatherly knew him: he participated in the Bikini test. If Eatherly had any cards identifying himself as Paul Chenchar we were unable to find them.

He did, however, have several cards identifying him as Claude Eatherly; and in a plastic case he had nine cards identifying him as Francis A. Baker, 1942 Alta Vista Street, Houston, Texas.

"F. A. Baker" is another of Eatherly's aliases. There was and is a real F. A. Baker. At a football game in Houston in October, 1954, Mr. Baker either lost his wallet or a pickpocket lifted it. Eatherly somehow got possession of the cards in the wallet: driver's license, social security card, auto insurance card, hotel and gasoline credit cards, etc. He later told police that he acquired the cards from "an unknown female he met in a Houston bar."

On November 27, 1954, he entered Mayer-Israel, Inc., 714 Canal Street, New Orleans, and selected a topcoat. The price of the coat was $61.75, and he asked if he could pay by check. He was taken to the store's credit office where a Mrs. Tatum examined the cards of Francis A. Baker and accepted the check. It was drawn on City National Bank, Houston, and signed "F.

A. Baker." Eatherly left the store wearing the coat. Deposited in a New Orleans bank, the check "bounced" from Houston marked EVIDENTLY DRAWN ON US IN ERROR. The police were notified; and Mr. Mayer and Mrs. Tatum described "F. A. Baker."

Near 5 P.M. on December 1, 1954, Eatherly entered Coleman E. Adler & Sons, jewelers, 722 Canal Street, and selected a man's ring selling for $611. It was a white-gold ring with one large stone and two smaller stones. Eatherly stated that he wanted to give a check for $250 on the City National Bank of Houston as a down payment. He offered to pay the balance in eight notes of $40 each and a ninth note of $41.25. He showed the F. A. Baker identification cards, said he lived at 1942 Alta Vista Street, Houston, and that he was employed as a salesman for W. H. Betz Company, of Houston. He gave this information to the store's credit manager, Edwin F. Moise.

Mr. Moise telephoned the Houston bank; but as Eatherly had guessed, the bank's switchboard had been turned off at 5 P.M. Mr. Moise then telephoned the Houston Credit Bureau which reported that F. A. Baker, of 1942 Alta Vista Street, had a "good credit rating." On that assurance Mr. Moise accepted the $250 check, along with the nine notes, and delivered the ring to Eatherly.

In 1962 Mr. Moise, now employed elsewhere, recalled the incident.

"Eatherly? Sure, I remember him," Mr. Moise said. "He was a cunning one. But he trapped himself by talking too much. He made one statement which enabled me to catch him. Milton Adler, one of the store's owners, brought him to me just after five. I had a hunch he was a con man. I'm always suspicious of guys who come in after five P.M. after banks can't be reached. But when I got that good credit rating I decided to let him have the ring. But he disturbed my sleep that night: I kept feeling he had 'taken' me. So promptly at nine the next morning I telephoned the Houston bank, and of course they didn't know Mr. Baker of Alta Vista Street. I informed both Milton and Walter Adler, the store's co-owners. We also informed the police.

"Then I remembered something," Mr. Moise continued.

113

"There had been a three- or four-minute delay while the Houston Credit Bureau was checking its files. Eatherly was sitting there at my desk, and to make conversation I had asked him what brought him to New Orleans. He replied that he was in New Orleans 'to spend a few days playing the horses.' The racing season was on at Fairgrounds Race Track, and many Texans come to New Orleans for the races. The minute I remembered this, I suggested to Milton Adler that I go to the tracks and look for him. 'I'll bet I can find that rascal in thirty minutes,' I said. Milton Adler didn't think I had a chance to find him, but Walter Adler thought it was a good idea, and he sent me to the track in a taxicab."

"Now don't tell us you found him," Mr. Gurvich said.

"I sure did," Mr. Moise said. "I searched the grandstand two or three times and I was about to give up when I went up to the mezzanine and was eating a hamburger when I spied Mr. 'F. A. Baker' in line at one of the betting windows. I grabbed a cop and the two of us confronted him. He put on a good act. He was a cold-blooded operator. He first denied ever having seen me before. The cop took him downstairs to the track manager's office and called two city detectives. To the detectives he admitted he had bought a ring, but he claimed that his name was F. A. Baker and that, by mistake, he must have drawn the check on the wrong bank. He said the ring was in his room at the St. Charles Hotel. The detectives searched him and found a pawn ticket, dated that morning, December 2, 1954, from Reiner's Loan Office. The pawnbrokers had loaned him $154.50 on the ring. He had ninety dollars cash on him."

Eatherly was lodged in jail. He was wearing the topcoat he had "purchased" at Mayer-Israel; Mr. Mayer and Mrs. Tatum identified him. During the next few days a total of nine "F. A. Baker" checks reached the police, each check representing a swindle similar to the two described. One store received a check, but luckily escaped loss. On October 26, 1954, Eatherly gave an "F. A. Baker" check to the D. H. Holmes Department Store (formerly Dalton's) in Baton Rouge. While the credit manager was examining the check, something apparently frightened Eatherly because he dashed away, saying he'd "be back in a few minutes." When he didn't return, the check was delivered to the police.

The nine "F. A. Baker" checks were sent to the FBI laboratory, and all nine were found to be in Eatherly's handwriting. The police telephoned the real F. A. Baker; he revealed that he had lost his identification cards at the football game, and he was happy to get them back.

The St. Charles then charged Eatherly with "beating a hotel bill" for $61.60.

On Christmas Day, 1954, Eatherly sat in the New Orleans city jail awaiting trial for forgery. He could have gone free on a bond of $1500. But no one appeared to post bond.

In 1962, while we were investigating Eatherly in New Orleans, Mr. Gurvich quite unexpectedly found the wallet which Eatherly was carrying when he was arrested at Fairgrounds Race Track on December 2, 1954. This wallet was in a file in the office of the Detective Bureau, New Orleans Police Department. Normally it would have been returned to Eatherly when he was released from prison. Why it was not returned to him we could not determine.

You can learn much about a man by examining his wallet. Here are some of the contents of Eatherly's wallet while he was "playing the races":

Instrument Pilot Certificate, U. S. Air Force. Expires March 22, 1947. Based: Roswell, New Mexico. Total pilot time to date: 2694. Last 12 months 277.

Driver's License, Texas Dept. of Public Safety, No. 2810318, expiration date, October 2, 1955. Address 3217 Thomas, Midland, Texas.

Identification Card: Employes Federation, Humble Oil & Refining Co., 1952, Crude Oil Department.

Unemployment Card, Texas Employment Commission. Contact date: October 2, 1953. (This is a record of claims for unemployment benefits.)

Unemployment Card, Texas Employment Commission. Contact date: June 10, 1954, Midland.

Sears Roebuck Easy Payment Plan Receipt Book, 6800 Harrisburg, Houston, February 18, 1953.

Counter checks, various banks.

A scribbled memo: Sans Souci Hotel, Miami, May Gallagher.

Bankbook, Midland National Bank, Midland, Texas. No dates. No stampings. Example of ink insertion: Balance $6,654.22. Deposit $12,000.00 Total $18,654.22.

From these items in Eatherly's wallet, and from the "F. A. Baker" criminal acts, readers who are not versed in the ways of petty criminals can begin to understand Eatherly's manner of deriving money from worthless checks. Forgery and passing worthless checks are not simple crimes in the United States. They require planning, ability at deception, and a considerable degree of intelligence.

To pass a check a person must identify himself. The larger the check, the more impressive must be the identifications. If you will examine Eatherly's identifications—the cards he carried in his own name—you will note that he had nothing which would commend him to an intended victim. His Air Force Pilot Certificate would have been excellent had it been up to date; but it expired March 22, 1947. The same was true of his card identifying him as an employee of Humble Oil Company. This card was for 1952. Would a credit manager be impressed by unemployment cards?

Note what Eatherly had tried to do before he left Midland. He had obtained a bankbook into which he had written figures showing a bank balance of $18,654.22. But that bankbook was worthless. Any credit manager would have noted that it was not genuine.

This meant that for Eatherly to pass checks he had to have some other man's identifying cards. This is why he had obtained the cards of F. A. Baker. But even with the Baker cards, and with Mr. Baker's good credit rating in Houston, Eatherly could not exchange checks for cash. He had to follow the "MO" of selecting merchandise, persuading a merchant to accept a check, getting possession of the merchandise, then converting the merchandise into cash by either selling it or pawning it.

This was the "mode of operation" followed by a man during a year in which he was diagnosed as "neurotic, with an anxiety reaction"; and during a year in which his psychiatric treatment included sixty hours of insulin coma.

As Claude Eatherly, alias Paul Chenchar, alias F. A. Baker, sat in jail awaiting trial in New Orleans, the question was: Would he go back to the hospital in Waco, or would he go to prison in Louisiana?

Ten

CLAUDE EATHERLY spent thirteen months in prison in New Orleans, from December 2, 1954, to Christmas Day, 1955. These months were the lowest point of his experience. Neither of his brothers visited him. Because neither he nor anyone else had yet suggested that he was suffering from guilt feelings over Hiroshima, he had no pacifist friends and no journalist friends. No New Orleans reporter took any note of him.

Three months passed before he came to trial on the forgery charges, and during this period his brothers might have freed him on bond, but they could not because there were several "holds" against him from Texas cities.

What is a "hold"? When a man with an FBI record is arrested in the United States, the news of his arrest becomes known quickly to all law enforcement agencies. If the man is "wanted" in places other than where he has been arrested, the authorities in those places notify his jailers that when and if they are ready to release him they are *not* to release him but "hold" him for delivery to the other places.

For Eatherly to go free, first the State of Louisiana had to release him, and second, those "holds" against him had to be "dropped." So freeing Eatherly from this predicament in New Orleans would be difficult, particularly since he had neither money nor friends working for him on the outside.

The task was assumed by an attorney named Joseph Gowan. Other prisoners had suggested to Eatherly that Mr. Gowan was the sort of lawyer who might help him, and from the jail Eatherly wrote to the attorney.

Mr. Gowan is an unusual man. He practices yoga, and frequently lends aid to prisoners who have little money. He began visiting Eatherly, who paid him $200 from his compensation money mailed to him from the Waco hospital. Eatherly told Mr. Gowan that he wanted to go back to Waco, and he urged the lawyer to work toward getting all charges dropped so he could return to the hospital.

Mr. Gowan began an extensive correspondence. He urged Eatherly's wife and brothers to try to help. He tried to persuade the Texas district attorneys to "drop their holds against Eatherly," and he urged the VA to try to help. In addition to this correspondence, Mr. Gowan began talking with various authorities in New Orleans, trying to persuade them to give Eatherly a break and let him return to Waco.

In 1962, Mr. Gowan recalled his experience with Eatherly. "Generating sympathy for Eatherly in New Orleans in 1955," he said, "was a tough proposition. Whenever you go to a judge or a district attorney, trying to get a break for a prisoner, the first question that always come up is children. Is the man trying to support his children? Are minor children depending on this man for support? If you answer no to that question, then the next question is a job. Does he have a job? Is he trying to make a living? And when you are compelled to answer no, he has no job, he has left his family, he isn't trying to support his children, he's only a drifter with a long record for swindling, and with 'holds' against him, how can you argue that he ought to be given a light sentence and set free? Won't he be back in jail next week or next month? Eatherly's criminal record was a particular handicap because his first arrest had been in New Orleans in 1947 for 'gun-running'—for violation of the Federal Firearms Act. When a judge or district attorney picks up a long FBI record and the first entry he sees is 'Federal Firearms Act,' how can you expect much sympathy?

"Other things worked against Eatherly," Mr. Gowan continued. "He had been an officer in the service, not an Enlisted Man. He even drew compensation and didn't have to work like other men for 'something to eat.' There was nothing underprivileged about him. Then his Mode of Operation . . . all that sly swindling . . . even his being arrested at a race track, showing that he was swindling not to get something to eat or to feed hungry kids, but to get money to gamble with . . . all such things worked against him."

I asked Mr. Gowan if he considered a plea of not guilty by reason of insanity.

"Sure, I considered it," he said, "but such a plea seemed hopeless for several reasons. The forgery case was to come before Judge Fred Oser in the Criminal District Court; and the judge, plainly, had no sympathy for Eatherly. If a jury would support it, the judge intended to send Eatherly to Angola—the State Penitentiary at Angola, Louisiana. There was no money to hire psychiatrists to prove that Eatherly was insane, and the VA diagnosis of Eatherly would not support a plea of insanity. The VA diagnosis was anxiety *neurosis,* not insanity: Eatherly was legally sane and culpable. And Eatherly's forgeries didn't resemble the work of a crazy man. No jury would have found him crazy. And even if I could have freed him in New Orleans on an insanity plea, he would have been returned to Texas to face felony charges. The Texas district attorney who wanted him most was not going to send him to Waco but to Huntsville." (The Texas State Penitentiary.)

In the face of all those difficulties Mr. Gowan worked for limited objectives. First, to keep Eatherly out of Angola; to try to persuade Judge Oser to let Eatherly serve his time in the parish (county) prison. This required a special concession because, under Louisiana law, if a prisoner is sentenced to more than a year he must be sent to Angola and not held in any parish prison.

There was no trial. On March 23, 1955, Eatherly appeared before Judge Oser and pleaded guilty to forgery. Sentencing was deferred until March 28th when Judge Oser sentenced him to eighteen months' imprisonment. But to allow him to stay in the parish prison, the judge agreed that if he would work—"really work"—he would be credited with serving "two days for one" and would be eligible for release in nine months.

After that success Mr. Gowan redoubled his efforts to "get the Texas holds dropped" so that when Eatherly was released in New Orleans in December, 1955, he could go back to the Waco hospital instead of to a Texas jail and then to the Texas penitentiary. But one district attorney held out so stubbornly that on December 1, 1955, Eatherly was still facing a "hold."

In that extremity Mr. Gowan sought political help. A powerful political figure in Texas was the late Speaker of the House, Sam Rayburn. His home was at Bonham, Texas, in Fannin County, which adjoins Grayson County; and Grayson County was in the Speaker's Congressional District. So Eatherly, having entered the Air Force from Grayson County, might be called one of Mr. Rayburn's constituents. About December 15, 1955, Mr. Rayburn returned to Bonham from Washington for the Christmas holidays. Mr. Gowan traveled from New Orleans to Bonham where he asked Mr. Rayburn for help.

From Bonham went the powerful telephone call to the stubborn Texas district attorney, and the last "hold" on Claude Eatherly was dropped on Christmas Eve, 1955. This allowed Eatherly to be released in New Orleans and to travel, unmolested by police, to the Waco hospital.

According to the record which later was presented twice in court by VA psychiatrists, Eatherly flew "directly" from the New Orleans prison to the Waco hospital on January 5, 1956. But when Mr. Gurvich and I dug into the record, we found that Eatherly left the prison on Christmas Day, 1955. What happened during those "lost" days involves sex and the Christmas Spirit.

The Christmas Spirit infects jailers in the United States, and on Christmas Eve there is a saying that every man who can be out of a jail is let out. By Christmas Eve, 1955, Eatherly had made friends among his jailers, and they were trying to let him out on Christmas Eve. But the Texas "hold" was not "dropped" in time for him to be "processed" out of the prison on Christmas Eve. So they let him out on Christmas Day.

There had been an agreement that he would not "hang around" New Orleans where the horses were running again and where the Sugar Bowl Classics (football, etc.) are celebrated from Christmas to New Year's. Louisiana authorities wanted to see him safely across the Texas line; they didn't want to risk his getting back into a Louisiana prison. So it was agreed that he'd be escorted by police to the New Orleans airport and onto the nonstop plane for Dallas.

But sex reared its head. In the United States, prisoners are not generally allowed sexual access to women in the Latin manner, but New Orleans is a Latin city. Eatherly had been in jail a year, Moreover, he was headed for a VA hospital where presumably his sexual opportunities would be limited. So, it being Christmas and all, shouldn't he be allowed a little "soldier's comfort"? Especially since he had met a divorcée in jail, a woman who was not a prisoner but who had come to the jail regularly to visit another inmate. He wanted to "spend Christmas" with her.

Eatherly's persuasiveness led to some relaxation in police vigilance. He was allowed to spend extra days in New Orleans, and most of these days seem to have been spent in the Monteleone Hotel which is in the French Quarter.

That Eatherly was able to leave jail and get into the crowded Monteleone during Sugar Bowl Week indicates either that he was still a convincing man or that his police friends also influenced the hotel for him.

When Eatherly left New Orleans he was escorted by the police, not from the jail to the airport, but from the Monteleone to the airport. By then, I was told, "he had beat the Monteleone a big bill," and by law he should have been jailed again in New Orleans. But how could those police jail him without revealing that they had disobeyed orders and neglected to put him aboard the plane on Christmas Day?

How did he behave in prison in 1955? Did he manifest any mental disorder? Mr. Gurvich and I sought information on his behavior during his one year plus twenty-three days in prison.

He worked in the prison as a "hallboy." This means he was a combination messenger and order-keeper—much like a bellboy in a hotel. He delivered messages to inmates, advised inmates of visitors, escorted imates to and from the area where they talked with visitors or their lawyers. He quickly became a "trusty." He was never allowed outside the prison, but inside the prison he enjoyed considerable freedom. He was not locked in a cell, either during the day or at night.

Most of the jailers, sheriff's deputies, and police who came to know him were former enlisted men in the service; many of them had been army sergeants. When we showed them photographs in 1962, almost without exception they nodded, recalled him pleasantly, and inquired as to where he was and what he was doing. But they recalled nothing specific about him—nothing more than that "he was around here a while and he got along fine."

We questioned the prison physician and the prison pharmacists, all of whom remembered him well. We told them that the VA doctors had given him sixty hours of insulin shock only six months before he came to New Orleans. The VA doctors had had him on tranquilizers. So didn't he request tranquilizers in prison? Didn't he at least ask for an aspirin?

We were given this general reply. That while Claude Robert Eatherly was in the New Orleans Parish Prison he appeared to be a healthy and well-adjusted man, both mentally and physically. He was involved in no dispute or fight and he evidenced no nervousness. Not once did he request medical attention or medication. He ate heartily, took exercises, kept himself neat, performed his work capably. He slept near other prisoners, and prisoners frequently complain of other men snoring or having nightmares or being restless during the night and disturbing their sleep. But no one ever heard any such complaint about Eatherly. He was a well-behaved prisoner; he served a minimum sentence because of good behavior. Everybody who knew him liked him, and he left the prison with the good wishes of everyone.

Eleven

ON January 5, 1956, Claude Eatherly voluntarily returned to the Waco hospital for his fourth admission. The hospital was his bank; his compensation was deposited there by the VA and dispensed to him at the discretion of the administrators; and he had a balance of several hundred dollars.

His wife wrote to the hospital, inquiring as to his condition and suggesting that in view of his inability to avoid trouble on the outside the VA should reconsider its diagnosis and perhaps try some other method of treatment.

On February 20, 1956, his wife received this reply:

DEAR MADAM:

Your husband was admitted to this hospital on January 5, 1956.

We are pleased to inform you that he has been showing progressive improvement in his mental reaction. We now have him on a new medicine called thorazine which is helping him more than any other treatment he has received in the past. His brother Joe Eatherly from Van Alstyne, Texas, came to the hospital on Sunday, February 19, 1956, and took him out on a 72-hour pass. As you know your husband had some difficulty in New Orleans. According to our records he is suffering from a nervous condition called anxiety reaction; however, from time to time he shows symptoms which are more severe than just plain nervousness and anxiety. Those symptoms are leading him into many difficulties with which you are acquainted.

At the present time he is very friendly, cheerful, agreeable and is very anxious to get better, go home and take care of his family.

We trust that in another month or so he will be able to leave the hospital either on trial visit or a discharge.

Please be assured that we are doing everything possible to help your husband.

WALTER L. FORD, M.D.
Director, Professional Services

Two weeks later the hospital informed his wife that Eatherly wished to leave the hospital, and that while the doctors thought he should remain a while longer, the hospital could not hold him against his wishes and therefore he was being scheduled for release on March 16, 1956.

His wife immediately wrote back and asked the hospital authorities how, in view of his recent prison experience, they could release him so soon? Shouldn't he be held for more thorough treatment? Wasn't he likely to commit crimes again and be returned to prison?

On March 20, 1956, his wife received this reply:

DEAR MADAM:

This is to advise you that your husband, Claude R. Eatherly, was given a leave of absence for fourteen days in the custody of his brother, Joe Eatherly, on March 11, 1956.

It was agreed that if Claude is unable to make an adjustment at home during his short visit with his brother, he will be returned to the hospital. If he refuses to come voluntarily there is a possibility that he may have to be committed on a 90-day commitment. We left this matter up to his brother.

We understand how you feel about your husband and your concern for his behavior difficulties on the outside. We also think that his brother Joe is aware of Claude's problems. We hinted in our letter to you before that your husband's difficulties are more than just anxiety neurosis. He may be developing a more serious mental reaction than just plain anxiety neurosis as evidenced by behavior reactions away from the hospital. Whatever diagnosis he may receive we believe that he needs constant care and supervision either through hospitalization or through some friend or relative who will be responsible for him on the outside while he is on trial visit or leave of absence.

Regarding his detention in this hospital, as you know we cannot hold him against his will unless he is committed here by court and

125

that is the reason why we had scheduled him for discharge against medical advice on March 16, 1956, and notified you of that fact.

Please be assured of our effort to do all we can for your husband.

WALTER M. FORD, M.D.,
Director, Professional Services

Two months later, May 18, 1956, his wife received another —and most significant—letter from a new doctor:

DEAR MRS. EATHERLY:

I don't think it is possible to explain Claude's mental illness in such a short letter as this.

Giving him a diagnosis of anxiety reaction or neurosis is very easy but to explain the reason for this anxiety is very hard. It seems that his problem is that of growing up emotionally. He has not completely matured. He wants to stand up on his two feet and face responsibility, he wants to live up to his expectations, he wants to be a good father and husband, but realizing his inadequacy, insecurity and emotional immaturity he goes to pieces, so to speak, and develops all sorts of symptoms and reactions.

I believe that he has grown up some with the help of medicine and psychotherapy he received here. You probably know by now that he went home on a trial visit in the custody of his brother, Joe, on April 24, 1956. We only hope that he will continue to grow and improve.

Very truly yours,
O. P. CONSTANTINE, M.D.,
Physician in Charge of Case

This letter is significant because it reveals the entry into the Eatherly Case of Dr. Oleinick Pavlovitch Constantine.

From Eatherly's first admission to the hospital in 1950 until 1956, the doctor chiefly responsible for his diagnosis was Dr. Samuel H. Ross. The doctor who administered insulin coma to him in 1954 was Dr. Robert B. McElroy. But when he returned to the hospital in 1956, Dr. Constantine became physician-in-charge of his case. Dr. Constantine became more: he became Eatherly's friend and adviser. With Dr. Constantine, Eatherly developed the closest relationship he ever had with a VA psychiatrist.

Dr. Constantine was to become one of Eatherly's psychiatric

interpreters to the courts, and ultimately was to become his chief psychiatric interpreter to the press.

The foregoing letters reveal further developments. There are hints that Eatherly "may be developing a more serious mental reaction than just plain anxiety neurosis." There is the suggestion that a 90-day commitment may be needed. *Without a court order,* the Waco hospital can hold no patient against his will for more than *four days.* Eatherly had never been under court order at the hospital. Even though he had been guilty of numerous "worthless check" offenses in Texas, had been jailed several times, had twice been returned to the hospital by sheriff's deputies, he had never been "committed" even temporarily, and he had always been free to leave when he insisted on leaving. Now the VA suggested this might have to be changed.

Moreover, the VA had decided that henceforth Eatherly should have "constant care and supervision either through hospitalization or through some friend or relative who will be responsible for him on the outside while he is on trial visit or leave of absence." Since his wife was in the process of divorcing him and would no longer accept such responsibility, it was being accepted by Joe Eatherly. Claude Eatherly, with Joe Eatherly as his custodian, had left the hospital for three days on February 16, 1956; for fourteen days on March 11, 1956; and for an indefinite trial visit on April 24, 1956.

This last date must be remembered.

"On these visits," Joe Eatherly told me, "my brother was living with me, my wife and two children in our home at Van Alstyne. He spent some of the nights at the old home place with our father. He behaved normally. He slept well. My wife and children liked him; he liked them. Everybody in town liked him and was pulling for him."

With his brother's help, Claude Eatherly obtained a job. Perrin Air Force Base is at Sherman, Texas, sixteen miles north of Van Alstyne. On June 26, 1956, Claude Eatherly went to work at the base as an aircraft dispatcher.

"This was the most hopeful thing we had been able to do for him," Joe Eatherly said. "Now he had an interesting job— one he knew how to perform. He was back at an air base dealing with pilots and airplanes."

Therefore, on August 6, 1956, the eleventh anniversary of Hiroshima, Major Eatherly was living where he had been born and reared, and he was working for the United States Air Force. No reporter interviewed him on that anniversary; and as far as I could find, his name had not appeared in any newspaper since 1948, in the last report in New Orleans on the Marsalis affair.

In 1952–53 the motion picture *Above and Beyond* had been made and released. This was a successful film, financed by Metro-Goldwyn-Mayer, starring Robert Taylor and Eleanor Parker, and written, produced and directed by Melville Frank and Norman Panama. Beirne Lay Jr. helped Mr. Frank and Mr. Panama write the script. This film was presented throughout the free world as the story of the training of the 509th Composite Group and the flight of the *Enola Gay* to Hiroshima. The Air Force approved the film. Mr. Taylor portrayed Colonel Tibbets, the Hero of Hiroshima, and Miss Parker portrayed his wife. Other "key figures" were portrayed by name. As part of the film's promotion "every man who was involved in the attack" was found and publicized in his "home community."

Claude Eatherly was neither found nor publicized. No one connected with the film made any *use* of him. When I discovered this, I recalled one of his statements to me: he wanted to be *used*. *Above and Beyond* was a big commercial effort to *use* Hiroshima, but no one had used Claude Eatherly. The writers had not talked with him, or portrayed him, because drama required concentration on the stars . . . on the few men who "dropped the bomb" and who "witnessed this single greatest event in human history." The promoters and publicists had not used Eatherly because they had not found his name among the thirty-two who "witnessed the attack." Only "witnesses" had been adjudged useful to the publicists.

So all the fears which Eatherly had expressed to Jack Bivans on Tinian had become reality. Eatherly had said: "Books will be written about Hiroshima. Movies will be made. And nobody is ever going to know we were there unless we tell them." All this had come to pass. Several books had been written; the big movie had been made; Hiroshima had become history—and history had overlooked Claude Eatherly.

I had been unable to find any evidence that, eleven years after Hiroshima, Claude Eatherly had ever felt any emotion over his role except that of disappointment at not being used—regret at being overlooked by the historians and the publicists. Not once to anyone—not to his wife, or his brother, or any crew member, or any cellmate, or any nursing assistant, or any psychiatrist— had he ever suggested that his mental disorder might stem from Hiroshima. He had expressed guilt feelings over his treatment of his wife and children; but not once, as far as I could find, had he associated guilt feelings with anything he did during the war.

In all their diagnostic examinations, in all their psycho-therapy, in their conversations with him after insulin coma, the psychiatrists had found no evidence that his disorder was related to war experience. To satisfy the legal requirement for compensation—and because he and his children needed finan-cial assistance—someone in the VA, in 1953, had labeled his disorder "service-connected." But Dr. Constantine had written to his wife on May 18, 1956: "His problem is that of growing up emotionally. He has not completely matured."

One other important point. On the eleventh anniversary of Hiroshima, when he was nearing his thirty-eighth birthday, Claude Eatherly had never been called crazy, insane or psy-chotic—three words with the same meaning. His diagnosis was *only* anxiety neurosis . . . a mental ailment . . . a recurring mental disturbance . . . but it was what the psychiatrists called "only a neurosis" and not a "serious crippling disorder" which would bring into question his legal culpability. Not once, as far as I could find, had he ever claimed, or had anyone sug-gested, that he was out of touch with reality, or that he didn't know right from wrong. The various criminal charges against him in the state of Texas had been "dropped by agreement"— but not by agreement that he was insane, only by agreement that he was a VA responsibility and that he would return to Waco instead of beeng imprisoned. In the state of Louisiana he had pleaded guilty to crime and been punished with no "sug-gestion of insanity."

On August 6, 1956, Claude Eatherly was said to be living normally with his brother's family and working every day for the Air Force as an aircraft dispatcher. His sanity had never been questioned. Since April 24, 1956, he had been on a successful "trial visit" away from the hospital.

Eighteen days after the eleventh anniversary of Hiroshima, on August 24, 1956, Claude Eatherly was summoned to the Grayson County Sheriff's office in Sherman, Texas, and there he met George T. Heaberg Jr., a detective for the United States Post Office Department. The detective had evidence that during the night of April 30, 1956, Eatherly, with two accomplices, had broken into post offices at View and Avoca, Texas. Eatherly admitted complicity in these burglaries, signed a statement of admission, and was released in the temporary custody of his brother. This development attracted no publicity, and Eatherly returned to his job at Perrin Air Force Base.

These burglaries had been committed six days after Eatherly left the hospital on the trial visit mentioned in Dr. Constantine's letter. They had been committed nineteen days before Dr. Constantine wrote the letter in which he reaffirmed the diagnosis of anxiety neurosis and immaturity. They had been committed two months before Eatherly went to work at Perrin Air Force Base. Joe Eatherly had not known of the burglaries when he was seeking the Air Force job for his brother because the federal detective had spent four months investigating before he confronted Claude Eatherly.

When I reached this point in my investigation, and when I read the confession which Eatherly signed for Mr. Heaberg, I understood that August 24, 1956, was a turning point in his life.

He had confessed to a serious federal crime. In the United States there are state crimes and federal crimes, state courts and federal courts, state police and federal police, state prisons and federal prisons. Federal crimes are those "against the United States"—crimes like treason, violation of the Firearms Act (as in the Marsalis affair), tax evasion, counterfeiting, and crimes "against the mails." Traditionally, any crime "touching the mail" is serious; and federal officers do not "drop charges" as readily as some state officers do.

According to his confession, four days after he left the Waco hospital, on April 28, 1956, Eatherly received a telephone call from another veteran he had met at Waco. In response to this call he traveled by bus from Van Alstyne to Abilene, Texas, where he and two other veterans hatched a plan to forge a series of post office money orders and cash them in order to provide Eatherly a stake of $2500 for gambling at Las Vegas, Nevada. To accomplish these forgeries they needed money order blanks and a rubber validating stamp used by postal employees to make a money order cashable.

Again according to his confession: seeking the validating stamp and the money order blanks, Eatherly and his accomplices, on the night of April 30, 1956, burglarized the small post office at View, Texas, near Abilene. They obtained the validating stamp but missed the money order blanks. (The postmistress had taken the blanks home with her.) So during the same night they broke into a larger post office at Avoca, Texas, but again they missed the money order blanks when Eatherly failed in repeated efforts to open the safe. Next day Eatherly returned to Van Alstyne without his brother, or anyone else, he thought, knowing of the burglaries.

These burglaries had failed but they were nonetheless burglaries; and once Eatherly had signed the confession, what would happen to him was as predictable as sunrise. No American who is convicted of burglarizing a post office escapes punishment. Eatherly was free, in his brother's custody, on August 25, 1956; he was still a civilian employee of the Air Force; but at the next meeting of the federal grand jury in the Abilene district he would be indicted. Time would pass—months, perhaps even a year—but inevitably he would stand trial in a federal court. And just as inevitably, he would be convicted and sent to a federal prison for not less then one year and probably for three years.

In 1962 I understood the perilous position Eatherly was in on August 25, 1956. The question was: Had Eatherly in 1956 been sufficiently in command of his faculties to understand his position?

According to the VA psychiatrists, he was in sufficient command—he was legally culpable. Eatherly was in the same position he had occupied in New Orleans: his VA diagnosis would not support a claim of insanity.

So, with these post office burglaries, had Eatherly been "seeking punishment," as writers later were to insist? Or did Eatherly still hope to avoid punishment for the burglaries?

Short of death, about the only way he could hope to avoid federal prison was to claim, for the first time, that he was insane. More correctly, he had to claim that on April 30, 1956, he *had been* insane, "out of touch with reality, unable to distinguish right from wrong, psychotic, insane." Not only did he have to claim this, but he had to support his claim with what the courts call "expert testimony."

Would the VA psychiatrists come into federal court and disavow their diagnosis of anxiety neurosis as of April 30, 1956? Would they tell a federal judge and jury that Eatherly on April 30, 1956, had been much sicker than they had reported to his wife on May 18, 1956? If the psychiatrists testified that on April 30, 1956, Claude Eatherly had, in their true but unannounced opinion, been psychotic, then how could they explain their releasing him on April 24, 1956, for an "indefinite trial visit"?

How could Eatherly persuade a federal jury that he was insane, or that he had been insane on April 30, 1956, if he continued to live normally with his brother and to work every day as an aircraft dispatcher? Would not such sane behavior belie a claim of insanity?

In short, for his own welfare and protection, did not Claude Eatherly, in September, 1956, need to be diagnosed as psychotic?

I asked myself these questions, as, step by step, I reconstructed his experience and tried to understand it.

In the early evening of September 28, 1956, Eatherly left his father's farmhouse armed with a .410 shotgun. He drove to Denison, Texas, which is also in Grayson County, ten miles north of Sherman. Unmasked, he walked into a small grocery store and found the grocer alone. He held the gun on the grocer and forced him to empty his cash register and put the money in a paper sack. Eatherly then reached into the sack, took a few coins, and deliberately turned around and walked out of the store leaving the sack and about $80 on the counter. He drove back to the farmhouse where, about two hours later, he was arrested by the Grayson County Sheriff.

Next day the probate judge of Grayson County formally committed Claude Eatherly to the Waco hospital "for a period of 90 days"; and on October 1, 1956, the sheriff again delivered him to the hospital.

The employment records at Perrin Air Force Base show that Eatherly's work was called satisfactory from June 26, 1956, until September 29, 1956, when "for some unexplained reason he ceased appearing for work."

The Denison grocery robbery was a turning point in Eatherly's criminal activities. From his first arrest—in the Marsalis affair in 1947—through all his check offenses, and including the two post office burglaries, his offenses could be classified as ordinary crimes committed for the purpose of obtaining money unlawfully.

But the Denison grocery robbery was what the police call a "stunt" or "attention-seeking" crime. Eatherly didn't take the sack of money, so he didn't commit the crime for the ordinary purpose of obtaining money unlawfully. His purpose then was extraordinary. The psychiatrists call such a crime "a bizarre antisocial act." Several writers later called the Denison robbery a "punishment-seeking" crime. They said Eatherly committed it for the purpose of seeking punishment for the greater crime of Hiroshima.

When I reached the Denison robbery in my investigation, I asked myself these questions: Was Eatherly's purpose at Denison to seek punishment? Or was his purpose to avoid punishment? Or was the crime purposeless?

I concluded that his purpose was to get back in the hospital and thereby try to avoid federal punishment for his post office burglaries. I noted that to commit his "bizarre crime" he had driven about thirty miles from the farmhouse to Denison, which is on the Texas-Oklahoma line. He could have found a small grocery store with a shorter drive, at Denton, Texas, or at McKinney. But had he chosen Denton or McKinney, he would have been jailed by a strange sheriff because they are in other counties. His case would have come before a strange county judge. They might not so readily have delivered him to Waco. But Denison, though distant, is still in Grayson County, on its northern edge; and after a "bizarre holdup" in Denison, Eatherly was arrested by a friendly sheriff who had delivered him to Waco before, and his case came before a friendly county judge.

Back at the hospital, Eatherly reported to the physician in charge of his case, Dr. Constantine. He brought the doctor up to date on his behavior since April 24, 1956, when he "went on trial visit." He described the post office burglaries as well as the bizarre Denison holdup.

What happened?

A month later, in November, 1956, Dr. Constantine changed Eatherly's diagnosis from anxiety reaction to "schizophrenic reaction, chronic and undifferentiated type, a major psychotic disability."

The VA accepted this diagnosis; and in January, 1957, awarded Eatherly "100 percent service-connected disability compensation." His wife began receiving $118.50 a month for the children; he began receiving a similar amount, making a total of $237 a month, the maximum disability compensation.

The VA went further. They rewrote Eatherly's medical history by making his new diagnosis "retroactive for one year." This meant that he had become psychotic on January 5, 1956, when he reentered the hospital from New Orleans; and therefore he was psychotic, suffering from schizophrenia, on the night of April 30, 1956, when he burglarized the post offices.

This "retroactive" decision also gave Eatherly another windfall. In January, 1957, in a lump sum, the VA paid Eatherly enough to give him "100 percent" all the way back to January 5, 1956.

On January 11, 1957, a federal grand jury meeting in Abilene, Texas, indicted Eatherly for the post office burglaries. The federal district attorney notified him of the indictment and advised him to prepare to stand trial.

Twelve

DURING the twelfth year after the bomb fell, Claude Eatherly at last became useful to writers. To learn exactly how he became useful, I studied transcripts of testimony, court records, official correspondence, newspaper and magazine stories, a television film, and a script for a proposed motion picture.

Eatherly's post office burglaries of April 30, 1956, were committed within the jurisdiction of the Abilene Division of the District Court of the United States for the Northern District of Texas. This district court also has an Amarillo division and a Fort Worth division; and presiding over all three divisions, then and now, is the Honorable Joe E. Estes, United States District Judge, whose headquarters is in Fort Worth. In 1957 the United States District Attorney for the Northern District of Texas was Heard L. Floore, also of Fort Worth. When, on January 11, 1957, a federal grand jury indicted Eatherly for the burglaries and thereby instituted the case of *The United States of America versus Claude R. Eatherly,* Mr. Floore bore the responsibility of bringing the defendant to trial before Judge Estes and a jury.

When a defendant is in a mental hospital, as Eatherly was in January, 1957, to bring him to trial a district attorney must first establish with "expert opinion" that the defendant is "presently sane to the extent of being able to cooperate in his own defense." The question is not guilt or innocence, not whether the defendant was competent or incompetent on the day he committed the crime—only his present mental condition. Is he presently able to understand the charges against him and to assist in defending himself against these charges?

Accordingly, March 1, 1957, Mr. Floore wrote to the Waco hospital asking for "expert opinion" as to whether Claude R. Eatherly "will be able to stand trial at Abilene during the month of April, 1957."

When this letter reached the hospital, Eatherly was on a ward supervised by Dr. Ross. The physician in charge of his case was Dr. Constantine; but he was on Dr. Ross's ward. Since Dr. Ross had known Eatherly since 1950 and had been responsible for his first diagnosis, Dr. Ross was instructed by Dr. McMahan to prepare the answer to the district attorney's letter. Dr. Ross wrote:

DEAR MR. FLOORE:

It is our opinion that Mr. Eatherly is competent to aid in the preparation and conduct of the defense of the charges against him.

We feel that he will be able to stand trial at Abilene during the month of April, 1957.

(Signed) SAMUEL H. ROSS, M.D.

That letter was approved by the hospital administration, and when it reached Mr. Floore on March 8, 1957, he had a warrant issued for Eatherly's arrest. A U. S. marshal arrested Eatherly at the hospital and lodged him, as a federal prisoner, in the McLennan County Jail, Waco.

Then, since Waco is not in the Northern District of Texas, Mr. Floore ordered him moved "to the jurisdiction of the court." This meant that Eatherly would be moved eighty-seven miles, from Waco to the Tarrant County Jail, Fort Worth, from where he would be moved to Abilene on his trial date.

It was during the movement from Waco to Fort Worth that coincidence entered the Eatherly Case.

A deputy United States marshal named Robert C. Smith, of San Antonio, Texas, happened to accompany the marshal who moved Eatherly. Mr. Smith was not on duty: he was in Waco, and he went along for the ride. Eatherly rode in the back seat; the two marshals in the front seat.

At some point during the trip a low-flying airplane attracted attention, and the conversation turned to airplanes. Mr. Smith recalled that in 1945 he was a sergeant and assistant line chief in the 509th Composite Group, United States Air Force. The prisoner then recalled that in 1945 he was a major in the 509th, and that he commanded a B-29 called the *Straight Flush*.

"Well, I didn't know whether to believe him or not," Mr. Smith recalled in 1962. "I wasn't sure I remembered any Major Eatherly, but then I thought I did remember the name. When he said some things which indicated he was on Tinian, I decided he might be telling the truth. And I thought it was a hell of a note: me a former sergeant being a federal marshal, and him a former major being transferred from a nuthouse to a prison to stand trial for robbing post offices."

Eatherly and the two marshals reached the Tarrant County Jail, Fort Worth, during the afternoon of March 18, 1957. After the prisoner had been lodged in a cell, Mr. Smith told several of the jailers and a trusty that the prisoner claimed to be "a Major Eatherly," and that he might have had "something to do with the atom bomb."

That evening a reporter for the Fort Worth *Star-Telegram*, Jim Vachule, visited the jail on his usual round. As Mr. Vachule (Vah-hooley) looked over the list of new prisoners, the trusty who had talked with the marshal mentioned Eatherly and what Mr. Smith had said. Again coincidence played its part: Mr. Vachule, too, had been in the Air Force. As a B-29 crewman he had been on Guam at the time of the atomic attacks on Hiroshima and Nagasaki.

"You have been a crime reporter," Mr. Vachule told me in 1962, "so you know how it is. Eatherly was being lodged temporarily in that portion of the jail which Tarrant County rents to the federal government. A reporter almost never finds a story among such federal prisoners. Most of them are being held for trial for transporting stolen cars across state lines. When I heard about the marshal bringing this prisoner up from Waco, I might have ignored it except I had been in a B-29 outfit on Guam. So I was interested enough to go to Eatherly's cell and talk with him. He was in bad shape. He smoked a pipe constantly and nervously. He appeared highly emotional and confused. He appealed to me as an old Air Force buddy to help him."

"He wanted to get out of jail?" I asked.

"Sure he did. Above all, he wanted to avoid going to a fed-

137

eral penitentiary. He wanted to go back to the hospital at Waco."

"Did he win your sympathy? Did you want to help him?"

"Well, first," Mr. Vachule answered, "let's say that I'm paid to find and write human interest stories that people want to read. I don't like jails enough to visit them as a welfare worker: I was there as a paid reporter with a job to do. Some of what Eatherly told me I knew was incorrect. But other things he said proved to me that he had been a B-29 pilot. If it was true that an Air Force major who had been at Hiroshima had now turned to a life of crime . . . well, I thought that was a good story . . . one worth working on. Then, yes, I think it was true that if he was telling me the truth I was willing to help him stay out of jail. I told him I'd try to help him. So I hopped to it. I held up the story for two nights while I worked, trying to dig up the facts. The hospital wouldn't give me anything, nor would the Air Force here in Texas. The federal district attorney, Heard Floore, didn't know anything about Eatherly except what the indictment said. Van Alstyne is about eighty miles from Fort Worth, in our circulation area—but Eatherly's brother Joe resisted publicity and wouldn't give me the time of day. But I was able to find some other members of the 509th who confirmed that Eatherly had been a pilot at Hiroshima and Nagasaki. I then wrote the first story that ever appeared about Claude Eatherly after he had become a mental patient."

Mr. Vachule's first story appeared on Page One of the *Star-Telegram* on March 20, 1957. The *Star-Telegram* may be the most influential newspaper in Texas. It was long owned by a prominent national figure, Amon Carter; and it circulates in Grayson County as well as at the Waco hospital. It is read each day by psychiatrists, federal judges, federal district attorneys, and citizens of Van Alstyne. A story about himself on Page One of the *Star-Telegram* was more important to Claude Eatherly than a story in *The New York Times* or *The Times* of London.

I studied Mr. Vachule's story, trying to imagine what its effect had been on Eatherly, on the psychiatrists, and on the officers of the federal court.

Here is the story:

WORLD WAR II HERO IN TROUBLE
PILOT ON FIRST A-BOMB MISSION
BROUGHT TO JAIL BY OLD COMRADE
by Jim Vachule

The Air Force pilot who led the world's first atomic bombing mission into Hiroshima was in Tarrant County Jail Wednesday—charged with a crime against his country.

He is Claude R. Eatherly, 38-year-old resident of Van Alstyne.

Eatherly, a decorated hero of World War II, is accused of breaking into post offices at View and Avoca in West Texas.

He was transferred here from the Veterans Hospital in Waco to await trial in Abilene next month.

Nervously puffing on his pipe in a jail cell, the former Air Force major and B-29 pilot reluctantly described to a reporter his part in the Hiroshima bombing.

His crew was one of four assigned to fly reconnaissance ahead of the bombing plane over several potential target cities.

Eatherly's mission was to go to Hiroshima.

Finding bombing conditions there suitable, he flew back to a rendezvous point with the other scout planes and the bomb-carrying plane, Col. Paul Tibbets' "Enola Gay."

Together the five bombers made the historic raid on Hiroshima.

"I was calm and not worried at all . . . not a bit nervous," Eatherly recalled Wednesday.

He said he didn't know the details of the atom bomb at the time but said he was aware he was participating in "something big."

After the explosion, Eatherly's plane and the others circled, taking various scientific measurements and observing the results as well as they could.

A few days later he performed the same assignment when the second bomb was dropped on Nagasaki.

For his wartime services Eatherly was awarded the Distinguished Flying Cross and other honors.

But things haven't been so good since for him.

He spent a good part of the past seven years in and out of mental hospitals undergoing treatment for a condition of extreme nervousness.

Then came his troubles with the law.

He and another man were arrested last spring and charged with breaking into the West Texas postoffices.

"We were both out of the hospital on a 90-day trial period.

I don't know why we did it . . . we didn't need money," Eatherly said, explaining that he draws a $237 monthly pension from the government because of his mental disability.

The one-time hero said he wanted it understood that he is not blaming his mental condition or his troubles on his war experience.

"I do feel though," he added, "that I should be in a hospital rather than in jail."

Attendants at the Waco hospital said Eatherly had been adjudged in condition to come here to face trial.

"It's best to have this kind of problem cleared up before attempting to treat a mental patient," a doctor at the hospital observed.

The doctor also noted that Eatherly's record showed that he had had previous troubles with the law.

U. S. Attorney Heard Floore ordered the man brought here to be held for trial.

Floore said Eatherly has never been legally adjudged to be mentally ill. He has always entered the hospital voluntarily, the attorney added.

Floore said he wants to take the case to court to settle the issue of whether Eatherly should be hospitalized or made to stand trial.

Wartime comrades expressed amazement when they learned of Eatherly's confinement here.

One of them, Col. Ralph R. Taylor Jr., now stationed at Biggs Air Force Base in El Paso, told the STAR-TELEGRAM by telephone he was a close friend of Eatherly.

Taylor was commander of another of the five planes making the bomb run on Hiroshima.

"He was a carefree kind of fellow . . . very stable. He never had any problems," said the colonel.

Taylor pointed out that the five pilots assigned to the mission were selected from the entire Air Force especially for the job.

"You had to have an outstanding service record and pass a most rigid security test."

Eatherly's role in history also was recalled by John W. Porter, owner of an automobile agency here. He was a lieutenant colonel in the 509th Bomb Group, the outfit organized especially to deliver the A-bomb.

He, too, remembered Eatherly as a topnotch officer.

Most astonished of all, though, was Robert C. Smith, assistant line chief and staff sergeant in the 509th.

Now a U. S. deputy marshal in San Antonio, it fell to Smith to bring Eatherly here from the Waco hospital.

The two got to discussing the war on the way here and recognized each other.

Unable to believe what his eyes and ears told him, Smith had to return to San Antonio and look up Eatherly's picture in the 509th's yearbook before becoming convinced that he had jailed a former hero and officer in his own outfit.

Next day, March 21, 1957, the *Star-Telegram* continued developing its Eatherly story on Page One:

HERO TO PLEAD INSANITY
IN POSTOFFICE BREAK-INS

A World War II Air Force hero who is accused of breaking into two West Texas postoffices said Thursday at a preliminary hearing before U. S. Commissioner Van Orden that he wants to plead insanity.

The former major and B-29 pilot, 38-year-old Claude R. Eatherly of Van Alstyne, led the history-making atomic bomb attack on Hiroshima.

He was brought here Monday from the Veterans Hospital in Waco to await trial in Abilene on April 17.

Appearing somewhat confused when he first arrived in Van Orden's office from county jail, Eatherly said he did not want to contest the case.

But upon learning that this meant entering a plea of guilty and throwing himself on the mercy of the court, he said he wanted a lawyer so he could plead insanity.

Van Orden set bond at $500 and scheduled a final hearing for 2 P.M. Friday.

Eatherly and members of his family contend that he is a victim of schizophrenia, or split personality.

U. S. Attorney Heard Floore, on the other hand, says he is prepared to submit evidence at the trial next month that Eatherly is legally sane.

Doctors at the Waco hospital, where the former bomber pilot has spent many months since his discharge from the Air Force in 1947, declined Thursday to give details about his case.

Eatherly's last trip to the hospital was on a temporary 90-day commitment ordered by Grayson County Judge J. N. Dixon after the one-time war hero was arrested in Denison as a suspect in grocery store robberies there last September.

The temporary commitment expired early this year but Eatherly remained in the hospital voluntarily until his arrest Monday.

Grayson County Sheriff Woody Blanton said he was advised last fall that Eatherly needed treatment and that he was not in condition to be arrested at that time.

The robbery cases were presented directly to the grand jury and no action was taken, Blanton said.

A check with Strategic Air Command Headquarters in Omaha, Nebraska, Thursday revealed that Eatherly was considered one of the top World War II Air Force pilots.

He and his crew were chosen from the entire Air Force to fly reconnaissance ahead of the atom bomb-carrying plane on the Hiroshima mission.

Finding weather conditions suitable for the big drop, he met at a rendezvous point with the bomber "Enola Gay" and joined in the actual bomb run flight.

Records at Omaha also showed that Eatherly was honorably discharged in 1947 after participating as an observer-pilot in the first postwar atomic tests at Bikini in 1946.

Eatherly's future appeared Thursday to hinge on whether he is found mentally ill.

A schizophrenic, a psychiatrist explained, is a person who is "thrown off the track" by an unusual or changing condition to which he is unable to adjust his thought processes. An escape mechanism which permits him to escape reality then takes hold of him.

The following day, March 22, 1957, the *Star-Telegram* ran a two-column staff photo of Eatherly on Page One. He was standing beside an Air Force recruiting poster, and the camera angle also caught a U. S. Mail truck. The cut lines were:

A THIN LINE—*Claude R. Eatherly, veteran former combat pilot who flew on the first atom bomb mission in history, poses beside two posters that tell a significant story in his life. A decorated Air Force hero in World War II, he is now charged with breaking into two U. S. postoffices.*

Here is the story which accompanied the photo:

CHARGED IN BURGLARIES
BROTHER POSTS BOND FOR HIROSHIMA HERO
by Jim Vachule

Former Air Force hero Claude R. Eatherly was released from jail here Friday and headed for his East Texas home to try to patch up his tragic postwar life.

Eatherly, 38-year-old bomber pilot who participated in the atomic bomb drop on Hiroshima, was freed on $500 bond posted by his brother, Joe Eatherly of Van Alstyne.

The ex-pilot, who held the rank of major and was considered an outstanding officer in World War II, is charged with breaking into postoffices at View and Avoca in West Texas.

His story of glory and tragedy came to light here Thursday when it was discovered he was in county jail and a check was made on details of Eatherly's war record.

Since receiving an honorable discharge in 1947, Eatherly has been in and out of government hospitals for mental patients. Sometimes, between hospital confinements, he has been involved in troubles with the law.

Accompanying Joe Eatherly here were Rev. James Duckworth, pastor of the First Baptist Church at Van Alstyne, and Grayson County Attorney Boyd Newman, of Sherman.

Newman said he came to the hearing as an observer to familiarize himself with the federal case.

Eatherly indicated during a preliminary hearing Thursday before U. S. Commissioner Van Orden that his defense in the postoffice cases will be to plead insanity.

U. S. Attorney Heard Floore ordered Eatherly brought here from the Veterans Hospital in Waco, where he had been since fall, to stand trial in Abilene April 17.

A check Friday with the Veterans Administration regional office in Dallas revealed that the one-time B-29 commander draws government compensation for a service-incurred neuropsychiatric disability. His monthly compensation check, a VA spokeman reported, is based on an 80 per cent disability.

The 80 per cent disability rating was arrived at on the basis of his military records and a study of his case by VA doctors.

"His case is very difficult and complex . . . one of the most involved that we have had," a spokesman in the regional office said.

Both Newman and Rev. Mr. Duckworth, Eatherly's family pastor, offered to post the bond.

The county attorney said a doctor at the Waco hospital told him Eatherly will never get well.

"That's why I was so surprised when charges were filed against him," Newman said.

Extremely nervous and reluctant to discuss his war experiences while he was in jail here, Eatherly left Fort Worth in apparent good spirits.

With those three stories on successive days, an influential newspaper established a distorted image of Claude Eatherly in the places which were important to him: in his home county, at the college he had attended, at the Waco hospital, and in the federal district where he was a defendant in the case of *The United States versus Claude Eatherly.*

No one could hope to understand Eatherly without knowing this fact: that for twelve years he had gone unmentioned in all accounts of Hiroshima because he had not been a witness to the attack or the destruction. But the news stories buried this fact and changed it. He had been a witness! The *veteran former combat pilot* was the Hiroshima Hero . . . hero . . . hero . . . hero: the word *hero* was used eight times in the stories. The Hiroshima Hero was one of only *five* pilots selected from the *entire* Air Force to *lead* the attacks on Hiroshima and Nagasaki. After reconnoitering the target, the hero had led in the *Enola Gay* and *joined in the actual bomb run flight.* Then he had circled, taking measurements and observing details. Three days later he had been the same hero at Nagasaki. And for all this heroism the hero had been decorated, not with a relatively modest decoration like the Air Medal, but with nothing less than the Distinguished Flying Cross.

These news stories created the impression in every reader's mind, possibly including Eatherly's, that since he had won the Distinguished Flying Cross, he had left the Air Force as a publicized hero. Therefore, it was as a publicized hero that he had developed mental illness and "turned to crime."

The truth seems to be that when Claude Eatherly began evidencing mental illness and "turning to crime," he was a disappointed and immature man who thought he had been overlooked. Instead of being a *veteran former combat pilot,* he was a veteran former patrol pilot who had lied to cover his embarrassment at never having been in real combat. Instead of being the Hero of Hiroshima, he was a man who had been disappointed at being left out of the attack on Hiroshima. Instead of being the Hero of Nagasaki, he was a man who had been more disappointed at being entirely left out at Nagasaki. Instead of going to Bikini in triumph as the news stories implied, he had gone to Bikini after being disappointed at failing to win the competition to make the bomb drop. He had been disappointed again at failing to win a Regular Commission in the Air Force —and disappointed again at being expelled from the Air Force for cheating—and disappointed again when, after dreaming of being paid $100,000 for bombing Havana, he had been arrested for participating in a criminal conspiracy.

That was the real truth about Claude Eatherly—the truth that psychiatrists, as well as ordinary people, needed to know if they were to understand and help him. Perhaps it was the truth which he himself needed to know if he was to maintain contact with reality. But in 1957 the most influential newspaper in his environment *established* that he had evidenced mental illness and turned to crime *after* being acclaimed a Hero of Hiroshima and after receiving the Distinguished Flying Cross.

To what extent was Eatherly responsible for this distorted image? Apparently he supplied the misinformation: the reporter says he did. But why should the reporter have believed Eatherly? He had been brought from a mental hospital. He was scared. He was facing a prison term he said he wanted to avoid. He was "reluctant" and "obviously confused." He wanted the reporter to help him get out of jail; and apparently the reporter did help him do that. He was released on bond for a few days. But how can another distorted image help a man who is plagued with distorted images?

The news stories caused questions to be asked of the Veterans Administration. Not only Mr. Vachule but other reporters had begun telephoning the Waco hospital and the Dallas regional office. The spokesman for the Dallas regional office was saying in print "the one-time B-29 commander draws government compensation for a service-incurred neuropsychiatric disability."

145

But Eatherly was saying in print "I want it understood that I am not blaming my mental condition on my military experience."

If Eatherly was correct, he was drawing compensation illegally; and who in the VA was responsible for this illegality? The reporters were asking: how and where during Eatherly's military service did he incur a neuropsychiatric disability? The spokesman was replying: "The 80 percent disability rating [the spokesman had not learned that this had been raised to 100 percent three months earlier] was arrived at on the basis of his military records and a study of his case by VA doctors." But that reply was no answer. The reporters insisted: *where* in his military record is there a basis for awarding service-incurred neuropsychiatric disability compensation?

The Waco hospital had supplied the U. S. Attorney, Mr. Floore, the "expert opinion" that Eatherly mentally was able to stand trial. But Eatherly was announcing that he would plead insanity. Would the VA doctors who had pronounced him ready for trial support his insanity plea? Would they say he was insane when he burglarized the post offices but he was now sane? After awarding him 100 percent service-incurred neuropsychiatric disability compensation, how could they *not* support his plea of insanity?

Until these news stories were published, the VA psychiatrists had never heard of Eatherly being "at Hiroshima" and they had regarded his case as a simple case of a man not being able to grow up. Now the spokesman in the Dallas regional office was informing the public that "his case is very difficult and complex . . . one of the most involved that we have ever had."

The news stories also posed problems for Mr. Floore. Readers would conclude that the hero should be treated in a hospital and not brought to trial. How could the U. S. District Court legally try a hero who was 100 percent mentally disabled? The Grayson County Attorney had traveled to Forth Worth and expressed amazement that the U. S. Attorney would proceed against a man in Eatherly's mental condition. The County Attorney said the Waco doctors had told him that Eatherly would "never get well."

Moreover, a Baptist preacher had traveled from Van Alstyne

to Fort Worth to offer, from his meager resources, to post bail for Claude Eatherly. The preacher was amazed at the U. S. Attorney's action; and when a Baptist preacher is amazed in Waco, Dallas, Fort Worth or Van Alstyne, Texas, public figures take heed. Because Baptists dominate that area: Waco's Baylor University belongs to the Baptists.

On March 28th the issue of *Newsweek* Magazine dated April 1, 1957, went on sale in Waco and Fort Worth. Mr. Vachule's stories had been forwarded to *Newsweek,* and that national magazine, with its overseas circulation, had broadcast the false image around the world. (See Chapter One.) *Newsweek* had not bothered to check a single detail reported by Mr. Vachule. The Hiroshima Hero was a super-pilot . . . a hero-in-handcuffs . . . the picked pilot who had reconnoitered and selected and rendezvoused and led and witnessed and surveyed at both Hiroshima and Nagasaki . . . and the hero had been awarded the Distinguished Flying Cross.

Since *Newsweek* maintains a "research staff" in the shadow of the Pentagon in Washington, how could any psychiatrist or U. S. Attorney doubt that *Newsweek* presented the truth? And how could any *Newsweek* reader in Britain, Germany or Japan doubt that he was reading truth?

As I will show subsequently from a court record, on March 29th a telephone conversation was held between the U. S. Attorney's office in Fort Worth and the hospital in Waco. A conference seemed indicated to consider recent developments. So on April 1st Mr. Floore drove to Waco. Three doctors had been selected to represent the hospital in the conference with the U. S. Attorney. One doctor was Dr. Ross, who had written the opinion that Eatherly was ready to stand trial. Another was Dr. Constantine, the physician currently in charge of Eatherly's case. The third was Dr. McElroy, who was the administrative superior of the other two doctors.

This conference lasted five hours, with the U. S. Attorney facing the three doctors. Dr. Ross reviewed Eatherly's medical record from 1950 and reasserted his opinion that Eatherly was legally competent and ready to stand trial. But Dr. Constantine, in the light of events, had changed his mind. He argued at

147

length that Eatherly was not legally competent to stand trial *at that time.* Dr. McElroy was on the fence for three hours, then began siding with Dr. Constantine and against Dr. Ross.

The U. S. Attorney was critical. Eatherly was free on bail, and neither doctor had seen him since March 18th. What had happened to change anybody's mind about the defendant's present mental condition? The attorney heatedly reminded the doctors that only on their advice had he proceeded toward bringing Eatherly to trial. Yet now, apparently, they wanted to vote two out of three to change their advice.

This conference had a bizarre result. By a vote of two out of three, the psychiatrists suggested that the federal court send Eatherly back to the hospital for an examination. They felt that perhaps they had not examined him carefully enough before giving the U. S. Attorney the opinion of March 8th. Dr. Constantine emphasized that Eatherly was a "masked schizophrenic, and therefore able to hide his symptoms to a remarkable degree."

On April 5, 1957, a motion was filed with Judge Estes by Mr. Floore. The motion was set forth in part;

The United States Attorney further respectfully advises the Court that there is some question as to the mental condition of the said Claude Eatherly, and that certain psychiatrists who have heretofore examined and treated the said Claude R. Eatherly in the Veterans Administration Hospital in Waco, Texas, have advised the United States Attorney that there is a question as to whether or not the said Claude R. Eatherly is now mentally able to assist in the preparation of his defense; and as to whether or not the said Claude R. Eatherly is now insane;

THEREFORE, the United States Attorney is of the opinion that the said defendant should be transported to the Veterans Administration Hospital at Waco, Texas, in order that the medical authorities employed at that institution may make an observation and examination of the said defendant, and after having made such examination and observation, make a written report to this court of their findings.

THEREFORE, the United States Attorney moves that this Honorable Court enter an order . . .

On that same day, April 5, 1957, Judge Estes ORDERED the marshal to take Eatherly back to the hospital, and ORDERED the psychiatrists to make an examination and report FORTHWITH.

On April 6, 1957, Eatherly was admitted officially, for the fifth time, to the hospital "by court order."

On April 12, 1957, this letter was transmitted:

HONORABLE JOE E. ESTES
United States District Judge,
Post Office Building,
Abilene, Texas.

DEAR JUDGE ESTES:

Mr. Claude R. Eatherly was admitted to the Veterans Administration Hospital, Waco, Texas, by court order, on April 6, 1957, for a period of neuropsychiatric observation and examination. Since February of 1950 Mr. Eatherly has had four previous admissions to this hospital. He is rated by the Veterans Administration as being service-connected 100% from World War II on the mental disability of schizophrenic reaction, chronic undifferentiated type, a major psychotic disability. The present findings indicate that the veteran is of unsound mind and the schizophrenic process remains active and progressive. At this time he is not considered to be so mentally incompetent as to be unable to understand the court proceedings against him. While he is unreliable, unpredictable, and his thinking is disorganized, nevertheless he should be able to offer some assistance in his defense.

He was discharged from the hospital on April 12, 1957, upon termination of observation and examination as requested by court order. He departed from the hospital in the custody of his brother, Joe Eatherly.

> Sincerely,
> ROBERT B. MCELROY, M.D.
> Chief, Acute Intensive Treatment Service
>
> O. P. CONSTANTINE, M.D.
> Physician in Charge of Case

After receiving that report, Judge Estes ordered a hearing at Fort Worth on April 17, 1957. This was not to be a trial; only a hearing on the question of "present competence of the defendant." The judge ordered Eatherly, Dr. McElroy and Dr.

Constantine to be present, along with counsel for both Eatherly and the United States. The hearing was brief—Eatherly said nothing; the doctors did little more than affirm what they had said in their letter—after which Judge Estes issued this order:

Upon consideration of the report of examination and testimony by Doctors Robert B. McElroy and O. P. Constantine, qualified psychiatrists of the Veterans Administration Hospital in Waco, Texas, it appears to the Court that the accused, Claude R. Eatherly, should be recommitted to the Veterans Administration Hospital in Waco, Texas, for further observation, examination and report;

It is hereby ORDERED that the said Claude R. Eatherly shall voluntarily appear at the Veterans Administration Hospital in Waco, Texas, on April 18, 1957, for observation and examination and remain there for such purpose until December 16, 1957; and that upon completion of said observation and examination by said psychiatrists, they shall submit to this court a written report containing the result of said examination and observation.

Said psychiatrists will report whether in their opinion the said Claude R. Eatherly is then insane or otherwise so mentally incompetent as to be unable to understand the proceedings against him or properly assist in his own defense, and whether in their opinion the accused Claude R. Eatherly, if released, would probably endanger the safety of the officers, the property, or other interests of the United States.

The hospital record shows:

Claude R. Eatherly's sixth admission occurred April 18, 1957. He was admitted on the order of a United States District Court for observation and examination. He was discharged on December 7, 1957, by court order.

This means that for nearly eight months following April 18, 1957, Claude Eatherly was on a closed ward in the hospital and could not be reached in person by any reporter. However, on May 2, 1957, Mr. Vachule was able to score another beat. He persuaded Dr. Constantine to give him a report on Eatherly's progress. Dr. Constantine gave more than a progress report: for the first time he volunteered an answer to the troublesome question as to where and how the Hiroshima Hero, while he was in the Air Force, had incurred a neuropsychiatric disability.

Here is the story from Page One of the *Star-Telegram*:

HAUNTED BY HIROSHIMA?
GUILT COMPLEX BLAMED
IN WAR HERO'S CRIMES
by Jim Vachule

Could a guilt complex arising out of his participation in history's greatest mass killing have driven Air Force Hero Claude R. Eatherly into a postwar life of irresponsible crime?

Psychiatrists treating the one-time B-29 pilot aren't positive, but they think Eatherly's role in dropping the first atomic bomb on Hiroshima may be in large part responsible for his present mental disorder.

It was Eatherly's plane that flew reconnaissance over Hiroshima and then led the bomb-carrying plane over the target on that fateful day that hastened the end of World War II.

Eatherly, 38-year-old Van Alstyne resident, was jailed here in March on a charge of breaking into postoffices last spring at View and Avoca in West Texas near Abilene.

He was to have been tried on burglary charges, but after news stories disclosed his distinguished World War II record and his subsequent background of mental illness, federal officials asked that he be committed to the Veterans Hospital at Waco.

Eatherly entered the hospital April 18 and since has been undergoing extensive examinations and treatment.

Dr. O. P. Constantine, one of the hospital psychiatrists assigned to the case, reported Thursday from Waco that Eatherly has shown some signs of responding to treatment.

The doctor said in his opinion Eatherly will continue to improve.

"But," he added, "I can't say if he will ever be a completely new man."

Dr. Constantine said he wanted the public to know that because of a severe condition of mental illness Eatherly was not responsible for his acts at the time he broke into the postoffices.

"Prior to his wartime experience," said Dr. Constantine, "Eatherly was everything a man should be.

"He was one man in a thousand . . . loyal and dependable. He had high moral principles, and all the qualities of leadership."

It was an accumulation of horrifying war experiences climaxed by his participation in the first atom bomb drop that induced Eatherly's mental condition, the doctor said.

"From time to time he experiences feelings of extreme guilt, imagining himself responsible for the mass killing at Hiroshima," Dr. Constantine said.

This condition, continued the doctor, causes him to lose the characteristics of leadership and dependability that he had to have to become one of the top pilots in the Air Force.

Instead, he becomes almost like putty and can be talked into doing just about anything, Dr. Constantine said.

"Anyone can influence him. He loses all will power," the doctor added.

This, explained the psychiatrist, was the condition Eatherly was in when he and another man broke into the postoffice.

When I found that story in 1962 I was so astonished that I quickly read it a second time. It constitutes a remarkable performance by a doctor involved in a criminal proceeding. The case of *The United States of America versus Claude R. Eatherly* was pending. As an expert witness in the case, Dr. Constantine was an officer of the court. It was the court's responsibility to determine Eatherly's mental condition on the night of April 30, 1956, when he burglarized two post offices. The place for Dr. Constantine to express his expert opinion was in a district court of the United States where he could be cross-examined. Yet far in advance of the trial Dr. Constantine "wanted the public to know that because of a severe condition of mental illness Eatherly was not responsible for his acts at the time he broke into the post offices."

Had Dr. Constantine made those statements in court, here are sample questions he might have been asked:

Doctor, if you thought Claude Eatherly was so severely ill on April 30, 1956, when he burglarized the post offices, will you please tell the court why on April 24, 1956, you released him for an indefinite trial visit?

And Doctor, if you thought he was so ill on April 30, 1956, will you please tell us why on May 18, 1956, you wrote his wife that he was suffering only from an anxiety neurosis and that his principal trouble was not being able to grow up?

And Doctor, you have testified that Eatherly's mental illness

152

was *incurred* while he was in the Air Force . . . and you say that it was incurred by an accumulation of horrifying war experiences climaxed by his participation in the first atom bomb drop. So, Doctor, I hand you Eatherly's official Air Force service record, and I ask you to point out to the court *one* horrifying war experience prior to August 6, 1945.

And Doctor, if Eatherly experiences feelings of extreme guilt, imagining himself responsible for the mass killing at Hiroshima, why do you suppose that on March 18, 1957, to Mr. Vachule, Eatherly so vehemently denied that his military experiences contributed to his postwar mental difficulties?

No such questions were asked Dr. Constantine because he wasn't in court, Eatherly was unavailable for questioning, and the reporter who was quoting Dr. Constantine lacked the information on which to base such questions.

Over and over I returned to this question: Why would a Veterans Administration psychiatrist make such statements to a reporter about a defendant in a case pending in federal court? The VA declined to answer this question and refused to allow me to ask Dr. Constantine. So I could only reconstruct the situation and see if I could find an answer.

Following publication of the *Star-Telegram* stories, VA officials in Texas were under severe pressure to explain publicly how and where Claude Eatherly had incurred, while he was in the Air Force, a 100 percent neuropsychiatric disability. And where does a Hiroshima Hero get mentally disabled if not at Hiroshima? Had Eatherly been mentally disabled to the slightest degree prior to Hiroshima, he would have had no role in the Hiroshima mission. The war ended eight days after Hiroshima; and Eatherly's last wartime flight was made two days after Hiroshima. So if Eatherly had not suffered some emotional wound at Hiroshima which ultimately disabled him, where could he have incurred such a wartime disability?

Dr. Constantine made the public explanation. Eatherly's disability, he said, was the result of "an accumulation of horrifying war experiences" which now caused him "to imagine himself responsible for the mass killing at Hiroshima." Thereafter, Dr. Constantine became the VA's principal spokesman to the courts and to the press. All other VA spokesmen took their cues from him. So two questions must be asked:

One, did Dr. Constantine make his public explanation after being instructed to do so by his superiors in the VA? And two, was Dr. Constantine correct in saying that Eatherly suffered an emotional wound from his role at Hiroshima—a wound which resulted in a guilt complex and mental disability?

The answer to the first question seems to be yes. I find it unbelievable that the doctor would have spoken to the public without prior consultation with his superiors. And no superior has ever challenged his statement.

The answer to the second question? Each reader from this point will have to reach his own answers. I'm not a psychiatrist, so I can't debate psychiatric conclusions with a VA psychiatrist. All I can do is report the developments which followed.

On Friday, May 24, 1957, the Fort Worth *Star-Telegram* published a photo of a smiling Mr. Vachule; and the cut line said he was smiling because he was $500 richer. Here is a portion of the accompanying story:

SHOW NEXT FRIDAY NIGHT
FORT WORTH REPORTER
WINS "BIG STORY" PRIZE
by Elston Brooks

The eyes of the nation next week will be on Fort Worth, and more particularly on a STAR-TELEGRAM reporter.

Jim Vachule, 34-year-old county courthouse reporter for the morning STAR-TELEGRAM has won television's "The Big Story" award. He will be honored on the NBC show next Friday night at 7:30 P.M. on Channel 8.

The video show will tell the part he played in the recent story here about the forgotten war hero who was arrested for postoffice burglary. Vachule found the burglar actually was a former Air Force major who had selected Hiroshima as the target for the world's first A-bomb blast.

They are calling the video drama "Hiroshima Plus Twelve."

"Of course I was trying to pick up extra dough out of the story," Mr. Vachule told me. "NBC had sent a lot of publicity to newspaper offices, urging reporters to send in their best stories and compete for The Big Story Award. They had this series where the gimmick was to *award* a reporter $500 for the best story of the week. Then they'd present the story as true with only a little *dramatization* added. Even before Dr. Constantine had given me the guilt complex, I had sent the first three stories to NBC. And they grabbed it *like that!*"

"How did you like the TV drama?" I asked.

"Well," Mr. Vachule sighed, "to put it mildly I was flabbergasted. I had been vaguely aware that some television shows use dramatic license, but I wasn't prepared for what they did to my Eatherly story. I had hoped they would emphasize the work I did in digging out the facts. But their production dealt primarily with the mental illness aspects of the case. I believe the saying is: the *true* story was *very highly dramatized.*"

Claude Eatherly viewed NBC's "Hiroshima Plus Twelve" on May 31, 1957, while sitting with thirty other patients in a closed ward at the Waco hospital. Joe Eatherly watched it with his family at his home in Van Alstyne. Dr. Constantine watched it with his family at his home in Waco. I purposely have never seen the film. I wanted to know what one average viewer, looking at the drama once in 1957, might have seen and remembered. So in 1962 when the program's sponsor, the American Tobacco Company, agreed to show the film for this book's purposes, I asked one "average viewer" to look at the film once, then walk away and later write me a memorandum as to what she remembered. My "average viewer" was Miss Nancy Seward, a stenographer for G. P. Putnam's Sons, who had not read any portion of my manuscript and who knew little of the story.

On November 30, 1962, Miss Seward sent me this memo:

The film opened with the announcement that *The Big Story* was a creation of Pyramid Productions; executive producer was Everett Rosenthal; producer and director were Robert Lewis Shayon; script was by Jerome Coopersmith.

Twelve years after Hiroshima the name Peter Morgan rang a bell with Jim Vachule, Texas reporter. Pete had been arrested for a postal robbery. Jim remembered that a man named Peter Morgan had been in the Air Force unit which was responsible for dropping the A-bomb on Japan. Jim also remembered that those men had been chosen specifically for their good character. So *that* Air Force Peter Morgan would not be involved in any crime. The man in jail must be *another* Peter Morgan. But Jim, being a real reporter, must satisfy himself. He goes to the jail cell where Peter Morgan denies everything. Peter says he was never in the Air Force, never had any A-bomb experience, and Pete orders Jim to "get out of here and leave me alone."

But Jim, with his proverbial reporter instinct, is only made more curious. He must probe. In order to find out more about Peter's personal life and true identification, he contacts the Veterans Administration for help. Here he finds that Peter has spent time in the Waco Veterans Hospital which is a mental institution. And at the hospital a psychiatrist, Dr. Edward Nichols, describes the situation like this: He says that before the war Pete had had such a healthy and sensitive attitude toward life that the reality of having to do things during the war against his moral code . . . such as killing . . . this had created or touched off a deep conflict in Pete.

Because Pete was a member of the unit which dropped the first A-bomb, he imagined himself to be responsible for 75,000 deaths.

"Pete Morgan," Dr. Nichols says to Jim, the reporter, "thought that he himself was responsible for all those deaths. So he yearned to atone for this act, he wanted to be punished for it. Instead, society treated him as a hero. This made Pete's sense of guilt even more intense. There was only one outlet left for him. He had to commit antisocial acts . . . crimes . . . in order to be punished for what he believed to be unbearable personal guilt."

"In effect," Dr. Nichols concludes, "Pete Morgan has been driving his shame into his unconscious. Conscious, Pete doesn't recognize his war crimes, but unconsciously he does, and he wants to be punished."

The doctors feel that Pete must not be put in jail but must be brought back to the hospital for treatment.

Meanwhile, however, Pete Morgan has been released on bail by his brother with whom he had been living prior to his arrest. The brother is named John Morgan. And John Morgan tells police that he is very proud of his brother . . . for his unselfish character . . . for his athletic prowess. Pete once won an award for the Cotton Bowl Football Game . . . and Pete won an award for saving people's lives by running into an oil refinery when it was in blazes in Denison, Texas.

Now Jim, the reporter, rushes to Pete's brother to try to persuade him to seek psychiatric help for Pete. Meanwhile, his being arrested has aroused this huge sense of guilt in our pilot. He has decided to go up to the family shack for a while because "they all think I'm guilty." He's never going back to Fort Worth again for that reason.

When Jim, the reporter, arrives at the brother's home, Pete has flown the coop . . . he has gone to the shack. The brother says he never once suspected or knew of Pete's illness and complex.

After Jim, the reporter, explains everything that Dr. Nichols has told him, and after a bit of trauma on the brother's part, they both take off to retrieve Pete and convince him of his need for psychiatric help.

The last scene takes us to the shack where Peter is holed-up, guns emplaced, ready to shoot it out with the law. His brother coaxes him to relax by explaining that he has just found out that he was sick. Peter then reveals his reason for never telling his brother about his mental troubles.

"I never wanted you to be ashamed of me," Peter says.

His brother is quick to use psychology. He responds: "Pete, I'm more proud of you now than ever."

A headline of the Fort Worth *Star-Telegram* informs us: U. S. ATTORNEY DROPS CHARGES AGAINST BOMB HERO.

The Narrator explains that the Hero received treatment instead of punishment, and for this reason the Big Story Award was given to Jim Vachule of the *Star-Telegram*.

Vachule comes on and accepts his Award. He says that Chief Psychiatrist Nichols has just flashed this message to him: THE PATIENT IS RESPONDING WELL TO TREATMENT AND WILL CONTINUE TO IMPROVE.

In brief: cops-and-robbers, hearts-and-flowers, the never-say-die Reporter saves the War Hero from jail, and the Chief Psychiatrist is going to teach the Hero how to find peace.

Many questions occurred to me when I reflected on that television show and its effects on Claude and Joe Eatherly.

Why had their names been changed? The usual announced explanation is that are names are changed to *protect*. To protect whom? Claude and Joe Eatherly? Every newspaper reader from the Waco hospital to Van Alstyne had been told that the show was the televised story of Claude Eatherly. The Fort Worth *Star-Telegram* was named in the show. The reporter was rewarded by name. Any viewer who didn't know the real names but wanted to know, had only to write a letter or lift a telephone. So who was protected by the device of fictitious names? The exploited or the exploiters?

Name-changing is only one trick in a bag of tricks to reduce legal risk . . . to enable exploiters to commercialize a claim of truth while remaining free to fabricate.

There are laws in the United States regarding the right to portray living persons. As long as a writer is truthful and free of malicious intent, he has great latitude in writing *about* living persons in the United States. But no one has the right to portray living persons with actors without their consent.

Did the television exploiters portray Claude Eatherly? If so, why hadn't they sought his permission? Why hadn't they shown him the script? Why hadn't they considered the effect of their commercial effort on him?

Claude Eatherly, in the mental hospital, was embarrassed by the show. Did his exploiters help him toward learning to distinguish fact from fancy?

I asked him: "Why do you think they spent all that money on that television show?"

He replied with a hard, cynical sneer: "Money, money, money! The bastards were making money out of me!"

Was his answer correct?

Did the television exploiters portray Joe Eatherly? His neighbors and business associates thought they did. Then why hadn't the exploiters sought his permission? Why hadn't they shown him the script? Why hadn't they considered the effect of their commercial effort on him?

When I asked Joe Eatherly about the show, he looked at me in pain and anguish. "Why did they do it?" he asked. "How could they do it? Didn't I have enough trouble trying to help my brother without Jim Vachule trying to win The Big Story Award and without NBC using my brother and me to sell cigarettes? The show was a silly lie which held my brother and me up to ridicule. Our neighbors wanted to know what year Claude Eatherly won the big prize in the Cotton Bowl football game. They wanted to know how come I hadn't known about Claude's mental illness until a reporter came and explained it to me. And if Claude Eatherly was such a hero in 1945, how

158

come nobody had ever heard he was a hero until 1957 when the *Star-Telegram* and *Newsweek* and NBC told us he had been a hero? Is that the way people write *news* and spread *truth* in America!"

With that television show on May 31, 1957, a questionable image was conveyed to millions of unsuspecting Americans. Most of these Americans didn't know Eatherly's real name, but they had been told a truth—that an Air Force hero had been driven to mental illness by his guilt feelings over Hiroshima. The hero yearned to be punished for Hiroshima. But because his society would not punish him for Hiroshima, the hero had resorted to forging checks and robbing post offices to compel his society to punish him.

Claude Eatherly himself had had little part in creating this questionable image. He had supplied a reporter distorted information about his role at Hiroshima. But he had insisted that his postwar crimes were not related to his military experiences. Thereafter, he had sat in confinement and read and watched while his questionable image was being built and conveyed both to him and to the public.

Eatherly had sat silent in confinement and read Dr. Constantine's announcement that he was suffering from guilt feelings over Hiroshima. Then he had sat silent in confinement and watched and listened while television's "Dr. Nichols" explained *to Eatherly* as well as to millions of Americans that the hero's forgeries and robberies were his efforts to win punishment for the larger crime of Hiroshima.

Now, how could Eatherly dispute what the psychiatrists were saying? "Dr. Nichols" had informed both Eatherly and the public that any denial by the hero that he felt guilty over Hiroshima would be irrelevant. Why? Because the hero *did not know* that he felt guilty over Hiroshima. His Hiroshima-guilt had been driven into his unconscious, and only a psychiatrist could discern that Hiroshima-guilt had caused the hero to forge checks and rob post offices.

How can one mental patient oppose doctors and dramatists who can command the pages of *Newsweek*, the wires of the Associated Press, and the coaxial cables of NBC?

Had the television show helped Claude Eatherly? To end their show happily, the dramatists had flashed the headline: U. S. ATTORNEY DROPS CHARGES AGAINST BOMB HERO. Eatherly knew that was a lie. In truth the U. S. Attorney was only waiting for the bomb hero to improve. The television show ended with the announcement: "the patient will continue to improve."

The more the patient improved, the more certain he was to stand in the dock.

Readers will now note carefully what I have called *distorted* and what I have called *questionable*.

I have labeled as distorted all published information about Claude Eatherly which is at variance with available records which would be accepted as evidence in any court in the free world. That Eatherly witnessed the attacks on Hiroshima and Nagasaki, or the destruction after the attacks; that he received the Distinguished Flying Cross; that he was called a hero prior to 1957; that he made a *legal* attempt to commit suicide; or that he scorned his compensation as blood money—all such statements are distorted and I can prove they are distorted.

But as for the psychiatric opinion that Eatherly suffered an emotional wound at Hiroshima, that he feels guilty and seeks punishment for Hiroshima—I have called this opinion *questionable* because, as I shall explain, it was *questioned* and opposed by other VA psychiatrists who had examined Eatherly over a period of years.

Readers will understand that I cannot know or prove that any psychiatric opinion about a human mind is either true or false. I can only report contrary opinions, records, statements and developments.

From what I will now report, each reader must reach his own conclusions as to conflicting psychiatric opinion. Each reader must come to his own judgment of Eatherly, Dr. Constantine, TV drama, motion picture scripts, and all the writers who have made the Eatherly Case into an international *cause célèbre*.

160

Thirteen

AT this point in my investigation it seemed clear to me that the Eatherly Case had become an international *cause célèbre* because of two developments:

One, because someone in the VA, in 1953, had called Eatherly's mental disability a *service-incurred* disability. This action by the VA had been interpreted, in 1957, as being official recognition that Eatherly had suffered an emotional wound at Hiroshima. And,

Two, because Dr. Oleinick Pavlovitch Constantine had, in 1957, announced that Eatherly was suffering from guilt feelings over Hiroshima.

So before I considered Eatherly's trial for the post office burglaries, in which Dr. Constantine testified at length, I paused and examined the doctor's background. Why had this doctor, in 1957, been able to peer into Eatherly's subconscious and detect Hiroshima-guilt, while other doctors, in 1950 and thereafter, had failed to detect it?

On one of my visits to the hospital I shook hands with Dr. Constantine in Dr. McMahan's presence. Fair, stocky, strong-faced, amiable, he is unmistakably Russian. In appearance and manner he reminded me of General Zhukov. Dr. McMahan told him I had come to "get to the bottom of the Eatherly Case and put everything on the record." Dr. Constantine said he had always assumed this would be done, sooner or later. He told me he had been responsible for changing Eatherly's diagnosis. Then Dr. McMahan reminded us of the VA edict against conversation between me and VA psychiatrists. Dr. Constantine shrugged and wished me well.

In the face of the edict, to try to understand Dr. Constantine, I had to dig into records and depend on conversations he held with Ray Bell, the Waco newsman who assisted me. At Baylor University, in the files of the student paper, Ray Bell found *The Daily Lariat* of Friday, September 23, 1932. On page two is a full-length photo of a handsome, smiling, stocky, vigorous, blond young Ukrainian in his polished, knee-length boots, baggy pants, and colorful sash. The story says:

FIRST BAPTISTS TO
HEAR RUSSIAN TALK

BAYLOR STUDENT, ATTIRED IN
NATIVE DRESS, WILL DISCUSS
RELIGIOUS CONDITIONS

Constantine Oleinick will have firsthand information when he appears in native costume and discusses religious conditions in Russia at 7:30 o'clock Sunday evening at the First Baptist Church. Oleinick enrolled as a premedic student in Baylor University this fall. He plans to enter Baylor medical college at Dallas next year and finish work which should prepare him for medical missionary work in Russia.*

Mr. Oleinick received his master's degree from the University of South Carolina and has spent a year at the seminary in Philadelphia. He has practically finished a book dealing with past revolutionary and present Russia.

The young Russian is a man who has lived through the terrors and hardships of the Russian revolution and the downfall of the church there. This downfall he attributes to corruption in the churches and the government.

In *The Daily Lariat* of Tuesday, September 27, 1932, appeared this leading editorial:

CONSTANTINE OLEINICK

Few men can describe war in more striking terms than those who heard the roar of guns and the screams of dying soldiers during the

---

* Baylor's medical college is now in Houston; but in 1932 it was in Dallas.

great catastrophe of 1914–18. Even more vivid is the description of one who as a little child was caught between blazing enemy lines, deprived of a father through conscription, and lost from his mother.

This is the account of Constantine Oleinick, young pre-medic student in the University, as he related his life story at First Baptist Church Sunday. It is a story direct from war-torn Russia of that period, a true story from his native land.

As a nine-year-old boy Constantine fled to the forest with his sister, who was seven years old. They climbed trees to escape wild animals. Like the denizens of the forest, they lived on roots, grass, and anything which nature provided. All the while they could hear the frightful shells as they screeched past their little peasant home.

The editorial continues with details of how young Constantine Oleinick was persecuted as a Christian in Red Russia, and how he was discovered and brought to America by Baptist missionaries. It concludes with:

When his education in America is completed, Oleinick will return to Russia to journey from village to village and minister unto his people, physically and spiritually. He will preach the word of God and the cause of peace. A man could be no greater than he who overcomes apparently insurmountable obstacles for the uplifting of an oppressed people.

The Waco *Times-Herald,* on Monday, September 26, 1932, published a column-long report on Constantine Oleinick's address at the First Baptist Church. The report ended with these paragraphs:

"But you cannot bind the religious souls of the people by laws and regulations," Mr. Oleinick said, "and the more the sincere Christians in Russia have been persecuted the more rapidly they have increased in numbers. There are at least five million Baptists in Russia today . . . and God is not going to permit Himself to be legislated out of Russia."

The young minister has made a reputation for himself as a lecturer while studying in the east. When he completes his medical education at Baylor, he will become a medical missionary and return to his native land to give his life working among his people.

He was a 9-year-old child at the outbreak of the Russian Revolution, and he gave a vivid description of the privations he, his family, and millions of others suffered as the result of the World War.

He pleaded that the American people and others of the world learn the futility of war, and he urged his hearers to pray for world peace.

"Yes," Dr. Constantine told Ray Bell, "I was one of the boys after the Russian Revolution who drifted from place to place. They found me in Warsaw, Poland. My father was a Protestant. He reared me as an evangelical student, or Baptist. Actually, it was all one group over there, Evangelical Christians. The people of the Baptist Missionary Union came in, found me as a student with an evangelical background, and decided to send me to the United States to be educated. Sort of like the present exchange students program except it was operated by the Baptist Missionary Union. I had a guardian, Dr. G. A. Broady, from Plains, Kansas. He's dead now. He and his wife were doctors. They became my guardians because I was only seventeen. They sent papers to the American consul in Warsaw and guaranteed that I would not become a burden on American society. I arrived in the United States with one dollar in my pocket, barely speaking English. I was told I'd have a better chance of making friends if I went South. That's how I got to South Carolina.

"My parents were Ukrainians," Dr. Constantine continued, "and Ukrainians are different from persons in any other country. The language is not Polish or Russian: it's Ukrainian. The Ukrainian people have a separate culture. They are like Texans: boastful, nationalistic, very proud of their country. I guess that's why I belonged in Texas, and why I like it here. I came from South Carolina to Texas with Dr. George Truett, who was the greatest preacher and the greatest man I have ever known. He said: 'You come to Texas with me, for Texas is wonderful.' I came with him to Dallas and Waco, and he was behind me all the way. The Truett Memorial Hospital in Dallas is named for him and I did some intern work there. Once, while I was an intern, he had pneumonia, and I was privileged to help care for him.

"No," Dr. Constantine concluded, "I'm not an ordained minister, but I once had a license to preach. I thought that

164

when I finished my education I'd go back to the Ukraine, but by 1938 it had become very difficult to return to Russia. I changed my name the day I was naturalized. The judge asked me what I was called, and I told him 'Constantine.' So the judge suggested I let Constantine be my last name instead of my first. That's why I have been O. P. Constantine ever since, and few people know that the O.P. stands for Oleinick Pavlovitch. In 1939 I had permission from our State Department to bring my family to America. But the war broke out. Today I have one sister and one brother who are still alive. My sister is a doctor in the Ukraine. She writes to me. She told me only that our family 'perished' during the German invasion."

Dr. Constantine, thoroughly Americanized, prospered in Texas. The late Dr. George Truett, long of Dallas, was a distinguished American and a distinguished Baptist, so any protégé of Dr. Truett was off to a good start at Baylor and Waco. Dr. Constantine was in the Army during the war, but he did not go overseas. He was assigned to a hospital at Rochester, New York. He is a Mason and a member of the American Legion. He is an impressive man with a brilliant family. His wife, born in Big Springs, Texas, is an instructor in the English department at Baylor. His daughter, who was a student leader at Baylor, is married to a doctor in Austin, Texas; and his son is an honor pre-medical student at the University of Texas.

Ray Bell found Dr. Constantine to be aware of all the results of his action in the Eatherly Case. The doctor said he understood that when he announced in 1957 that Eatherly was suffering from guilt feelings over Hiroshima, he "made Eatherly an international figure," he "brought on all the television and Hollywood interest," and he "caused mail to start flooding into Texas from every point of the globe."

"There was no mention of guilt in Eatherly's case until 1957," Dr. Constantine explained to Ray Bell. "I was not aware of his being at Hiroshima until after he became my particular responsibility in 1956, and I don't believe I fully accepted that he was at Hiroshima until I read the first publicity about him in regard to the post office hearings."

That statement by Dr. Constantine removes from the field of controversy in the Eatherly Case the twelve years between

1945 and 1957. Here is a *truth:* during those twelve years Hiroshima was not a factor in any decision in this case. Eatherly had never had one Hiroshima nightmare; neither he nor anyone else had ever suggested that Hiroshima had contributed to his difficulties; and no psychiatrist or anyone else had considered it.

"When I really got down to studying Eatherly," Dr. Constantine continued, "I realized that the diagnosis of anxiety reaction was wrong. The doctors before me hadn't watched him closely enough. He would hide his mental illness. He knows how to hide it. The man is smart. He had hidden his true condition from other doctors who had examined him. The very first thing that struck me was that for some doggone reason he was seeking punishment to the very point of destroying his own life. He was trying to destroy himself. That was why he had tried to commit suicide. He was seeking punishment for *something!* I saw him as really ill, and I changed his diagnosis from anxiety to schizophrenia. I stuck my neck out. I called a spade a spade to the proper people. Eatherly was schizophrenic, and he was committing antisocial acts seeking punishment for Hiroshima."

That is a convincing statement by a reputable doctor whose conclusions may be correct. So why have I called Dr. Constantine's conclusions questionable? I have called them questionable, not because I question them—I'm not equipped to question them—but because they were questioned by an equally reputable VA psychiatrist.

I have mentioned that Dr. Samuel H. Ross was the VA psychiatrist first in charge of Eatherly's case in 1950; that Dr. Ross maintained a doctor-patient relationship with Eatherly from 1950 to 1957; that in March, 1957, Eatherly was on Dr. Ross's ward; and that in 1957 Dr. Ross spoke for the Waco hospital in advising the U. S. Attorney that Eatherly was mentally able to stand trial for the post office robberies. I have described a five-hour conference during which Dr. Ross took issue with Dr. Constantine as to Eatherly's diagnosis and condition.

A native of Pennsylvania, Dr. Ross was a graduate of the University of Detroit. He was a respected member of the psychiatric staff at the Waco hospital from 1947 until February 13, 1959, when at fifty-two he died of a heart attack at his home in

Waco. He was therefore unavailable for questioning in the preparation of this book. However, in 1957, after Dr. Constantine had announced to the public that Eatherly was suffering from guilt feelings over Hiroshima, and after Dr. Constantine had become the VA's spokesman in the Eatherly Case, Dr. Ross insisted on inserting his opinion in Eatherly's permanent VA file. A portion of Dr. Ross's opinion was read into a federal court record. Here it is:

Claude Eatherly is capable of very little emotional response to any problem. He has no moral feelings toward his wife or children or toward any human being that he meets. He is incapable of feeling responsibility or loyalty or moral obligation of any sort to any individual or group of individuals.

Dr. Ross was not alone in his conclusions. He was supported by other members of the Waco hospital psychiatric staff. One of these doctors told me that Dr. Ross insisted until his death that Dr. Constantine was wrong in believing that Eatherly felt guilty or sought punishment. I was told that Dr. Ross declared at a staff meeting: "Any suggestion that Eatherly feels guilty of Hiroshima is nonsense. Eatherly is incapable of feeling guilt. He is incapable of feeling obligation to his own children, to any individual, or to society as a whole."

A point on which Dr. Ross differed with Dr. Constantine was Eatherly's suicide attempt. Dr. Constantine insisted that this attempt was a genuine effort by a man trying to destroy himself —what the psychiatrists call "a punishment-seeking act." Dr. Ross insisted that the suicide attempt was "obviously bogus— an attention-seeking act, not a punishment-seeking act."

The absence of legal evidence that Eatherly ever attempted suicide seems to support Dr. Ross, not Dr. Constantine.

In the summer of 1957 Dr. Constantine took another step which increased Eatherly's income and which bears on the Ross-Constantine dispute.

Since 1953, when Eatherly was first awarded compensation, the VA had held him to be "incompetent in the matter of compensation." Therefore, the VA had never sent more than about half the total compensation to the hospital for him. The other half had been mailed directly to his wife for the care of the three minor children. But late in the summer of 1957 Dr. Constantine advised the VA that Eatherly's "psychosis is now in remission," and suggested that as a measure toward helping him toward responsibility, he be adjudged "competent in the matter of compensation."

Accordingly, the VA notified Eatherly's now-divorced wife that since Eatherly was "now competent" the VA would no longer mail to her $118.50 each month for the care of the children. Instead, the VA thenceforth would pay the entire $237 a month to Eatherly and "he will mail child support directly."

Did anyone in the VA expect Eatherly to "mail child support directly"? Dr. Constantine apparently did; Dr. Ross did not. And Dr. Ross was correct. Since the VA declared him "competent in the matter of compensation," Eatherly has never contributed a dollar to the support of his minor children.

In reporting these facts I am not debating with Dr. Constantine. I am only informing my readers that Dr. Constantine's conclusions prevailed in the VA. After 1957 Dr. Constantine spoke for the VA in the Eatherly Case and Dr. Ross did not. But Dr. Constantine's conclusions were not supported unanimously among the VA psychiatrists. They were instead ably and vigorously disputed.

After the television show of May 31, 1957, what happened to the Eatherly story?

"Well," Jim Vachule told me, "shortly after *The Big Story* broadcast I entered my Eatherly stories in a contest called the Newspaper Hall of Fame sponsored by a Hollywood producer named William Rowland. The purpose of the contest was to pick a newspaper story that could be made into a full-length documentary picture. The winning reporter was to be portrayed in the film by name and was to receive a $5000 cash award. In a surprisingly short time I began receiving telephone calls from Mr. Rowland in Hollywood advising me that my story would be the winner if all details, such as legal clearances, could be worked out. I supplied Mr. Rowland with considerable additional detailed information, and at one point I made a trip to Waco in an effort to obtain a release from Eatherly. But hospital authorities refused to let me see him because he was under federal court commitment awaiting possible trial at Abilene. Mr. Rowland paid my expenses to Waco, and he advised me that two well-known authors, Paul I. Wellman and A. B. Guthrie, were writing the script for the proposed motion picture. Because of the wide interest in the story and the obvious dramatic possibilities, I was hopeful that it could be produced as a motion picture from which Mr. Eatherly and I could share in the proceeds. I felt that he should receive the larger portion of these proceeds because, although we were both to be portrayed by name, the story was more his than mine."

The title given this proposed documentary motion picture was *Medal in the Dust;* and during the summer and fall of 1957, while Eatherly was in the hospital being treated in preparation for his possible trial, the script was being written. Eatherly and Dr. Constantine knew of this proposed film, because they knew of Mr. Vachule's visit. Also, Eatherly had begun receiving letters from "all over the world," and many of these letters insisted that not only must a film be made but also that books must be written to carry Eatherly's "message to the world."

As the date for Claude Eatherly's possible trial in federal court neared, Joe Eatherly, with a payment of $400, retained an attorney to defend his brother in the post office case. This attorney was Davis Scarborough, of the law firm of Scarborough, Black and Tarpley, of Abilene, Texas. On November 16, 1957, Mr. Scarborough advised Claude Eatherly by mail that his case in federal court would be called for a hearing on December 9th. Whether a trial would follow would depend on the "expert opinion" furnished the court by Drs. Constantine and McElroy. From the hospital Eatherly replied in a handwritten letter which I obtained:

DEAR MR. SCARBOROUGH:
Thanks for your letter of the 16th informing me that I must appear in Abilene the 9th of December. Dr. Constantine had a letter from the U. S. Attorney saying he would come to the hospital for a statement of my capabilities of assisting you in my trial.

I talked to Dr. Constantine for two hours today for his determination of my condition at this time. He talked as if he would say I was competent. He said he also was building his case to substantiate my illness at the time.

I would like to know if you think the case will go to trial? In case it does, I am confident the doctors will back our plea. I hope you can prevent a trial. I have a great deal of confidence in your ability to get it dropped.

Will I have to make bond again when I leave here? Please inform me what steps I must take to prevent a U. S. marshal from taking me from here and causing a lot more publicity.

The newspapers have continued to pester the doctors here as to my condition and when will I get out. My condition is greatly improved according to psychological tests and the doctors' opinion. So with your help I expect to be rid of this case in December.

Please keep me advised.

Sincerely,
CLAUDE R. EATHERLY

When I read that well-organized and sensible letter, I had difficulty believing that the writer was psychotic. Or indeed that he had been psychotic on April 30, 1956, when he burglarized the post offices. Moreover, the letter seemed to confirm my belief that Eatherly had found no joy in the publicity developments of March–May, 1957. The letter indicated to me that he had been embarrassed by Mr. Vachule's stories, by the *Newsweek* story, by Dr. Constantine's public pronouncements, and by the show on NBC. Certainly Claude Eatherly knew of Joe Eatherly's deep embarrassment, and the letter indicated to me that he shared it.

The letter further indicated to me that Claude Eatherly wasn't seeking the punishment of a federal prison; he wanted to avoid a trial if possible. But avoiding a trial became impossible on November 26, 1957, when Judge Estes received this written report.

Mr. Claude R. Eatherly was returned to the Veterans Administration Hospital, Waco, Texas, on April 18, 1957, by your court order of April 17, 1957, for further observation and examination. There has been improvement in the mental state of Mr. Eatherly. It is the present opinion that Mr. Eatherly knows right from wrong and is able to refrain from doing wrong. He is in contact with reality and mentally competent to understand the proceedings against him and to assist in his own defense.

ROBERT B. McELROY, M.D.
Chief, Acute Intensive Treatment Service

O. P. CONSTANTINE, M.D.
Physician in Charge of Case

On December 7, 1957, Claude Eatherly was officially discharged from the hospital by court order, but this time the court did not require a U. S. marshal. Eatherly was released in the custody of Joe Eatherly, and on December 9th he arrived in Abilene accompanied by both Joe and James Eatherly.

Fourteen

MY account of the federal court trial in Abilene on December 10, 1957, is based on the transcript of testimony which Ray Bell obtained for me in 1962 from the court clerk. I had expected to pay the cost of making the transcript from the shorthand notes, but fortunately we found that this cost had been paid by a German magazine, and Mr. Bell obtained a copy of the transcript for no more than the cost of running it through a facsimile machine. I also had access to the recollections of defense counsel, Mr. Scarborough, as well as to the recollections of Claude and Joe Eatherly.

The two small post offices had been burglarized by Claude Eatherly, Alvin D. Crews and Roy L. Mantooth. Eatherly had met Mantooth at the Waco hospital. They were about the same age. They also had approximately the same behavior pattern. Mantooth, too, had been in the Army during the Second World War, and after the war he had committed a succession of forgeries. But he had not claimed mental illness. He had been in and out of the Texas State Penitentiary three times; and once he had been sent to the Waco hospital.

In April, 1957, when Eatherly was to have been tried, Mantooth pleaded guilty to the post office burglaries, and was sentenced by Judge Estes to two years' imprisonment in the Federal Penitentiary at Springfield, Missouri. Alvin Crews pleaded not guilty, so his trial had been delayed along with Eatherly's.

In the trial of December 10, 1957, the case was *The United States versus Claude R. Eatherly and Alvin D. Crews*. The charge was breaking and entering two U. S. Post Offices. The pleas were: By defendant Crews, not guilty. By defendant Eatherly, not guilty by reason of insanity.

The chief witness for the "Government" or the "United States" was Roy Mantooth, brought back from the prison for the trial.

That Crews would be convicted and sentenced to two years was predictable. The judge, on the statement of the doctors, had held Eatherly to be legally sane on December 10, 1957. The only real question at issue was whether the jury, after hearing Mantooth and the doctors, would find Eatherly to have been insane on April 30, 1956.

Appearing for the United States was Mr. Floore; appearing for the defendant Eatherly was Mr. Scarborough.

After selection of the jury, Roy Mantooth was examined by Mr. Floore. Mantooth testified as to his prison background and stated that in the latter part of April, 1956, he was living with his brother, Curtis Mantooth, at Abilene.

Q Do you know the defendant Claude Eatherly?
A Yes, sir.
Q Will you point him out, please.
A (pointing) That is him there.
Q Describe the suit he's wearing, and his tie.
A He has a blue serge suit on and a two-tone tie.
Q When did you first know Claude Eatherly?
A I met him in '53 in the Veterans Hospital at Waco.
Q In the latter part of April, 1956, did you place a telephone call to Claude Eatherly in Van Alstyne, Texas, and talk with him?
A Yes, sir.
Q Tell me about the conversation.
A Well, he asked me what I was doing, and I told him I was bootlegging, selling whiskey.
Q Here in Taylor County?
A Yes, sir.
Q That is a violation of the State law, isn't it?
A Yes, sir.
Q Go ahead. What else was said?

173

A Well, he said . . . I forget just exactly what the conversation was; but I know it ended up I invited him to come down and look the situation over and see if he'd like to go in with me.

Q Did Claude Eatherly come to Abilene, Texas?

A Yes, sir.

Q On or about the 29th of April, 1956, did you receive a telephone call from the defendant, Claude Eatherly?

A Yes, sir.

Q As a result of that call, what did you do?

A I went to the Wooten Hotel where he was staying here in Abilene.

Q Did you have a conversation with him at the Wooten Hotel? If so, tell us about it.

A Well, he mentioned some kind of gambling system he needed money for, and I suggested we try to raise it by obtaining some money orders and cashing them.

Q What sort of money orders?

A Postal money orders.

Q Blank or filled out?

A Filled out.

Q How were you going to obtain them?

A The only way we could, by breaking and entering a post office.

Q Would they have been filled out money orders or money order blanks?

A They would have been money order blanks. We would have had to fill them out.

Q Did Eatherly express himself as to this plan?

A He thought the money order plan was a good idea. He was for it.

Q I now call your attention to the 30th day of April, 1956. I will ask you, sir, what you did that day. Did you do anything with Alvin Crews and Claude Eatherly?

A Yes, sir. We went out in my brother's car and drove around. . . . Claude, Billy and me. [Crews' nickname was Billy.] We went to View, Texas.

Q Where is View, Texas?

A About eight miles south of Abilene.

174

Q What did you do at View?

A Looked the place over and bought some cold drinks and ice cream.

Q What place did you look over, sir?

A Post office.

Q Do you remember where the post office in View, Texas, was situated?

A It was off to the right of the highway. I would say about a city block, off the highway near the railroad station.

Q Is it exclusively a post office or is another business carried on in the same building?

A It is a general store.

Q And is the post office a partioned-off part of the general store?

A Yes, sir.

Q Now you said you had some cold drinks. Where did you have those cold drinks?

A Inside the store.

Q While you were in there, did the three of you examine the post office portion of the building?

A Yes, sir.

Q And after you went back to the car, did you have a conversation with the defendant Eatherly with reference to money orders?

A Yes, sir.

Q Tell this jury about that conversation.

A Well, Eatherly said we'd need to know how to fill out a money order, so he gave me a $20 bill and told me to go back in and buy a postal money order.

Q And did you buy a money order?

A Yes, sir. Made payable to Claude Eatherly for $10.

It was this money order, purchased as a pattern, which trapped Eatherly. He later cashed it, and Detective Heaberg used it to catch him.

After the Government introduced this money order in evidence, Mantooth described how he and Eatherly had examined the money order, noted how the application was made out, how the money order itself was made out, and how a validating stamp was used in a square on the money order. They then understood that in order to forge and cash money orders, they must steal the application blanks, the money order blanks, and a validating stamp.

Mantooth further described how that afternoon they went to Avoca, also near Abilene. The post office at Avoca was larger, occupying an entire building; and again the three "cased" the post office and asked the postmistress if she sold money orders. She said she did. The three then returned to Curtis Mantooth's home to eat and drink. They had not intended to strike that evening, but the weather was "perfect": lightning, thundering heavily, pouring rain. So they headed for View.

Q About what time was it when you reached View?
A Around 8 p.m., 8:30 maybe.
Q What did you do?
A We broke in the post office.
Q Did you find the outside door locked or was it unlocked?
A It was locked.
Q Tell me what happened when you discovered the door to be locked, if anything happened.
A We broke open the front door with a tire tool and went in.
Q Who broke it open?
A Eatherly.
Q Who went in?
A Eatherly and I went in first.
Q What happened when you got inside the store building? Did you find the entrance to the post office enclosure open or locked?
A There was a little picket gate kind of over it. It was locked, had a chain run through it.
Q What kind of lock was it?
A Just an ordinary padlock.

The Government introduced the lock in evidence, and Mantooth said he had "twisted it off" with a screwdriver.

Q What did you do when you got inside the post office?
A Well, it had started to lightning pretty bad, and I saw the

176

validating stamp up where I saw the lady put it, and I took it and put it in my pocket.

Mantooth then described how he and Eatherly took "a bunch of tin drawers" out of the post office—drawers which Mantooth "had seen the lady take the money orders out of." The three assumed they had what they had come for, but when they examined the drawers in the car they found only "stamps and fountain pens and a little change." (The postmistress had taken the money order blanks home with her.) The three then returned to the post office, looked "high and low" and couldn't find the blanks. They then decided to drive thirty-five miles to Avoca, and they arrived there about 10 P.M.

Q What did you do when you reached the post office building at Avoca?

A We parked the car, and Eatherly opened the front door of the post office.

Q How did he open it?

A Pried it open with a tire tool.

Q Was he quiet or noisy when he pried open that door?

A Well, frankly speaking, he acted like a crazy person to me.

Q What did he do?

A He busted it open like it belonged to him. In fact, I cautioned him about it and said, "You make more noise than a Sherman tank."

Q What did he say, if anything?

A I don't know whether he said anything or not. He just didn't act like a normal person to me. He made too much noise.

Q What, if anything, happened after he broke that door open? Did anyone go in?

A He and Crews went in.

Q Did anyone then come back to the car?

A Well, after Eatherly had broke open the first door, he threw the tire tool back into the car. When he went in, he came right back out and said, "We got another door we got to go through," so he took the tire tool and banged that one open, making a lot of noise.

177

Q And then what happened?

A Crews came out and said, "There is a safe in there and a big one," and I better go in and look it over, so I went in and looked it over, and he asked me if I could open it, and I said, "No, I couldn't." And as I was looking it over, I was looking the building over, and I noticed that there was a window right opposite, and a light shining in right on the safe, and I noticed another window, and I could see a bed in there, so I told them I didn't want any part of it. I said I didn't want to get shot, and I told Eatherly again that he made more noise than a tank, and "you mess around here and we'll all get killed." Finally we all got in the car and drove off.

Mantooth related how, in the car, Eatherly kept insisting that he could open the safe, and kept demanding that they go back and let him try. They went back; Eatherly tried unsuccessfully; after which they "gave up" and Eatherly was let out of the car at the Wooten Hotel. Next day Mantooth picked Eatherly up at the hotel, drove him to the bus station, and Eatherly returned to Van Alstyne.

While Roy Mantooth was a Government witness, he obviously was not unfriendly to Eatherly's plea of insanity. Mr. Scarborough, trying to convince the jury that Eatherly was insane on the night of the crimes, cross-examined Mantooth as follows:

Q You met Eatherly in 1953 at the Waco hospital?

A Yes, sir.

Q How long were you there?

A Six months.

Q During that time Claude Eatherly was taking shock treatments, was he not?

A Yes, sir.

Q And you recognized him as being a very sick man, didn't you?

A Yes, sir.

Q Did you have any difficulties in carrying on a connected conversation with Claude in June, July and August of '53?

A Well, sometimes. Sometimes he liked to carry on conversation. He played baseball sometimes. But the next time he would be very quiet and remote, wouldn't want anything to do with anyone, get off by himself.

Q Get off to himself and have a faraway look in his eyes, would he not?

A Yes, sir.

Q He had a persecution complex, did he not?

A Yes, sir.

Q Thought that everybody was down on him, isn't that true?

A Yes, sir.

Q In your conversations with him, did you notice that he would be talking about something and just stop in the middle of a sentence and start talking about something else wholly unconnected?

A Well, I have been in several conversations with him when he would do that, and I would tell him "we wasn't talking about that at all; we was talking about something else. Let's finish the other story."

Mr. Scarborough then suggested that Mantooth had sought Eatherly deliberately in order to have an "obviously sick man" to front for him. Mantooth resisted this, claimed he had only wanted to "see Eatherly" when he telephoned him and "see if we could get together." Eatherly had ridden all night on a bus to reach Abilene at 5:30 A.M. on April 29th.

Q You saw Eatherly on the 29th and saw him on the 30th up until about 10 o'clock when you took him back to the hotel. You saw him the next morning, May 1st, when you took him to the bus station. Over those three days, tell this Jury whether or not Claude knew or was able to understand you fully at all times when you were discussing plans with him.

A Well, at first, it was pretty apparent that he knew what I was talking about; but then after we broke into the first place, well, I knew that he was in just as bad a shape as he had ever been in the VA hospital from the manner in which he broke into them.

Q You thought he was in just as bad a shape as when you saw him in '53?

179

A   Yes, sir. I realized it then. In fact, I said I didn't see how they ever turned him out of the VA hospital in the first place.

Mr. Floore then questioned Mantooth on redirect:

Q   Now about that noise that Eatherly made that night, Roy, what time did you all start drinking that day?
A   Well, we had two bottles, and I guess we drank most of them during the day.
Q   Eatherly was pretty drunk by the time you all got around to breaking into those post office buildings, wasn't he?
A   I was pretty drunk and I imagine he was.
Q   Could all of that noise Eatherly made . . . could it have been attributed to drinking?
A   If it had been me or Crews that was making the noise, I'd say so.

There was a brief recross-examination by Mr. Scarborough:

Q   What kind of gambling game had Eatherly figured out, what kind of a system?
A   Well, to tell the truth, I'm not smart enough to know. He didn't go into details, just said he had a foolproof system.
Q   Was it a crap table or roulette table?
A   I think he said roulette.
Q   He said he had a system that was foolproof; if he had $2500 he could run it up to a million?
A   I don't know that he said he could run it up to a million. He said it couldn't fail to work.

Curtis J. Mantooth, a resident of Abilene, the brother of Roy Mantooth, was called as a witness for the United States.

Q   How long have you known Claude Eatherly?
A   About five years. I met him in the hospital in 1953 when I went to visit my brother.
Q   Did you see him any time thereafter?
A   Yes, on a later visit to the hospital. My wife and I took him and my brother out of the hospital for a picnic.

Q Were Eatherly and your brother very friendly while they were in the hospital together?

A I would say they were.

Q When did you next see Eatherly?

A I believe it was in '55. He came into Abilene on a visit. He rented a room out at the Sunset Lodge, called me and my wife and invited us to visit him, and we went to see him.

Q How long did he remain in Abilene on that particular visit?

A I believe he spent that night and the biggest part of the next day.

Mr. Scarborough cross-examined Curtis Mantooth:

Q Now, Curtis, during the times that you were around Claude Eatherly, did you notice anything unusual or abnormal about him?

A Yes, sir.

Q Just tell the jury what it was that caused you to form that conclusion that there was something wrong with him.

A Well, I just . . . the first time I met him in the hospital, just from his actions, I mean he acted like he was in a daze or something, and he would . . . I mean like a while ago I said we took him out on a picnic, and once he would get outside the gates, he couldn't think of nothing but wanting to run off, and we had a hard time getting him back to the hospital, and he knew he had to have the treatment.

Q That was in '53 and '54. He was getting those shock treatments at that time?

A I believe so.

Q And, of course, none of those fellows looked forward to those treatments at that time?

A No, sir.

Q And when you saw him in '56, at that time did he still have a faraway look in his eyes?

A Well, he has always had it, and he . . . this particular instance, when he came to town and stayed at the motel out there, he even got in an argument with the landlord and had to leave and go to another motel because they wouldn't let him swim in the swimming pool after 10 at night.

181

Q Did you notice in talking to him that he would start in a conversation and stop right in the middle of it and start off talking about something else?

A Well, he just never did do much talking.

Q He seemed to be withdrawn most of the time?

A Yes, sir.

Q Had a kind of persecution complex?

A Yes, sir.

Mr. Floore had further questions on redirect:

Q What is a persecution complex, Curtis?

A I would say feeling guilty or let down about something.

Q You are not a psychiatrist, are you, Curtis?

A No, sir.

Q And you don't purport to be any psychiatrist, do you?

A No, sir.

Q And you don't really have the slightest idea about what a persecution complex is, do you?

A Well, maybe not with educated words; but I have got an idea what it is.

Q You said that Claude Eatherly always had a faraway look in his eyes. Look at his eyes now. Does he have that faraway look in his eyes?

A He looks like he has been sick.

Q But has he still got that faraway look in his eyes?

A No. I wouldn't say so.

Q How far away is the look in his eyes now?

Mr. Scarborough objected, and the Court sustained. Mrs. Curtis Mantooth had this brief exchange with Mr. Scarborough:

Q You say you met Claude Eatherly at the hospital in Waco?

A Yes, sir.

Q And when you met him down there, was he taking those shock treatments?

A Yes, sir.

Q And did you observe anything unnatural or abnormal about him when you were talking to him at that time?

182

A   Highly nervous type.

Q   And then when you saw him at your home here in Abilene, did you notice anything abnormal or strange about him?

A   He didn't seem as friendly. He didn't talk as much as he did when we met him in Waco.

In the dialogue between Mr. Floore and the post office detective, George T. Heaberg Jr., there is this exchange:

Q   Mr. Heaberg, when you questioned Claude Eatherly in the sheriff's office at Sherman, Texas, on August 24, 1956, did you find his memory clear?

A   Remarkably clear. I showed him the $10 money order made out to him. He told me that he had furnished the money; he had given a $20 bill to Mantooth at View, Texas, and asked him to go into the post office and purchase a money order for $10 so they would have a sample to use in filling out money orders after they obtained the money order blanks.

That was the Government's case against Claude Eatherly at Abilene. The Government rested; the defense called its first witness.

Fifteen

THE case for the defense at Abilene was made by Drs. Constantine and McElroy. Claude Eatherly did not testify. Sitting between his brothers, he faced the doctors and jury, watching and listening. This fact that he listened to all that was said about him, yet never spoke, struck me as the most interesting aspect of the proceedings. So as I studied the transcript I tried to imagine the effect of each exchange on Claude Eatherly.

Seven reporters, including representatives of the press associations, also watched and listened. They had come to hear Dr. Constantine expand on how Hiroshima had caused Claude Eatherly to commit forgeries and burglaries.

Mr. Scarborough called Dr. Constantine:

Q You are Dr. O. P. Constantine?
A Yes, sir.
Q Are you a graduate of a recognized school of medicine?
A I graduated from Baylor University College of Medicine in 1937.
Q Following your graduation, did you do an internship and then a specialization in some particular field?
A I interned in Baylor University Hospital in Dallas as a rotating intern. In 1938 I had a residency in the San Antonio State Hospital. Then I had a residency in the Department of Hygiene in the State of New York. I was at Columbia Medical Center in New York City as a neurologist. I am certified by the Department of Hygiene of the State of New York as a qualified psychiatrist. I am also certified by the

American Board of Psychiatry and Neurology. I am a fellow of the American Psychiatric Association. I was on the staff of several hospitals: in the VA hospital in Tucson, Arizona; Fort Lyon, Colorado; Canandaigua, New York, which was associated with the University of Rochester. I was—

Q Is your license to practice medicine duly—

A I am licensed by the State of Texas and the State of New York.

Q Do you have any official capacity with the Veterans Administration?

A I am a psychiatrist in the hospital at Waco. I am just a psychiatrist and a doctor.

Q How long have you been at the Waco hospital?

A Since 1949, but my specialty in psychiatry dates back to 1938.

Q Doctor, in connection with your duties at the Waco hospital, did you become acquainted with Claude Eatherly, the defendant in this case?

A He was assigned to me in January of 1956 as my . . . as my problem.

Q And when he was assigned to you, did you have the benefit of all the reports and histories and examinations and treatments— Did you have this man's complete military and medical record before you?

A I had access to all records in his case file, what the VA Rating Boards had done, everything pertaining to compensation, and some war records.

Q And, Doctor, in preparing to treat this man in 1956, was it necessary for you to familiarize yourself with all his past records, and weigh them, and go over them with him?

A Yes, sir.

Q Going back to his first admission in 1950, please tell the jury what you found, and what struck you as important, as you prepared to treat him.

A What struck me as very important was the fact that he was admitted to the hospital after an attempted suicide.

What struck me as important here was that Mr. Floore, the United States Attorney, did not object and demand that the defense introduce *legal evidence* of attempted suicide. Dr. Constantine's conclusion that there had been an attempted suicide was allowed to go into the record unchallenged.

Q And what did you conclude further, Doctor, from those records?

A Well, studying the records, I could see that there had been a marked change of personality, a marked change of behavior, a marked change of everything about this individual from what he had previously been to the onset of his difficulty.

Q When you talk about change of personality, will you tell us what you mean, Doctor?

A Well, in psychiatry, in studying about a human being, it is like in medicine: You see that a man is well and a normal human being in every respect; in fact, in Eatherly's case I felt he was a little bit above average, and then something happens that makes him just about the opposite of what he used to be.

Q And did you delve into his records to try to find out what it was that caused him to have that change in mental attitude and have that change in personality?

A Well, I don't know. I mean we don't know. We can't pinpoint the onset of a difficulty just like you can't pinpoint the onset of a physical disease like influenza or pneumonia. It starts gradually and finally develops into a full-blown kind of a disease or reaction or a psychosis.

Q Doctor, particularly I want to ask you if you found any evidence in his war experiences which, in your opinion, contributed to this change in personality?

A Well, I want to . . . I want to make an explanation before the Court, if I may.

Q All right, sir.

A Before, I didn't say very much about his past experiences because, well, it is a confidence between the patient and doctor; but since these things are in the open now . . . and in the papers now . . . and everything else . . . I just kind of feel that I should say a little bit more about him.

Q All right, sir.

186

A I kept quiet about it in the past, but I found out that he was well, well, sort of a . . . I don't want to say this . . . but I think he was sort of a war hero.

Q Yes, sir.

A Although I treated him as just an ordinary patient and—

Q You think that has had an effect on him, Doctor, being the war hero, as you described it?

A Well, it wasn't the war hero that had an effect on him; but I think what he went through as an airman had something to do with his present condition.

Q Particularly, Doctor, did you find him to be suffering from a guilt complex?

A Yes. It seems to me that from the beginning I felt that the man . . . the man depressed and despondent and discouraged and often crying and often depressed, and what struck me later on was the fact that he was asking for shock treatment.

Q He himself asked for that?

A He was asking for punishment. Now that is the way I interpret it. He wanted to have some kind of treatment to punish himself. Surely very few patients in our hospital, or any other hospital, are asking for shock treatment.

Q Most of them dread that, do they not, Doctor?

A That is right.

Q Want to avoid it at all costs. Here is a man who was asking for it!

A Asking for shock treatment, begging me almost every day to give him some kind of treatment that was very drastic; and when he had insulin shock treatment, it seems to me that he asked for it himself and somewhat enjoyed it. And I can't put it in words; but why should a man enjoy punishment? That was very startling to me.

Q All right.

A He wanted to be punished. In other words, he just wanted to be punished for something.

Q Yes, sir. In January of 1956 when you started out on this man, at that time did you find him to be a sick man mentally?

A I definitely did, and I want to read from my . . . if I may

187

. . . from my record. There has been discussion about differences of diagnosis and so forth; but in . . . I want to read it from the records.

Q Give us the particular date of the—
A This examination was made by me, signed by me. He was admitted to the hospital in January of 1956.
Q I think you will find it to be January 5th, Doctor. January 5th, 1956.
A 5th, 1956.
Q What was the date of your report?
A My examination was from January to the time I completed my examination on March 30, 1956.
Q And what did you conclude in your report, sir?
A Here is a statement that I discussed with Dr. McElroy and other members of the staff, and here is the quote: "Personality has undergone a definite change, so much so that if one were not familiar with his war record, he would be inclined to call this patient suffering from some kind of schizophrenic process."
Q That was in January, now?
A March.
Q All right.
A And the reason why I want to call him schizophrenic . . . I think I want to take the blame on myself somehow . . . very seldom . . . well, very seldom . . . you hate to call a man crazy, you know, and if you have a patient with you, and you don't want to call him insane or crazy or anything like that, and I just didn't have the heart to tell him, "Now you are in the language, in the legal language of some of the people, you are just plumb crazy or insane." I just didn't feel like I could do it.

Five of the seven reporters commented in their dispatches on how Dr. Constantine kept looking at Eatherly as he testified, and on how uncomfortable the doctor seemed to feel at having to testify in Eatherly's presence.

Q In other words, Doctor, you just didn't want to say bluntly to this man or his family, "You are crazy"?

188

A I did tell his wife though, that he was suffering from more than just anxiety.

Q Let me ask you about that, Doctor. As part of your procedure, do you require some member of the family to authorize severe treatments, such as shock treatments, before you give it?

A Absolutely. We don't go on with the treatment without permission of the family.

Q So the family was notified back in '53 and '54 of the giving of the shock treatments and the seriousness of the shock treatments?

A Absolutely.

Q Did you yourself write to this man's wife not once but twice and tell her of the seriousness of the man's condition?

A Not at that time, but I wrote her a letter in March of 1956.

Q March what, Doctor?

A March 20, 1956.

Q All right. That was before this alleged offense. What did you tell her then?

A And, of course, I had to be a little bit diplomatic and a little bit kind to her. I didn't want her to . . . but I still told her like this: "We hinted in our letter to you that your husband's difficulties are more than just anxiety neurosis. He may be developing a more serious mental reaction than just plain anxiety neurosis as evidenced by behavior reactions away from this hospital."

Q Did you write her after that, after March 11, 1956?

A In February of 1956 I see a letter signed by me . . . written to the patient's wife.

Q That again was before these alleged offenses took place?

A I don't know much about these offenses, because I don't think a thing about this post office business.

That remark must have startled Judge Estes. The United States had thought enough of the "post office business" to have a detective work on it for four months. Judge Estes had thought enough of it to sentence Roy Mantooth to two years in prison. And Claude Eatherly had been brought to trial at an uncommon amount of expense to the taxpayers of the United States.

Q All right, sir.

A I wrote to his wife, "According to our records"—that is February 20, 1956— "According to our records, he is suffering from a nervous condition called anxiety reaction; however, from time to time, he shows symptoms which are more severe than just plain nervousness and anxiety."

Q All right.

A That was before anything happened.

The letter which Dr. Constantine did not find and read to the court was his letter to Eatherly's wife on May 18, 1956. That was three weeks after the "post office business," and the doctor had reported Eatherly suffering from immaturity.

Q And, Doctor, by November, 1956, did you overcome your reluctance to call him just plain crazy . . . and did you come right out and make that diagnosis?

A From the very beginning, in March I made the statement that he was suffering from schizophrenic reaction, although I didn't want to go out on a limb, on the record, that he is plumb crazy, so to speak. I told Dr. McElroy and other members of the staff, "This man is not anxiety reaction; he is sick; there is no question in my mind."

Q All right.

A And I followed with the same diagnosis, with psychotic manifestations; and later in the year 1956, I told Dr. Mc-Elroy, I said: "Now there is no point for us to fool around and just call this man anxiety reaction. He is just as sick as he can be, and we have to do something about it."

Q All right.

A And Dr. McElroy said, "We have got to do something about it." And we came to the conclusion: "Let's change the record and make it plain that he is psychotic."

Q Now, Doctor, at that time did you know about any post office troubles at all that this man had?

A I didn't know any post office trouble until . . . until, I think, this year, something about when the papers came out that he had a post office trouble.

Q So at the time that you came around to this conclusion that you were going to have to make the diagnosis to show that he was psychotic, at that time you knew nothing whatever about this criminal offense that is alleged against him now?

A   I didn't know a thing about it.

Q   And when the Board changed his rating, the 100 percent rating was dated back to January 5, 1956, was it not?

A   Well, according to the record, yes, sir. But I didn't do it.

Q   That is done by the Board?

A   By the Board.

Q   But the Board acts after receiving your advice and counsel?

A   That is right.

Q   Now, Doctor, after you assumed him as your problem in 1956, did you take any electroencephalograms, or what the laymen commonly calls a brain wave, that you attach these gadgets to his head to see what a man's condition is?

A   Well, I must admit this much: that I didn't take it at the beginning. I suspected something was wrong somewhere; but you see you don't try to do all kinds of studies, because when you do all studies in the ward, you are just lost; but later on it came to me that here is a man who is all right and he is fine; he is a normal human being; he has a good war record; he is doing fine. All of a sudden something happens to him. And there was a possibility, I thought, maybe there was something wrong with his brain, with his electrical potentials of the brain . . . we call electroencephalogram . . . so I just had a hunch to take the test.

Q   Did you make several over a period of time so that you could compare them?

A   Yes, sir, I did.

Q   Tell the Jury what the result of that experiment was.

A   Now, an electroencephalograph is a machine, as probably all of you know. You connect about 16 wires to the brain from both sides to locate any trouble in the brain, organic or convulsive disorder or anything like that, and we connected . . . and we connected these wires to his brain to see if there was any. I knew there was something wrong, no question in my mind, is the reason why I ordered that, and we found out that his brain . . . we have several readings . . . eight readings . . . and the report comes . . . the first report came in as very confused and abnormal. Well, we thought that maybe it was an artifact or something wrong with the machine, so we ordered another one. The other one comes in. Now this one was dated . . . this one was taken on April . . . April 10, 1957, also a tracing. This is just an extract from about 10 feet long, maybe more, and it shows, according to the experts who read it, as borderline normal EEG.

The Texans who were members of the jury and who were pondering this psychiatric testimony were: Richard B. Lawrence Jr., of Abilene, foreman; William Ray Brown, of Rotan; Louis Agee, of Abilene; Donald Theodore Knight, of Abilene; Mitchell T. Broyles of Abilene; Fred Collett Martin, of Aspermont; Jerry Rosser, of Abilene; Homer T. McLeod, of Roscoe; Joseph K. Wallingfor, of Abilene; Z. Oswalt, of Abilene; James Warden Boswell, of Sweetwater; and James Thomas Solsbery, of Roscoe.

Mr. Scarborough continued examining Dr. Constantine.

Q That was in April of '57 that you took the EEG?
A Yes.
Q Now, Doctor, had there been some improvement from the time you took the first electroencephalogram until the time you took the second?
A Let me say another thing. We had another one made on May 9, 1957. We put him to sleep. You know, sometimes a man is awake and maybe his tracing could be distorted, you know, when a man winks his eyes or thinks about something. It makes him just a little bit different, have abnormality of reading, and we put him to sleep, and still . . . still the same thing came out . . . as a borderline.
Q That was May of '57?
A That was May of '57.
Q All right, sir.
A And when I had that test, I knew that we were dealing with something more than just . . . well, it gave me the idea that the man has some damage to his brain.

192

Q All right. Now, Doctor, the last one that you made, state whether or not you have . . . has the last electroencephalogram shown those waves to be normal limits?

A Well, I may say this much: That after . . . when I got those electroencephalographic tracings and the reports, I suspected that the man had some kind of abnormality of the brain which would make him do some of the so-called crazy things, and I put him on a special medicine called dilantin.

Q Now, when did you put him on . . . on dilantin, Doctor?

A As soon as I found out; as soon as I was convinced.

Q That was back in May of this year? [1957]

A It was after the Court had sent him to us. [April '57] And I put him on that medicine dilantin, in addition to thorazine, and I also gave him ritalin, and I had him on this medication continuously until just recently when I had these tests made again.

Q All right. Now what did the tests show just recently after giving him that series of treatments and using that medicine that you have described?

A Well, happily, and I hope it's going to continue to be this way, happily, this report says "Normal EEG."

Q All right. In other words you found an improvement, did you not?

A I notice improvement from the EEG standpoint, and also in his responses, in his alertness, in his thinking a little better.

Q And when you say "EEG," again you are talking about the electroencephalograph?

A Yes, sir. In other words, in comparing these waves, you can see that there is improvement in the tracing, and the impression by the man who read them says, "Impression Normal EEG."

Q Now, Doctor, of course, medicine is not an exact science, is it? It is kind of a process of elimination?

A It is pretty good. It is pretty good.

Q Well, I can see that doctors are good and very nice. Don't misunderstand me. But I mean you can't do it like an equation and say two times two equals four; it is a process of elimination sometimes to arrive at your diagnosis and the cause?

A You have to eliminate. You have to have several possibilities, and then you eliminate and eliminate and work hard and you come to a conclusion. Sometimes you don't come to a definite conclusion, but you know that the man is sick.

Q In other words, you might go up a blind alley a time or two and you come back?

A You have to come back. You have to consider brain difficulties or lung difficulties or heart, you have to consider at least 10 to 15 possibilities.

Q Doctor, what I'm getting down to is this: Do you think from your long period of examination and treatment of this defendant that you have gotten the man back to where, in your opinion, he will make a useful, normal citizen now?

A Now, well, if he takes the medicine that I gave him, and he has them in his pocket now, three types of medicine, and if he follows the routine, and it is just like a case of diabetes mellitus. A man with a diabetes condition, he follows insulin. If he follows diet and follows other things, he is going to be all right. Now if he doesn't take his insulin and if he doesn't follow the diet and if he doesn't follow other things, he will go into a coma. If he [Eatherly] continues with the same medicine and the same instructions, I think he is going to make a satisfactory adjustment.

Q All right. Now, Doctor, specifically, on April 30, 1956, when it is alleged that he committed the criminal acts, tell the Jury whether or not, in your opinion, the mental disorder and disease this man was suffering from, in your opinion, was the sole and only cause of his doing the antisocial acts?

A I don't see any other reason for it. Except for his mental illness.

Q In other words, Doctor, just in laymen's language, in your opinion, was he crazy on April 30, 1956?

A I hate to say so in his presence. He is my patient. I don't want to call him crazy. I think he was mentally ill, and if you want to, you call him crazy. I hate to use the word "crazy." But I think he was mentally sick. Yes, I guess I might say he was crazy, all right.

194

MR. SCARBOROUGH: Your witness, Counsel.
MR. FLOORE: Thank you.

The United States Attorney then cross-examined Dr. Constantine:

Q Doctor, you have testified that on April 30th he was mentally sick, and today you think he is all right?
A I didn't say he was all right. The man is sick, still sick.
Q But so long as he takes his medicine, he is all right?
A He is not all right.
Q He is not all right? What's wrong with him?
A He still has the same condition; he is improved; he is in partial remission.
Q You said he was crazy in 1956. Is he crazy now?
A I don't like to use the word "crazy."
Q I know, but you did use it with reference to the year 1956. Is he crazy now?
A I never use the word "crazy." I never use the word "insane."
Q You used it a moment ago.
A I did, because the Court commands that.
Q All right. Is he crazy now?
A Well, he is partially crazy, like myself maybe. Everyone is a little bit crazy.
Q Is he more than usually crazy, Doctor?
A He might be a little crazier than most of us. I don't know. But that is the language you use. I don't like to use it. He is still sick.
Q Is he dangerous to himself or others?
A At this time he is not dangerous to himself or others. The only thing I am afraid . . . a little bit for himself. If the guilt complex gets too bad and he becomes discouraged and despondent and refuses his medicines or neglects to take them, he is likely to . . . well, I can't predict; but he is more likely to harm himself than anybody else.
Q Now, Doctor, you said this man was mentally ill and crazy in April, 1956. Was he dangerous to himself and others in 1956?
A You have asked me two different questions. A man may be

dangerous to himself, he may have ideas of suicide; but being dangerous to somebody else is a different story.

Q All right, we'll separate the questions. Was he dangerous to himself in April, 1956?
A Yes.
Q Was he dangerous to others in April, 1956?
A You mean in respect to killing somebody?
Q Harming somebody, doing something which would harm somebody else, not necessarily killing them but harming somebody else.
A Well, by accident, I think he was dangerous to others.

At this point, in effect, there was a long argument as to why Dr. Constantine, admitting that Eatherly might have harmed someone, had "turned him loose" on April 24, 1956. The doctor insisted that the VA, as well as society, must take such calculated risks in order to give mentally ill persons a chance to recover. "Besides," said the doctor, "we must make room for others."

Mr. Floore continued his cross-examination:

Q Now, Doctor, you have mentioned a guilt complex. Could this man's family relations have anything to do with that guilt complex? You are familiar with his family setup, aren't you?
A I am, very well.
Q How many children does he have?
A Three.
Q Does he have a wife?
A No wife now. She divorced him. And there is a very interesting problem to that divorce, too.
Q How long has it been since he has lived with that wife and those children?
A He hasn't lived with that wife as a husband, oh, I would say, oh, since '53. When he had this insulin, he was sicker that time.
Q He hasn't supported that wife or those children for a long time, has he, Doctor?
A Well, every time . . . every time . . . I don't know. But

196

every time I see him on the ward he asks me to write a check for presents for his children and send some money to his wife; so I don't know what his financial situation is; but the other day he sent . . . how much was it? . . . he asked me to send $75 to his children for Christmas presents; and ever so often he sends some money for his children and his wife.

This statement was interesting because Eatherly's ex-wife has said she and the children never received a cent.

Q Ever so often. Now you know that in the summer of 1956, after this post office event occurred, he was holding a job as flight dispatcher at Perrin Air Force Field, he was a civilian plane dispatcher there?

A I understood for a very short time, yes.

Q Actually, wasn't he doing a good job there, from the reports you all had? You all kept him out and extended the 90-day visit, didn't you?

A Yes.

Q You thought he was doing fine, didn't you?

A He was making a satisfactory adjustment on the outside. He was not . . . we have a lot of patients on 'the outside who are making marginal adjustment . . . crippling, and stumbling and falling. We don't want them in the hospital. If we had them in the hospital, we wouldn't have any room, in the first place.

Q Even so, you know that while he was working at Perrin Air Force Base at Sherman, he wasn't sending money to that wife and children?

A I don't know.

Q Well, in the event he wasn't, would that tend to contribute to his guilt complex that you are talking about? The fact that he wasn't doing his duty as a husband and father? Does that make a man feel guilty?

A No, sir. Absolutely no. He had a guilt complex long before this trouble.

In the heat of cross-examination Dr. Constantine must have stretched an opinion here. In 1962 he clearly stated to Ray

Bell that there was no mention of guilt in the Eatherly Case until 1957.

Q Are you telling this jury that a man not contributing to the support of his own children, that that wouldn't make him feel guilty, or make his guilt complex any greater?

A Positively not.

Q All right. What else *would* contribute to that mental condition? You have said his mental difficulty was *partly* due to a guilt complex . . . partly brought about by a guilt complex. What else brought it about?

A Well, I don't want to say this one. But since all this is now in the newspapers, about his atomic bomb, dropping of the atomic bomb and so forth—

Q Doctor, let me stop you right here. I'm not referring to the man's antisocial acts. I don't want those acts mentioned. This man is being tried for one particular crime.

A All right. But the man said to me many times, on the verge of tears and despondency, that he felt responsible for killing 100,000 people in Hiroshima. Now, I haven't told this before; but that's the way he would tell it.

If that was true, why had Eatherly on March 18, 1957, insisted to Jim Vachule that his war experience had nothing to do with his mental condition? Why had Dr. Constantine, in addressing the public through Mr. Vachule in May, 1957, failed to mention that Eatherly claimed he felt guilty? And since Eatherly's psychosis was said to be in remission at the trial, why didn't the defense call him to the stand and let him describe his guilt feelings for the benefit of the jury?

The United States Attorney continued:

Q All right. Was there anything else that contributed to that guilt complex?

A Well, that was one, and then the sense . . . a general sense of failure, feelings of inferiority. But feeling that he had killed all those people stood out as the most important symptom.

Q All right.

198

A There were several. There was something else. I hate to tell this Court; but when he became mentally sick—

Q Now, Doctor, please don't mention any antisocial acts.

A I will not.

Q Thank you.

A But he . . . Can I ask my patient if I may tell this one?

THE COURT: Go ahead.

THE WITNESS (*to Eatherly*): You think I ought to tell them about your feeling about not being manly, and so forth?

The record does not indicate that Eatherly *spoke* a word here, but apparently he nodded because Dr. Constantine thought he had obtained Eatherly's permission to proceed.

A He told me, and without my solicitation, that he lost his . . . after he became sick he lost his manliness. Now that is as far as I can go. And this loss of manliness is a very, very, very important part in a man's feeling toward his wife.

After examining Dr. Constantine at some length on how exact psychiatry can be, and how reliable it is, the United States Attorney returned to schizophrenia:

Q Doctor Constantine, how long would it take you to ascertain whether or not one of your patients is suffering from schizophrenia?

A How long? I am pretty good on it, not because I'm smart or anything, but because I've had a lot of experience.

Q Well, how long does it take you to make up your mind whether or not a man is schizophrenic?

A I've had cases where I could tell in five minutes.

Q Can you also tell in five minutes whether the schizophrenia is active or in remission?

A No, not in five minutes. But if I see a man from day to day and watch him closely and he begins to show some interest in life, reasoning is a little better and his reactions are

199

normal, and if he doesn't show bizarre ideation, when he shows a little insight into his troubles, understands his difficulties, then I say he is improving.

Q   And when a man's schizophrenia is in remission, he is capable of refraining from doing something that he knows to be wrong?

A   That is right.

Q   And he can distinguish between fact and fancy?

A   Between that which is real and that which is not real, yes.

I noted the following exchange with particular interest. It touches on the ironic situation where once a man is "awarded" 100 percent compensation, he can't afford to "get better" because his compensation might be reduced.

Q   Now, Doctor, something has been said with reference to the VA Compensation Board award to the defendant Eatherly. He is still receiving 100 percent disability, isn't he, right now, even though his disease is in remission?

A   We haven't made the report yet. When we make the report, they'll do something about it.

Q   You intend to make a report right away?

A   I'll write him up as soon as I get home and report his present condition. I haven't had time yet. He left last Saturday.

When Dr. Constantine told the jury "when we make the report they'll do something about it," did not the jury understand that Eatherly's compensation would be, or might be, reduced? Didn't the listening defendant note this threat to his economic welfare? Why didn't the VA Compensation Board subsequently reduce Eatherly's compensation?

This concluded Dr. Constantine's testimony.

Dr. Robert B. McElroy was called to the stand by Mr. Scarborough. When I studied Dr. McElroy's testimony, I thought it was more objective than Dr. Constantine's. Dr. McElroy, I thought, testified as the detached expert witness; while Dr. Constantine testified as the advocate of the defendant who sat facing him.

Q Detail your experience for us briefly, Doctor?

A I graduated from the University of Texas Medical School in 1936. I interned at the United States Public Health Service Hospital. Since 1939 I have been in psychiatry. During World War II, I was chief of a neuropsychiatric section of an Army hospital overseas. Since 1950 I have been a diplomate of the American Board of Psychiatry and Neurology. Since 1955 I have been chief of the Acute Intensive Treatment Service, Veterans Administration Hospital, Waco, Texas.

Q Doctor, you have been the person in charge of the case of Claude R. Eatherly, have you not, sir?

A Dr. Constantine has been in charge of the case.

Q But under your supervision?

A Yes, sir.

Q So the ultimate responsibility in this case has rested with you, and you have consulted frequently with Dr. Constantine concerning the case?

A Yes, sir.

Q Were you ever the case doctor in charge of Claude Eatherly?

A On one occasion. In 1953 when he had insulin coma therapy. I was his case doctor when he came in on December 19, 1953, and was discharged on May 19, 1954.

Both doctors had been ordered to bring "all pertinent records" to the trial. Dr. Constantine testified from his own record; while Dr. McElroy, as the administrative superior, held the hospital record in hand as he testified and frequently read from it. He also explained terms to the jury. In response to questions he made these replies:

A In a psychotic reaction the individual loses contact with reality. There are changes in the emotional response, changes in association of ideas. The individual may develop delusions. A neurotic reaction is a mild type of emotional disorder.

A When Claude Eatherly arrived at the hospital on February 23, 1950, he was diagnosed as suffering from a neurotic reaction (*reading from the record*) . . . anxiety reaction, manifested by insomnia and mild somatic complaints. He was discharged because he had received maximum hospital benefits.

A On the second admission: (*reading*) Anxiety reaction, chronic, manifested by restlessness, irritability and somatic complaints.

A On the third admission: (*reading*) Anxiety reaction is increased, manifested by increasing emotional tension, flattening of affect and bizarre ideation. Patient was given large doses of insulin—standard treatment for schizophrenia—showed improvement.

A On November 28, 1956, the diagnosis was changed to schizophrenic reaction, which is considered a maturation of the previous anxiety reaction. This was the first psychotic diagnosis given to Claude Eatherly.

Q In other words, Doctor, schizophrenia is not something that develops overnight?

A Many factors enter into it.

Q Knowing all you do about this man, when, in your opinion, did the schizophrenia tendency commence?

A Probably sometime after World War II. He began to show evidence that he was undergoing a personality change, that he wasn't functioning as well as he had previously functioned.

Q And when schizophrenia develops, does it commonly go and come . . . be active for a while, then be in remission?

A Most of the cases in the Waco hospital are schizophrenics, and we have a turnover of about 1500 a year.

Q Doctor, assuming a psychotic situation like schizophrenia, is a person often incapable of distinguishing between fact and fancy, that is, a past event and what he thinks might have occurred in the past?

A That is true. He may live in a world of fancy.

Q Could he tell you a story which he believed to be absolutely true but which in fact was absolutely false?

A He may think he is telling the truth, but there may be no basis for the story.

Dr. McElroy, reading from the record, tried to clarify for the jury the question of compensation.

Q Doctor, this service-incurred disability that you refer to, it is due solely to his mental condition, is it not? And not to having an arm off or something of that sort?

A As far as I know, he received no physical wounds. He had been adjudicated (*reading*) . . . as service-connected on his emotional disorder, experience overseas.

Q His experience overseas was dropping the bomb; he was the pilot of the plane that dropped the bomb over Hiroshima?

A I don't think he dropped the bomb. He was in a reconnaissance plane.

Q And that's what caused his service-connected emotional disorder?

A The doctor in charge of the case, or myself as chief of service, we do not make such judgments. The adjudication is made by the local Veterans Administration office. They have the man's military service records, and they have our records, and other information gathered by their case workers. On their findings, apparently, Eatherly's emotional disorder was adjudged service-incurred, and they awarded him 100 percent.

For me that testimony shed little light on the mystery of why and how Eatherly was awarded service-incurred disability compensation. Dr. McElroy not only insisted that he and the doctors did not make the award, but he also used the word *apparently* in trying to explain what the local VA office might have done. He read from the record that Eatherly had been "adjudicated as service-connected on his emotional disorder, experience overseas." But the Air Force medical record mentions no such "disorder." So how could the "local VA office" have used "emotional disorder, experience overseas" as a basis for awarding service-incurred compensation in 1953?

From Dr. McElroy's overall testimony I concluded that he was avoiding Dr. Constantine's position on Eatherly's guilt complex, punishment-seeking crimes, and how Eatherly had incurred his disorder. The U. S. Attorney must have sensed this because, remembering his five-hour conference at Waco, he insisted that Dr. McElroy put into the trial record the fact that disagreement existed at the hospital regarding Eatherly.

Mr. Floore questioned Dr. McElroy:

Q Now, Doctor, on March 1, 1957, I wrote a letter to the VA hospital, which you have there, and in which I asked for an opinion as to whether Claude Eatherly was able then to assist in his own defense. On March 8, 1957, I received a reply which you have. I direct your attention to that letter, and I will ask you to read it, sir.

A I would like to say that this letter was not written by me. It was written by a doctor on one of the other wards . . . where Eatherly was at that time.

Q Yes, sir. That was Dr. Samuel H. Ross. Now will you read the letter, sir?

A (*Witness reading*) "It is our opinion that Mr. Eatherly is competent to aid in the preparation and conduct of the defense of the charges against him. We feel that he will be able to stand trial at Abilene during the month of April, 1957."

Q Now, Doctor, immediately after I received that letter, you are aware that I had a warrant issued for Mr. Eatherly to bring him in to stand trial?

A The chain of events indicates that.

Q It was after I received this official and expert advice from the VA hospital that I had the warrant issued, set the case for trial, and prepared for trial? Is that correct, sir?

A Yes, sir.

Q And thereafter, on or about the 1st day of April, 1957, I made a special trip to Waco to see you and Dr. Constantine and any other doctors who had participated in this case.

A That is true. The other doctor was Dr. Ross.

Q Yes, sir. And we had a discussion lasting several hours. And as a result of that discussion, didn't I advise you that I intended to inform the Court that there were serious disagreements among the doctors as to Claude Eatherly?

A That is true.

I noted in the trial record that at this point there was a heated argument over the admissibility of evidence of disagreement among the VA doctors. The United States Attorney contended that the jury had a right to know that Dr. Constantine was voicing only a prevailing opinion at the VA hospital, and that "strong and capable contrary opinion" was in the VA record.

MR. FLOORE: If the Court please, I am endeavoring to show this jury that psychiatry is not exact, and that in the same VA institution, in a period of less than six weeks, in response to the identical question, the United States Attorney was given directly conflicting answers. Dr. Constantine and Dr. McElroy were only one party to that conflict. We think we are entitled to show this conflict to the jury. It bears on the weight and credibility of the opinion testimony.

When the Court sustained Mr. Floore in this argument, Dr. McElroy read Dr. Ross's opinion of Claude Eatherly from the hospital record:

DR. MCELROY: "This patient has no moral feelings toward his wife or children or toward any human being that he comes in contact with. He has no feeling of responsibility or moral obligation to any individual or group or to society as a whole."

Mr. Floore then put the question of Hiroshima-guilt to Dr. McElroy:

Q Now, Doctor, in the light of Dr. Ross's opinion, would you say that guilt feelings over killing people at Hiroshima caused Claude Eatherly to develop a mental disorder, caused him to attempt suicide in 1950, and caused him to break into post offices seeking punishment for his guilt?

Dr. McElroy must have known that, with that question, the United States Attorney was endeavoring to discredit most of Dr. Constantine's testimony. Here is Dr. McElroy's answer:

A There would be multiple factors involved. Perhaps that would be considered one factor.

Mr. Scarborough, for the defense, scored a last point with Dr. McElroy:

Q Doctor, have you yourself interviewed Claude Eatherly in the past few months?

A I have. And I have seen him almost daily on my rounds.

Q Please tell the jury whether or not, in your opinion, this man is now capable of making a useful citizen and of finding his place in society.

A If he is able to maintain his improvement, he should be able to make an adequate social adjustment.

At the conclusion of the trial the jury found Alvin Crews guilty. He was sentenced to two years in a federal penitentiary. He surrendered to a U. S. marshal to begin serving his sentence. Roy Mantooth was returned to a federal penitentiary to continue serving his sentence.

Claude Eatherly was found not guilty, and was free to return to Van Alstyne with his brother. He was not in the custody of his brother. He had no custodian, no guardian. He was as free as any other citizen of the United States.

Sixteen

AFTER I had studied the Abilene transcript and tried to see Claude Eatherly as Roy Mantooth saw him or as Dr. Constantine saw him, I examined the press association reports and tried to imagine Eatherly's human problems as he returned to Van Alstyne on December 11, 1957. What did he think? How did he feel? How did he plan to live? Was he capable of planning?

I asked Davis Scarborough, who had defended him, for an appraisal of him after the trial. Mr. Scarborough, of Abilene, calls himself a "plain vanilla country lawyer," but he is able and prominent. He served in the Navy during World War II and is a licensed pilot. His father, Dallas Scarborough, was a legendary West Texas criminal lawyer.

"I didn't feel as if I knew him," Mr. Scarborough said. "In my several conversations with him, preparing his defense, I never felt I was able to get through to him. He'd answer my questions freely, but I was never convinced that I had been taken into his confidence. I never believed he was telling me what he was thinking. I saw no evidence of any guilt complex in him: he didn't appear apprehensive over what might happen. He had the appearance of other men I have represented who had mental problems to the extent of being habitual criminals. I was convinced that the post office burglaries would not be the last of his antisocial acts. He had mental and emotional problems which would cause him to run afoul of the law later. I told him so."

"How did you happen to take his case?" I asked.

207

"The publicity had nothing to do with it," Mr. Scarborough replied. "I took the case back in March, 1957, without ever guessing that publicity would develop. The County Attorney of Grayson County telephoned me and said he was a close friend of Claude Eatherly's brother. The County Attorney said he didn't think Claude Eatherly needed to go to a federal pen, and the County Attorney asked me if I would help. As a favor to the County Attorney, I agreed. Because the man was said to be sick, the fee was nominal: four hundred dollars. One of the Eatherly brothers paid it to me—I don't recall which one. I talked with both James Eatherly, of Midland, and Joe Eatherly, of Van Alstyne. They are fine men.

"And I'll say this for Claude Eatherly," Mr. Scarborough added. "He had no shortage of friends. As soon as it was published that I was representing him, I got letters and calls from all over the country from men who had been in the 509th with him and who wanted to help in any way they could."

An Associated Press story, filed from Van Alstyne, ran inside many papers in Texas, Louisiana, Arkansas and Oklahoma on December 13, 1957. With this story a number of papers ran a one-column photograph which had been distributed by a picture service:

FLYER RETURNS
TO HOME TOWN AFTER
ACQUITTAL

VAN ALSTYNE, TEX. (AP)—A flyer once acclaimed as one of the world's greatest was back in the old home town today trying to pick up the pieces of a shattered life.

He is Claude Eatherly, a former major and a man hand-picked to usher in the atomic age.

Eatherly's plane was one of four which led the *Enola Gay* over Hiroshima. Nestled in the bay of the *Enola Gay* was the atomic bomb that changed the world's warfare in an instant.

Today Eatherly is out of jail and looking for a job, after a divorce, drunken sprees, a series of trips to mental wards and an acquittal only last Tuesday on post office burglary charges.

Doctors say he is obsessed by a guilt complex . . . that he feels responsible for 100,000 deaths in the Hiroshima bomb drop.

If he is well, and doctors say they can't tell, it probably is the first time since 1950, when he first went to the Waco Veterans Hospital for mental treatment.

Dr. Robert McElroy and Dr. O. P. Constantine, psychiatrists at the Waco VA Hospital, say he has a guilt complex and a split personality.

Dr. McElroy told the Abilene jury that acquitted Eatherly his work in the atomic bomb drop would be "one factor involved" in the guilt complex.

After his acquittal Tuesday, Eatherly told a newsman he would "try to go to work if someone will give me a job."

How could Claude Eatherly find a job in 1958? Who would hire him? He was no longer the man who worked at Perrin Air Force Base in 1956. Then only an employment officer, but none of his co-workers knew of his military, criminal or medical past. Now, he was locally famous—and famous as a hero, a criminal, and a nut.

For the first time in his life he had claimed insanity; and the psychiatrists, to free him, had been compelled to abandon protective words like psychotic and schizophrenic, and to state in open court that he had been "plumb crazy" in 1956 and without warning might become "plumb crazy" again. The psychiatrists had admitted that he might harm someone, that his freedom was a risk which society must take to give him a chance to recover. Who wants to hire a man like that?

If he couldn't find a job, how could he occupy himself? In the hospital, attendants tried to help him occupy himself by occupational therapy, educational therapy, baseball, swimming pools, punching bags and motion pictures—a whole program devised by experts to keep men occupied until the hour for their sleeping potions. Alone, how could Claude Eatherly occupy himself in Van Alstyne in 1958? He could help his brother sell oil products, but how much could he help?

Perhaps the psychiatrists had supplied a partial answer when they kept using that term "flattening of affect." It means a decline of the ability to respond to life; an abatement of feeling, emotion and desire with a corresponding increase in capacity to endure boredom. Flattening of affect is what gives a face "that blank or faraway look" which one witness tried to describe at the trial. So perhaps Claude Eatherly required less occupation then normal men.

His fame offered him new occupation. Some of the people who had heard of him began to discuss him, and write about him, and tell their friends about him. So he had begun to receive mail. Letters reached him easily. A letter addressed to him only at Van Alstyne, Texas, or Grayson County, Texas, reached him, as did letters addressed to The Military Hospital, Waco, Texas.

These letters urged him to occupy himself in "spreading your message." They urged him to make speeches, and help write books, and help make motion pictures, and "publicize what you stand for." Many of the letter writers saw Eatherly becoming a great voice, a savior of the world from nuclear holocaust. Even the modest letter writers insisted that he must devote himself to "promoting the cause of world peace."

Here is the first letter I received about Eatherly, in 1958, from a woman in New Zealand.

DEAR MR. HUIE:

You are aware that I consider your book *The Execution of Private Slovik* to be the most important anti-war story since *All Quiet on the Western Front*. Now I have just read a magazine article about Major Eatherly . . . how he has been tortured by his memories of Hiroshima and how he has turned to crime in search of punishment.

Here, sir, is a remarkable opportunity for you. With your worldwide audience, and your skill as a dramatist, you could help Major Eatherly become one of the great influences for peace in our time.

I urge you to go to the military prison in Texas and see Major Eatherly and begin helping him. You can make Major Eatherly into a marvelously effective instrument for promoting peace.

In 1958 I tossed that letter into my huge Crackpot File and did not acknowledge it because I knew that no Major Eatherly had been at the attack on Hiroshima. And my conversations with Eatherly in 1962 convinced me that by 1958 he understood that the letter writers wanted him to be not merely what he was, but whatever they needed or wanted him to be. They wanted him to be the man who either dropped the bomb or selected the target, who then repented, who suffered nightmares of guilt and anguish, who refused his pension, and who then turned to crime both to seek punishment and to publicize his crusade against nuclear destruction and for world peace.

Eatherly had seen what television dramatists wanted him to be. He had read what Jim Vachule and *Newsweek* wanted him to be. He had heard what Dr. Constantine wanted him to be. At the post office each week he found letters from "good people all over the world" telling him what they wanted him to be.

Now he would see what Hollywood wanted him to be.

I have reported that in 1957 Jim Vachule entered his Eatherly stories in a contest called the Newspaper Hall of Fame sponsored by a motion picture producer named William Rowland; that Mr. Rowland promptly notified Mr. Vachule that his story had "won" and that he would receive $5000, and Eatherly would receive $10,000, as soon as "details could be worked out." I have also reported that when I first talked with Eatherly he showed me a contract he had signed in January, 1962, with this same Mr. Rowland.

What I now must make clear is that the "promotion" of Mr. Rowland's proposed film, *Medal in the Dust,* was a continuous, rising-and-falling effort from 1957 to 1962. The film has not yet been produced; it may never be produced; but it seems clear that Claude Eatherly's hopes became involved in this promotion effort.

The effect on Eatherly, and on the Eatherly Case, of this effort to promote a film on his life cannot be overestimated.

Those of us who are experienced in Hollywood promotion efforts know that five years is not an extraordinarily long time for a film idea to be "promoted" before it finally attracts the money and the distribution contract necessary for its production. We know all the ups-and-downs, delays, disappointments, and compromises. So we discipline our emotions. We refuse to become excited until we are paid. But when Claude Eatherly, knowing none of this, was shown a book with an engraved title—a two-inch-thick, loose-bound mimeographed, professional-looking shooting script, all dialogue complete, with camera directions, by-lined by Paul I. Wellman and A. B. Guthrie Jr.—a finished drama in which the star was named CLAUDE ROBERT EATHERLY, and supporting characters were named JOE EATHERLY, JIM VACHULE, DR. ROSENWALD, and Eatherly's former wife by her real name—Eatherly assumed from this "book" that shortly a big film would be a reality, and that shortly he would be paid $10,000 and a big percentage of profits.

When Eatherly read in a Dallas newspaper that the Texas war hero, Audie Murphy, was being "considered" to play Eatherly in *Medal in the Dust,* Eatherly believed it. He next read that he was to be paid $250,000 for his "dramatic life story." Why didn't someone warn him that such items were only promotion tricks?

Most cruel to him probably was the fact that he seems to have assumed that the script should be defended by him as his true story! In order to help the film, and in order to assure his receiving between $10,000 and $250,000, he seems to have assumed that he must begin telling his visitors and correspondents that what the script depicted as true was in fact true!

I studied *Medal in the Dust,* and then I wrote to Paul Wellman about it. He replied cordially that the script was "of course mainly drama laid over the facts of Eatherly's life." He added, "Bud Guthrie had nothing to do with the writing; I wrote it; Bill Rowland put Bud's name on it, along with mine, to assist the promotion."

Claude Eatherly knew nothing about the film business. So in 1958 he assumed that if he was to become a rich crusader against nuclear holocaust, he should begin playing the role written for him.

Reading *Medal in the Dust* in my office in Alabama in 1962, then comparing it with what was published about Eatherly between 1958 and 1962, was a sobering experience for me.

A skilled craftsman, taking Jim Vachule's published stories and "additional material," had woven a drama which had some chance of being promoted into a film. It may yet become a film. The finished script, with numerous copies available, in a sense was "published." Because, as part of the promotion effort, the script was shown to a number of articulate people in the film world. Most important of all, it was shown to Eatherly at a time when he had begun answering letters "from all over the world."

Thus this script indirectly became the *source* for factual stories.

Throughout my investigation I had wondered at the source of Eatherly's "refusing his pension as blood money." Let me quote from *Medal in the Dust*.

JOE EATHERLY is explaining his brother to the REPORTER:

JOE: Another thing. His stealing . . . it's to get a little money to buy himself a meal, or maybe a bottle. But he doesn't need that money.

REPORTER: (*amazed*) He doesn't?

JOE: No. He's got money. The government pays him $264 a month for total mental disability (*beat*) But it just piles up in the bank here. He won't touch it. He looks on it as blood money.

REPORTER: It must amount to thousands by now. . . .

JOE: It does. But it will lie there. And there's another quirk that not many people know. When he does get a few dollars, he often doesn't even spend it on himself. He puts it in an envelope, and addresses it to Hiroshima, Japan, with a note, always the same, "I'm sorry."

Whether through Claude Eatherly or not, the "blood money" story was circulated. The French journalist Fernand Gigon heard it and wrote it as fact! *The Observer* in London, in reviewing Gigon's book, extracted it as fact. John Wain read the review after which he wrote his poem "A Song About Major Eatherly." The poem was published as truth by a firm like Macmillan; and it was read dramatically as truth over BBC!

And note this. Each of these authors and publishers thought he was being a "humanitarian" in writing and publishing this information. Each author and publisher was crusading for peace and understanding, and against nuclear warfare.

But did these humanitarians give any thought to Eatherly? He told me he didn't tell Mr. Gigon that he had refused his pension. But even if he did, do reporters accept as fact what they are told by a man who has just escaped prison by pleading insanity!

After "worldwide" publication that he had refused his pension as blood money, what was Eatherly supposed to do? Refuse his next pension check? Or begin feeling guilty if he accepted it? If he felt guilty before the humanitarians began publicizing him, how guilty do you suppose he felt when he pocketed his next pension payment?

Is this the way humanitarians do good?

Note what happened to the fiction that Eatherly sent money to Hiroshima. The German author, Robert Jungk, published that Eatherly did this! And he published it in his Introduction to the book by Gunther Anders as well as in the newspapers *France-Soir* and *Europèo*.

When I questioned Eatherly he insisted at first that he *did* send money to "the children of Hiroshima."

"Nonsense, Claude," I said. "If you have ever mailed a dollar to Hiroshima you have done it only in an effort to do what the humanitarians wrote that you have done. You know that."

He made no further comment.

When Eatherly saw the script of *Medal in the Dust,* the first page was a Foreword. But this was not a Foreword for the proposed film; it was a Foreword "for the trade"; for "promotion purposes." Here is what Eatherly read:

FOREWORD

The story of Major Claude Eatherly, the Air Force pilot who led the Hiroshima and Nagasaki atomic bomb attacks, then turned to a life of crime, is a true story documented in military and police files.

It is a story of unparalleled, universal importance, because for the first time it shows what the mass slaughter of the nuclear era can do to the military man who directs it. Its portent is such that every motion picture critic in the world will be *forced* to give this picture his most thoughtful, considered attention.

It is an action story . . . the story of the newspaper reporter, himself an Air Force hero, who finds the key necessary to rehabilitate Claude Eatherly and give him a new future. At the same time it is a love story, the story of a marriage saved on the verge of breakup.

It is an adult story, probing man's deepest motivations, his un-
spoken commitment to humanity. It is also a story with terrific box
office potential . . . a natural story for the film medium, and a
story with a "built-in" audience of millions of servicemen and ex-
servicemen, both in the United States and in other countries around
the world. All of them will want to *see* the inside, untold story of
what the world's first atomic bombing raid did to the mind and
heart of the man who actually led it. How it turned a national hero
into a common criminal.

PAUL I. WELLMAN

A. B. GUTHRIE, JR.

Eatherly then read the film's opening: a crime in progress.
This has been an effective film opening since *The Great Train
Robbery*.

1 FADE IN:

INT. SMALL DRUGSTORE NIGHT

CAMERA looks from rear of place, toward display window, in
which dim street lamps show typical display of corner drugstore,
and window sign in reverse: KIRK'S PHARMACY. Counters,
prescription department, perfumes and magazine racks, and so
forth dimly visible.

Beam of a flashlight suddenly throws a round circle of light on
counter, stopping on cash register. CAMERA HOLDS ON REG-
ISTER, and a man ENTERS SHOT FROM BEHIND CAMERA.
To us he is only a silhouette with beam of flashlight between
him and CAMERA. He approaches the cash register stealthily.
and begins to try to pry open the drawer with a small jimmy.

2 MED. CLOSE SHOT REVERSE ANGLE

Finding it hard to work jimmy with one hand, man places flashlight on counter so it will illuminate register, and takes both
hands to it.

His face is illuminated in harsh contrast by the slanting beam of
the flashlight, showing drawn and gaunt, with tired, tortured
eyes, and a three-or-four-day growth of beard. This is CLAUDE
EATHERLY. The slow, sure erosion of conscience has worn away
the once-sharp edges of his character, leaving it lax and loose. At a
faint, indistinct SOUND he starts nervously, listens. It is not

repeated. He devotes himself quickly to prying open the cash drawer.

3 EXT. STORE REAR DOOR ON ALLEY NIGHT MED. SHOT

A NIGHT WATCHMAN approaches, making his rounds. He tries the door, finds it unlocked. As he pushes it open carefully he hears the CLANG of the cash drawer, ringing as it is opened. He draws a gun and moves warily inside.

4 INT. STORE NIGHT MED. SHOT

As he enters, watchman pauses and looks around. He sees indistinct figure at the counter.

WATCHMAN'S VOICE: Get your hands up, there! I got you covered!

After that opening CLAUDE EATHERLY is jailed, and the REPORTER discovers that he was "the hero who helped drop the Big One—Hiroshima!" So the REPORTER sets out to explain CLAUDE so he can save him from prison and rehabilitate him through psychiatry.

At that point the film writer, as a dramatist, had to face commercial realities. Films cost money. They must entertain mass audiences. So an Air Force hero in a commercial film must be a combat hero. When we flash back to show that the hero was chosen to drop the big one only because he had already proved himself a great one, we must invent a granddaddy of an air fight—PILOT EATHERLY in a B-17 attacking a secret Jap radar station in the Philippines . . . all guns blazing . . . bandits at 3 o'clock . . . and Zeros exploding in the pilot's face. Such a fight sequence is a necessity for another reason: the producer can save money by splicing in "stock footage." All air fights look alike: the only difference is in what the hero does in CLOSEUP.

Claude Eatherly never saw such combat. But in *Medal in the Dust,* before he reached Tinian CLAUDE EATHERLY had flown thirty-two combat missions—bloody, hellfire missions—and this is important only because in subsequent, factual reports, CLAUDE EATHERLY's combat record became Claude Eatherly's record. (See Chapter One.)

I had wondered why the European authors pictured Eatherly

216

as a decision-maker at Hiroshima. Jim Vachule, *Newsweek,* and the press associations in the United States had used the trick word *led*—meaning that the *Straight Flush* flew in front of the *Enola Gay* and implying more—but European writers like Robert Jungk scorned such tricks and called Eatherly the commander of the Hiroshima raid. But wouldn't the commander and the decision-maker have been in the *Enola Gay*?

Medal in the Dust indicates how CLAUDE EATHERLY came to be the decision-maker. The briefing is underway at Tinian:

GENERAL: Major Eatherly, you will command a reconnaissance wing of four B-29s. Each plane will scout one of the four target cities. . . .

MED. SHOT—GENERAL

Unfurling map, using pointer to indicate targets.

GENERAL: (*continuing*) You will select the target, Major. Having established it, you will rendezvous with the *Enola Gay* over Iwo Jima . . .
(*indicating on map*)
. . . and lead her to that city. If in your opinion weather conditions are not suitable, you will cancel the operation. Do you understand?

That's how MAJOR EATHERLY assumed command. And in the script it is MAJOR EATHERLY in the thick of the attack, who barks all the commands into his radio: "Red Dog, this is *Straight Flush,* you will proceed . . ." Or fall back, etc, etc. The command post is MAJOR EATHERLY's cockpit.

Here is MAJOR EATHERLY's homecoming in *Medal in the Dust.* Compare it with Gigon and Jungk in Chapter One:

BACK TO JOE'S OFFICE   JOE AND REPORTER AS BEFORE

JOE: It was after Bikini that he resigned from the Air Force. He wanted no part of war and killing ever again.
(*beat*)
But he still wanted to fly.

REPORTER: Commercial?

JOE: Yes. The trouble was nobody else seemed to want him to fly.
(*beat*)
He came home, with his wife. I could see a big difference in him

217

right away. When the town heard he was coming home for good, they planned a sort of public reception. . . .

DISSOLVE TO:

EXT. STREET HIGH ANGLE FULL SHOT

With a banner flung across it reading:

WELCOME HOME, CLAUDE!

There is a crowd in the street, and a band is playing.

MED. CLOSE SHOT THE BAND

FEATURING the bass drummer, pounding on the drum on which we see:

VAN ALSTYNE H. S.

INT. CAR IN WHICH JOE IS BRINGING HIS BROTHER AND WIFE

With the crowd and band dead ahead.

EATHERLY: (*surprised and uneasy*) What's all this for, Joe?

JOE: It's for you, Claude.

He brings the car to a stop. People rush forward, but first to reach the car and open the door is MAYOR HAROLD WOLTMAN. He has an air of importance and a few notes in his hand.

EXT. CAR

WOLTMAN: (*seizing Eatherly by the hand*) Welcome home, Claude. All Van Alstyne's out to welcome you home.

EATHERLY: (*looking with dismay at the crowd*) What for?

WOLTMAN: You're a hero, my boy. Didn't you know?

Woltman, according to the script, has trouble quieting the crowd for the speechmaking, then he makes a speech.

WOLTMAN: (*recovering his aplomb*) Ladies and gentlemen, it is my privilege and honor today to welcome home Van Alstyne's most distinguished warrior from the greatest conflict in which our beloved country has ever engaged. I refer, of course, to Major Claude Eatherly . . .

218

He is interrupted by a great cheer, and the band strikes up again, and people rush to shake hands with Eatherly.

In the script the villains are the businessmen who try to exploit the Hiroshima Hero. They hire him to sell oil products, and to address the Elks' Club, and they embarrass him by insisting that he describe how he killed "all them Japs."

BACK TO JOE'S OFFICE   JOE AND REPORTER AS BEFORE

JOE: It was like that everywhere. Claude didn't want to trade on his reputation, but the company thought it was good business. (*beat*)
That was when he began to go to pieces. He tried to tell people that the Atom Bomb was the worst thing, the most terrible thing, that had ever happened to the human race.

REPORTER: (*feeling the pathos of it*) And they wouldn't listen?

JOE: Nobody would listen. Nobody at all.

REPORTER: And you think this . . . unsettled him?

JOE: There were other things . . . like that trip to Chicago. Claude didn't want to go, but his wife and I persuaded him. We thought it would do him good to get a little recognition. It was the worst mistake we could have made.
(*beat*)
Anyway, Claude and his wife flew to Chicago. . . .

In the flashback which follows the Air Force has brought MAJOR EATHERLY to Chicago to speak at the dedication of a hospital for some of the Japanese victims of Hiroshima . . . the Hiroshima Maidens . . . the girls with the burned faces. This is "good theater"—a boorish photographer posing one of the girls with MAJOR EATHERLY and asking the girl, with her horrible face, to "smile at the Major."
But what really "hits 'em in the gut" is when the GENERAL introduces the MAJOR to the crowd for his dedicatory speech:

GENERAL: (*as if continuing*) . . . and for the next speaker, we are privileged to hear from one of the men who actually took part in

219

the attacks against Hiroshima and Nagasaki . . . a young man who after distinguishing himself in the defense of his flag and his country, returned home, laid aside his sword for a metaphorical plowshare, and earned equal distinction as a leader in the civilian life of his community. . . .

Photogs begin to move from the press table into position before the speaker's table.

GENERAL: (*continuing*) This young man actually led these two historic missions, after having designated the targets himself. Our great nation is fortunate indeed to have men of this caliber . . . men capable of carrying these grave responsibilities. It is therefore with great pride that I have the extraordinary honor of presenting to you at this time . . . Major Claude Eatherly.

APPLAUSE. CAMERA IS STILL MOVING IN on Eatherly. He gets to his feet slowly, reluctantly, neglecting to pick up his speech (written for him by Air Force Public Relations) from the table. General Trent notices, grabs the speech and thrusts it into his hand with a reassuring pat on the back. Eatherly goes to the speaker's microphone like a man in a trance, and faces the audience. The room goes quiet. CAMERA IS NOW MED CLOSE AND STILL MOVING IN. Eatherly gazes at the audience with a bewildered, uncertain expression. His gaze fixes on the Hiroshima Maidens, and his eyes move from one to the other of them.

INSERT SHOT   EATHERLY'S POINT OF VIEW

CAMERA PANS THE HIROSHIMA MAIDENS. The audience, waiting for him to speak, begins to grow slightly restless. A self-conscious COUGH from somewhere in the back, echoes through the room. THROAT-CLEARING and FOOT SHUFFLING NOISES come up.

BACK TO SCENE

CAMERA STOPS ON CLOSEUP OF EATHERLY. For the first time since Hiroshima, the full realization of what happened there is hitting him. The effect is paralyzing to his will.

CLOSE SHOT   HIS WIFE

She looks at him in alarm.

CLOSEUP   EATHERLY

His face works as he tries to collect his thoughts. But he cannot. The enormity and horror of what he has done are too much.

EATHERLY: (*at length, blurting it out*) I . . . I'm . . . *sorry!*

In 1962 *Parade* Magazine, which is distributed in a number of Sunday papers in the United States, published a story which was prefaced with this Editor's Note:

Parade has spent nearly a year tracking down and checking details of this story. Reporters have talked to many of the chief characters . . . to Eatherly himself, who gives his version here for the first time.

Here is the first, complete, authentic report on the saga of Claude Eatherly.

After that introduction, the *Parade* story contains these sentences:

In conjunction with this experience [Bikini] came another that brought Eatherly to a fateful decision. The Bikini explosion had no sooner died down than he was called to the bedside of his dying mother. There a startling coincidence occurred.

As he knelt down by the bed, holding her hand, he noticed the Bible open on the table. "It was open," he recalls, "to the twentieth chapter of Exodus. The words 'Thou shalt not kill' leaped out at me. Then and there, for the first time, I realized what I had done."

Six months later Eatherly left the Air Force.

Here's how the scene appeared in 1958 in *Medal in the Dust:*

INT. HOSPITAL

Eatherly and Joe hurry along a hall, with a nurse showing the way. They come to a door. Nurse knocks and looks in. When another nurse, inside, sees who it is, she opens door wide and the two men enter.

INT. HOSPITAL ROOM   SEEN FROM EATHERLY'S ANGLE AT DOOR

Two doctors and two nurses are bending over the bed on which lies MRS. EATHERLY. In b. g., weeping, are PA EATHERLY and DOROTHY,

Joe's wife. The doctor in charge looks up, sees Eatherly and Joe and beckons them quickly forward as if there is need for haste.

MED. CLOSE SHOT   MRS. EATHERLY

She is a thin, fragile woman, who has been beautiful in her day, but is now near to her end. As Eatherly kneels at her bedside and takes her hand, she opens her eyes. There is a look of love and faint joy on her face as she sees him, but it is almost the last beat of her life.

CLOSEUP   EATHERLY'S HAND HOLDING HIS MOTHER'S HAND

For a moment there is a pressure of affection, and then the white hand of the mother goes limp. On the back of Eatherly's hand, holding hers, we see two teardrops fall.

WIDER ANGLE

Eatherly rises as the doctors confirm the fact that his mother is gone. Tears run down his face as he stoops and kisses her on the cheek. Then, with anguished grief, he turns away. His eyes fall on something o.s.

CLOSE SHOT   THE BEDSIDE TABLE

Upon it lies an open Bible. Eatherly's hand ENTERS SHOT and picks up the Bible.

WIDER ANGLE   EATHERLY

As he looks down at the Bible.

CLOSEUP   THE BIBLE IN EATHERLY'S HANDS

As he reads it, it is open at the twentieth chapter of Exodus, the Ten Commandments. CAMERA FOCUSES ON ONE LINE, the rest of the page being shadowed with gray. The line:

THOU SHALT NOT KILL.

CLOSEUP EATHERLY'S FACE

As a strange expression comes over it . . . an inward look, as it were, with pain and guilt in it.

WIDER ANGLE   EATHERLY

As he turns to Joe in uncontrollable sorrow sobbing.

222

When I compared *Parade*'s story with *Medal in the Dust*, I concluded that the sardonic gods must have chuckled over their winecups at *Parade*'s reporters. Those fellows labored a year to produce "the first complete, authentic report on the saga of Claude Eatherly" only to publish as straight-faced fact what appeared in a dramatized film script in 1958!

Is there really a reporter in the United States who could listen to Eatherly tell that "Bible story" without suspecting that Eatherly was repeating invention? And again: who's to blame? Eatherly or the reporters?

And note *Parade*'s "authentic effort" to report how Eatherly left the Air Force. In a whole year had it not occurred to at least one of that team of reporters that the cause of authenticity might be served by examining the Air Force record?

The publishers of *Parade* were so proud of their Eatherly story that they took a full-page advertisement in the trade journal *Editor & Publisher*, to boast of the authenticity their team of reporters had achieved in at last "presenting the truth about the tall, hollowed-eyed, violently controversial ex-Air Force major named Claude Robert Eatherly."

From start to finish, the *Parade* story was nonsense. Yet it was delivered to millions of American homes—and it was about Hiroshima.

Since I could find no evidence that Eatherly had ever had a nightmare, I had wondered where all the nightmare stories originated. (See Chapter One.) In *Medal in the Dust* I found a double dose of nightmares. Not only is CLAUDE EATHERLY afflicted with them, but so is the REPORTER. In his war the RE-PORTER bombed an orphanage—"just . . . little . . . kids!"—and this haunted him.

Nightmares are always effective in films. There is ACTION. The tormented guy is SCREAMING and writhing and sweating. Then his beautiful wife bounces out of the other bed, ter-rorized, in her shift, and the "production value" of sex is added to the scene.

Here is how the script introduces EATHERLY's wife:

223

INT. HOTEL ROOM

She is lovely, young, beautifully formed, in a charming dress with a full skirt showing off her tiny waist, sleeveless to display her pretty arms, and V-necked to reveal her perfect throat and upper bosom. She is putting on last touches before mirror. At a KNOCK on the door she gives herself a final quick inspection in the mirror, before and behind, then runs to open the door.

So *Medal in the Dust* is twice-fortified with nightmares. With both the REPORTER's WIFE and EATHERLY's WIFE bouncing around in their shifts, trying to wake their screaming, writhing, sweating husbands, there is real "gut drama." And in his nightmares EATHERLY screams: "Bail out! Bail out! Save the children!" This is the identical scream which was later reported as *fact* in some of the most reputable journals on earth.

Newsweek in May, 1959, reported: "Eatherly twice attempted suicide." (See Chapter One.) All the foreign writers agreed there had been two suicide attempts. That, too, was in the film script. After all, a sleeping pill suicide attempt is not suited to the film medium. There is no action. What can you show? A man taking a handful of pills? So here's how CLAUDE EATHERLY does it in *Medal in the Dust:*

INT. BATHROOM DAY MED SHOT

As he lurches to the wash basin, leans on it, and stares at himself in the mirror. The sight gives him the shudders. He puts his hand over his eyes to hide it and stands thus motionless but breathing heavily, for a long moment.

Finally he straightens, opens the medicine cabinet . . . the mirror is on the outside of the cabinet so CAMERA HOLDS SHOT and looks directly inside . . . as he takes out his safety razor. He closes the cabinet. For a moment he stares with increasing revulsion at his unshaved visage, with the lipstick (put there by a B-girl) across his mouth. Then, in a burst of self-hate, he smashes his fist into the mirror. It cracks.

He leans on the wash basin in despair, head bowed. Then, very slowly, he looks up, and with terrible resolution stares at himself in the cracked mirror. It is the stare of the accuser, the executioner.

He looks down at the safety razor in his hand. Deliberately he takes the blade out and holds it between his thumb and finger. Once more he looks at himself in the cracked mirror, then down at the blade. CAMERA MOVES IN FOR CLOSEUP OF DROPS OF BLOOD AS THEY PAN DOWN TO THE FLOOR.

                                    DISSOLVE TO:

INT. HOSPITAL CORRIDOR DAY-CLOSE SHOT SIGNAL LIGHT

That's how two suicide attempts became part of the Eatherly story "around the world." One attempt was the alleged sleeping pill attempt by Claude Eatherly. The other was the pictorial attempt by CLAUDE EATHERLY. One plus one equals two.

In psychiatry, however, the film script went its own way. The psychiatrist, Dr. Rosenwald, speaks "with a Ukrainian accent" but otherwise doesn't resemble Dr. Constantine. CLAUDE EATHERLY's robberies are not motivated by punishment-seeking. The explanation is that EATHERLY stole to buy his food and bottles rather than touch his blood-money pension. So there is no punishment-seeking in the script's psychiatry.

The script's psychiatrist motivates EATHERLY with "sibling rivalry in childhood." It is a variation on Cain and Abel. CLAUDE EATHERLY was an enthusiastic killer because imposed on the face of each of his Japanese victims was the face of his brother JOE, who had been his sibling rival. When CLAUDE finally gains insight into all this, he wants the JUDGE to send him to the VA hospital for psychiatric treatment. And Joe speaks out:

JOE: Just this . . . your Honor. There's something the Doctor here doesn't know . . . nobody knows but me. The thing that has broken Claude up is this. . . . He wants desperately to tell people . . . warn people . . . about the dreadful thing the Atom Bomb is. . . .
(beat)
And nobody will ever listen.
(another beat; intensely earnest)
Your Honor, if they would only listen to my brother . . . he might be *one of the great voices in the world today.* . . .

When I finished reading *Medal in the Dust,* I thought I understood what had happened when Claude Eatherly read it. He must have thought he had found a new purpose for his life. He wanted to see the film made, and he wanted to write or "help write" his autobiography to go along with the film. He wanted to devote his life to "world peace."

In May, 1958, Eatherly flew to Louisville, Kentucky, to attend the crew reunion which I described earlier through the recollections of four of the crew members. He sat in a box at the Kentucky Derby, played poker, and his crew members, after thirteen years, found him to be "just the same old carefree Skipper." By then almost a year had passed since the television show and since Eatherly had first heard of "movie interest." He had not yet been paid, so he told his crew members that he was opposing a film because there might be something in it his children shouldn't see. But when he returned to Van Alstyne from Louisville, he traveled to Fort Worth to see Jim Vachule, to inquire as to what was holding up the picture and what could be done to push it along.

On July 15, 1958, Eatherly went to Dallas, got drunk, and held up another grocery store in the bizarre manner of the Denison robbery. He forced the grocer at gunpoint to put the money in a paper sack, then walked out, leaving the sack.

On July 17, 1958, Dallas County sheriff's deputies escorted him back to the Waco hospital where he was officially admitted for the seventh time.

Seventeen

AFTER his seventh official admission, Claude Eatherly stayed at the hospital five weeks, until August 31, 1958, when he was "granted a 90-day trial visit in the custody of his brother." That trial visit is significant because it was the last such visit that his brother Joe would arrange. When on March 11, 1959, Claude Eatherly pulled another of his stunt grocery store robberies in Dallas, Joe Eatherly, too, "gave up." Joe refused to be his brother's custodian ever again.

"Joe lined up against me after that," Claude Eatherly told me.

Joe Eatherly told me: "My two children were growing up. My father was becoming very old at the home place. There is a limit to what a man can do for his brother; the time comes when he must put his own children first. I had no way to keep Claude occupied; and after he stayed around Van Alstyne three or four months, I had found no way to keep him from getting a gun and pulling one of his stunts in a grocery store. He hadn't shot anybody; but no man likes to have an unstable man point a gun at him. So when Claude pulled another stunt robbery in Dallas in March, 1959, I *had* to give up. I would go to see him; I would accept his collect telephone calls and listen to his pleas for me to come and get him; but I had been forced to the conclusion that he was a threat to people on the outside, so I had to oppose his freedom from then on instead of trying to get him out."

From July 17, 1958, until August 10, 1961, Claude Eatherly spent most of the time in the hospital. Some of this time he was confined in a closed ward, because on three occasions he

227

eloped or ran away without permission. He was kept in the hospital on 90-day commitments by either the Grayson County Court or the Dallas County Court, and when these commitments expired he was sometimes persuaded by his brother to remain voluntarily. The psychiatrists were unwilling to approve further trial visits without a custodian, and Claude Eatherly had run out of relatives who were willing to be his custodians.

I found two descriptions of him during this period in press association stories. On April 12, 1959, the United Press transmitted a story from Dallas containing these paragraphs:

DALLAS, TEX. (UP)—Veterans Administration psychiatrists will take over former Air Force Major Claude Eatherly, 40, probably on Monday and try to find out why leading the first atomic attack in history makes him want to be a bandit.

The Air Force mustered Eatherly out in 1947 and he has been in one jail after another and one VA hospital after another since. The newest charge against him was robbing a drive-in grocery in Dallas March 11th.

District Attorney Henry Wade got County Judge Lew Sterrett Friday to dismiss a charge of robbery against Eatherly on condition that Eatherly submit to treatment at the VA hospital in Waco.

"He's got hallucinations that the Japanese are after him," Wade said. "He's anxious to get back to the hospital."

Eatherly, pale and drawn, said he wants treatment and Sterrett signed an order committing him (for 90 days). He will remain in Dallas County Jail until the VA sends for him.

"I don't know what happens," Eatherly told a reporter in his jail cell. "At times everything just sort of goes blank. I usually feel them coming on . . . the blank spells, I mean . . . and when I do, I try to get to the hospital. I do feel I killed those people at Hiroshima. I tried to commit suicide twice, but it didn't work. The first time I swallowed poison and the police took me to the hospital."

He didn't discuss the second time.

On December 19, 1960, United Press transmitted a story with these paragraphs:

DALLAS, TEX. (UPI)—Former Air Force Major Claude Eatherly said Monday he is finally learning to "live with" a terrible feeling of guilt that he acquired from leading the first atomic bomb attack.

"I haven't had any sleep in 15 years," he said. "But my guilt complex has been getting better the last six months. All I want is a break."

Eatherly was picked up in Dallas Monday and is being held for the VA hospital at Waco, Texas, out of which he walked Nov. 22.

He said Monday in county jail that he thought of the carnage at Pearl Harbor when he led the attack on Hiroshima, where the bomb killed 78,000.

"After I saw the destruction at Hiroshima," he said, "I didn't want to go over Nagasaki. But I went."

He snapped his fingers. "The guilt complex came over me just like that," he said.

Eatherly was wearing a white jail uniform with a torn sleeve. He smoked cigarettes incessantly, and tears came into his eyes as he talked.

"Each time I get a little publicity it hurts me just that much more," he said. "I can't walk down the street without someone recognizing me. I could be a rich man. I've turned down half a dozen movie offers. But I don't want money. I just want peace. But there's no peace. They all recognize me. The cop [who arrested him] came right up to the car window, looked in, and said, 'Hello, Claude.' "

Eatherly said he is writing a book about how he feels.

"It is on the pacifist idea," he said, "I am writing about philosophy and my convictions about nuclear wars."

What may have been helpful to Eatherly was the development which followed the *Newsweek* article of May 25, 1959. (See Chapter One.) It was from that article that Gunther Anders learned of him. *Newsweek* later described Mr. Anders as a "German-born pacifist and writer who as a refugee spent World War II in California doing odd jobs, from carpentry to furniture moving. . . . Anders has published at least ten books in Europe on subjects which range from a biography of George Grosz to a major philosophical tract." After reading *Newsweek,* Mr. Anders wrote to Eatherly on June 3, 1959; and in Galveston in 1962, Dr. Thomsen, Eatherly's private psychiatrist, told me that the resulting correspondence between Mr. Anders and Eatherly had been good for Eatherly because it came when his family had given up on him, it gave him something to do, and it assured him that somebody, somewhere, still valued him.

Mr. Anders, from his home in Vienna, was writing about Hiroshima; he had visited Hiroshima; so he welcomed Eatherly's letters acknowledging that he was guilty of "the crime of Hiroshima." Mr. Anders placed Eatherly's letters in newspapers in Japan, Germany, France and Italy. Many persons then wrote to Eatherly, and perhaps these letters helped his damaged ego. They provided a new sort of occupational therapy for him: he could occupy himself at the hospital answering them and discussing "the cause of world peace."

The Eatherly letter which brought the most mail to Waco was one in which he "begged the city of Hiroshima for forgiveness." This letter ran on the front pages of the three larger newspapers in Tokyo; it was given a full page in *France-Soir*; it was prominently featured in many European newspapers. After such publication, many persons, particularly Japanese, wrote their forgiveness to Eatherly.

Mr. Anders sent this letter to the Hiroshima Maidens (the organization of injured girls) and the Maidens, in turn, wrote a generous letter of forgiveness to Eatherly. The letter was signed by thirty "girls of Hiroshima who received injuries in our faces, limbs and bodies from the atomic bomb." One member of the Japanese Diet wrote to Eatherly expressing forgiveness.

A German pictorial magazine, with a huge circulation, ran a series of ten articles on Eatherly, with many photographs; and that series brought a deluge of mail to Waco, including proposals of marriage.

Mr. Anders interested the German author Robert Jungk in Eatherly. Mr. Jungk had made several trips to Hiroshima and had written two "Hiroshima" books. So his articles on Eatherly promoted the story in Europe and Asia. Then he wrote the Forewords in the volumes in which the Anders-Eatherly correspondence was published in Germany, Britain and the United States. And in these Forewords Mr. Jungk presented the *facts* of Eatherly's life.

I studied what Mr. Anders and Mr. Jungk wrote, both in German and in English; and I studied particularly what Eatherly is represented as having written to Mr. Anders. From

Eatherly's letters as published, here is some of the information which he furnished his pacifist friends.

Gunther, my success has been great in Japan, and your writings and mine have been very effective. I can tell by the mail that my popularity and the curiosity of the people on the subject of nuclear armament has had its effect. As to my getting out, my other brother and my sister are coming to see me to try to get me out, but my doctor said it would be after the election. I don't know what I do that has so much effect in Washington, but they sure know where I am and they are doing a good job of keeping me locked up. . . .
. . . As to my autobiography, I have investigated the writer, Al Hirschberg, and because of his popularity over here, I have decided to use him. He is coming to see me in November and start work around the first of the year.
. . . I keep very little money as I have 19 children in foreign countries as their foster father. Each one costs me $10 a month.
. . . Forgive me for not answering your letter, but I have hoped and prayed that I would be released each day and I wanted to be able to write you telling of my release and the start of a new way of life. My doctor told me three weeks ago I could go home if my brother would come after me and sign a responsibility form. I talked to him over the phone, at first he promised to come get me. I waited two weeks then I called him again. He told me he didn't think I was ready; in other words, he refused to accept the responsibility for me. He does not share my views and has tried to prevent my work and writings for pacifist groups. He resents my popularity with certain groups and has prevented the hospital from giving me certain privileges and visitors. I did not want to tell you about this. It is very difficult to accuse my brother of this. I have found out about most of this only recently.
. . . I intend to go to Japan as soon as I finish my autobiography and the movie is made. I intend to have Robert Ryan play my part. I'm sure that we can raise the money so we can make the film as we want it. Audie Murphy offered me $250,000 for the screen rights, but I turned him down. I told him he was as phony a hero as I was.
. . . I have some bad news to tell you. My sister and two brothers came and the two brothers let the doctor talk them out of signing me out. They have applied for an indefinite commitment on me. I will, of course, take this to court and I will defend myself this time, as I found out that I have not been disbarred in the State of

231

Texas, only in the State of Louisiana. I'll demand a jury trial, and I'll use every tactic in the law books. I know my law.

. . . you will have to continue writing me here at the hospital. My request for a trial visit was turned down in Washington, so now you see how much I am controlled. My doctor says the public is too much concerned over me and that I am getting too much publicity for Washington to release me now.

. . . I have spoken before many pacifist groups in most of the States emphasizing the importance of discontinuance of nuclear build-up, testing and stockpiling. I have appeared on television with Christian leaders, but I am not wanted in our schools and universities. Only last month General Twining, Chief of Staff of the Air Force, tried to get me transferred to Walter Reed Hospital in Washington. His excuse was to get me better treatment. My doctor refused to let me be moved. He knew as well as I that General Twining's only reason was to try to prevent further publicity about me. It is very bad publicity for the armed services.

. . . The Air Force wrote another letter to the hospital wanting to know my condition and asking if they could do anything for me. They have me worried. But my doctor is going to try to keep me under his control.

. . . Last Wednesday I talked with my doctor and he told me I was in the unfortunate position of being so well known and famous, that I must stop my writings against nuclear weapons and using my influence in foreign countries. He said that he could do nothing to help me, that he and the hospital staff had to take orders from the Air Force and the State Dept. . . . I cannot leave because the Government has everyone on the lookout for me.

. . . As you know, Gunther, the Air Force is very worried and keenly interested in having me picked up and sacked away in the hospital.

. . . I have a very busy schedule ahead of me. Bob Hope Productions has asked me to sign a contract for a movie of my life. They intend to send me with the picture on a world tour.

. . . I have refused to talk to the lawyers of Bob Hope Productions until I leave the hospital.

. . . I still get lots of letters from Japan. Most of the people are encouraging me to come to Japan to lead the young people in the fight against nuclear weapons. I also had a letter from an Austrian priest in Kenya, Africa.

. . . I have lately been in contact with David McClure who wrote the story *To Hell and Back* for Audie Murphy, the US's most decorated soldier and now a movie actor. It seems that Audie is very interested in portraying me in a movie. I told him it could only be done if my convictions were carried out.

. . . I will ask a friend of mine, a famous writer, to write my story "as told by me" so I will not be stopped by censorship of the Air Force which dictates to this hospital what to do with me.

From such expressions by Eatherly as those, which he published, Mr. Anders concluded that the Eatherly Case was another Dreyfus Case—that a sane Eatherly was being unjustly called insane and imprisoned by the "military" because of having "repented Hiroshima." Trying to free Eatherly, Mr. Anders wrote an open letter to President Kennedy. Here are excerpts:

DEAR MR. PRESIDENT:

I am writing this letter, which simultaneously will be submitted to the international press, for the following reason: Is it not possible that, overburdened as you were with the tasks of the past months, you may have overlooked a certain case, more correctly, a moral scandal which you can't help inheriting upon taking over the reins of government; a moral scandal which threatens to go down in history as the Dreyfus Affair of the 20th Century . . . no, perhaps an even more fateful affair. For through the density of communications today, those who cause or even just tolerate a moral scandal can lose their good name and their trustworthiness more rapidly and more thoroughly than France had lost her good name in the course of the Dreyfus Case: I am speaking of the Hiroshima Pilot Claude Eatherly who, as you naturally know, had given the "go ahead" signal on both atomic missions.

. . . Since for one and a half years now I have been in regular correspondence with Eatherly, I possess and am treasuring a collection of letters which conveys not only a complete but a respect-inspiring portrait of this man.

. . . If Eatherly transgressed the law, he did it for a most plausible reason: While he was desperately trying to digest the effects of the action (Hiroshima) ; while slowly the decision matured in his mind to devote his life to doing his share in this work of salvation . . . while all this took place within Eatherly, he was celebrated as a national hero. There was no magazine without its patriotic "must": without the slick portrait of the dashing boy from Texas. This glamour and glory (in 1945–46) was just too much for him. And it is not difficult to deduce his so-called criminal acts from this painful discrepancy between guilt and glamour. As his participation in the Hiroshima Mission was not recognized as a crime, he had to devise other methods in order to enforce the penalty to which he felt entitled. There exists something like the "Right to Punishment"— Hegel has coined this expression—and if there is a criterion which defines the non-criminal, it is the fact that he insists upon this right. This is just what Eatherly has done: *Through his sham criminal actions he has tried to enforce that punishment which was not granted him.*

. . . The information which I have from Waco seems to leave no shadow of a doubt: the Air Force is exerting pressure on the hospital staff of the Veterans Administration Hospital in order to keep Eatherly interned indefinitely.

. . . The fact that Eatherly keeps his conscience alive and that he possesses the courage to feel guilty and stained by a crime mobilized and perpetrated by others, can by no means be classified as a "crime." What is due to him is respect and gratitude. And it is not only regrettable, but, I feel, for proud Americans it could be a cause of profound shame that at home he is considered a burden and a blemish, while respect is extended to him precisely there where hatred would be understandable: in Hiroshima and Nagasaki. For there he is honored with respect, even with love.

. . . Mr. President, it is not pardon or mercy for which I am pleading, but to consider two possible steps which may prove apt to rectify the Dreyfus situation.

1. Wouldn't it be worth considering to have Eatherly's mental state examined once more by a commission of psychiatrists and to make his further life depend on the decision of this commission? It seems to me that such a group should be composed in a way analogous to certain special commissions of the United Nations. I can see before my eyes a small international board consisting of recognized experts from various countries, for instance of a Swede, a doctor from India, a Pole and a Japanese. If you would grant such a request, I am sure you would greatly enhance the moral reputation of the United States.

2. I could imagine . . . for you are generally praised as a modern, informal, unbiased and totally unprejudiced man . . . that one day you could sit down together with Eatherly. Not only as *primus inter pares,* but as a brother with his brother. For the awe-inspiring burden of responsibility which now falls on your shoulders is not so different from that burden which Eatherly has carried on his

shoulders for years, and which he was scrupulous enough not to forget for one moment through these past fifteen years. And even if the man Eatherly who would face you would be a mere nobody (which isn't the case), the mere fact that he was sentenced to unknowingly and unwittingly committing such an act and that he has been dragging along the burden of this deed would make him into a tragic figure, into a symbol of today, into a man who is your equal, and not only because he was born equal.

Mr. Anders, in Eatherly's behalf, also wrote to a county judge in Waco (McLennan County, Texas). Here is an excerpt from the letter:

And now I shall try to paint the portrait of Claude as I see him, I am convinced that he is the victim of a completely new moral situation. Never before has there existed such an enormous gap between the possible effect of a man's acts and his small capacity of imagining this effect. Ever since Claude has seen the dreadful result of the Hiroshima mission, his whole life has consisted of his futile attempt to understand what he considers his "guilt" and to make this guilt clear to other people. All his partly nonsensical and criminal acts result from his frustration: He took recourse to deeds which are at least recognized as criminal acts in order to prove to his fellow men that he is not as innocent as they think him to be. To put it in a philosophical formula: *While ordinary people are guilty on account of their deeds, he committed the deeds in order to prove his guilt.*

Eatherly's life, to a large extent, has been a series of frustrated attempts to prove his guilt.

Time and again Claude and I have corresponded about his task to write his autobiography which, if he succeeds, will be a document of the frightful difficulties into which man can fall today as master-slave and slave-master of his technical world. Therefore I am convinced that Eatherly's condition is not an isolated and unique case. I consider it rather a first unprecedented and prophetic example which indicates to us how man in the technical age is bound to react after being entangled in actions which, in the most ambiguous way, are his and not his. In short: make him *guiltlessly guilty.* The decision about the Eatherly case is, in my opinion, not the decision about an individual crank, but about "man in the technical age."

235

Mr. Anders also corresponded with Ray Bell, the Waco newspaperman who assisted me. Two letters to Mr. Bell in March, 1961, contained these passages:

My "Open Letter to President Kennedy" has appeared in several languages. Some distinguished personalities, among them Nobel Prize scholars, were stirred by it to such a degree that they made the following suggestion: I should draft a short text which should be signed by them and then be handed over to the world press as a Letter to the Editor. I have written this text and now the action of collecting signatures is well under way.

. . . In an article which Lord Russell just sent me he refers to Claude's letters to me and goes so far as to say that if the one who wrote them is considered mad, then "I shall not be surprised if my last years are spent in a lunatic asylum, where I shall enjoy the company of all who are capable of feelings of humanity."

. . . Illustrated articles (in several installments) about Claude and his correspondence with me have appeared in big French and Italian papers and magazines (f. i. in *France-Soir and Europèo*).

. . . You see: The case lies naked before the eyes of the world and —I don't think to exaggerate—the thousands in Europe and Asia who are informed about Claude's fate are now waiting impatiently for a just disentanglement of this ill-managed affair. Moreover, the prestige of the U. S. abroad may be influenced by the outcome of this story.

. . . It is now certain that in the course of 1961 the correspondence between Claude and myself will appear in an abridged form in several languages. It goes without saying that I cannot edit my own correspondence, therefore Robert Jungk will take over the editorship and the biographical introduction. . . . The royalties will be divided 50-50 between Eatherly and myself. A bank account will be arranged in Hamburg, where the publishing house is located; and in a very short time a first advance payment of about $600–$800 will be deposited there under Claude's name.

. . . I got a letter from one of the staff members of Harvard University in which he informed me that my Open Letter to President Kennedy has been mimeographed and been circulated amongst the Harvard professors, and that now a great number of them are deeply interested in this case. This professor tells me furthermore that a student group in Southern Methodist University has published something about Eatherly. I'd appreciate your sending me a copy.

. . . I also would be very glad to learn whether you have succeeded in placing my Open Letter in an American magazine.

After I had read all that Mr. Anders and Mr. Jungk wrote about Claude Eatherly, I felt that, to some extent, I had failed Eatherly. From my first conversation with him, I had tried to explain the difference between a reporter and a philosopher. After reading Mr. Anders, I felt I had not tried hard enough.

In Chapter One I have quoted Mr. Jungk at length to show the image he held of Eatherly. When Mr. Anders imagined Eatherly, he began by imagining that in 1945 Eatherly "was celebrated as a national hero . . . there was no magazine without its patriotic must: without the slick portrait of the dashing boy from Texas."

When Mr. Anders imagined that Eatherly was being imprisoned by the Air Force for "repenting Hiroshima," he was ignoring what should have been obvious to him from Eatherly's own letters: that every agency of the United States had released Eatherly as often and as quickly as it could. By Eatherly's own letters, the only reason he was denied trial visits in 1959 and 1960 was that no member of his family would accept responsibility for him.

Joe Eatherly told me: "I blame the VA for the publication of my brother's letters by Anders. Claude was sick; his letters show how sick he was; yet the hospital allowed those letters to be mailed. It's cruel to take a sick man's letters and publish them. Anders subjected my brother to this cruelty. The hospital should have taken the risk of being accused of censorship, and should have prevented such letters from being mailed to an opportunist like Anders."

The trouble with all the writings about Eatherly, both in the United States and abroad, was that except for Jim Vachule and possibly *Newsweek,* no writer wanted to know the facts about Eatherly. Instead, each writer wanted to look toward Eatherly and see what he wanted to see.

My own feelings about the writings of Mr. Jungk and Mr. Anders were expressed by the reviewer from *The London Spectator* in a passage which, as previously reported, I showed to Eatherly.

Eatherly's letters are innocent. It may be an unreal, artificial innocence, a sign of unnatural withdrawal in a man of forty-two, but it angers me to see this innocence exploited. . . . I find this book, said to be based on Eatherly's letters, extremely distasteful. I find the idea of exploiting this unhappy, middle-aged man revoltingly cruel.

Eighteen

THE most revealing record in Claude Eatherly's tragedy is the tape-recording of his full-dress, public "lunacy hearing" which was held on a cold, gray, rainy day, January 12, 1961, in the McLennan County Courthouse, Waco, Texas.

I have the only copy of this tape; and that it was available to me, or to anyone, was due to the foresight of Ray Bell and to the compassion of County Judge Raymond Mormino who presided at the hearing. No record of any sort is usually made of such lunacy hearings; but because Mr. Bell regarded himself as a personal friend of Eatherly, he asked the judge for permission to set up the recorder. Judge Mormino could hardly have been unsympathetic with Eatherly. As a member of the United States Air Force, the judge in 1944 went down in a flaming B-26. Five of his fellow crewmen were killed, and his burned face, arms and hands have been restored in more than a hundred plastic-surgery operations.

When I was in Waco in 1962 the lunacy hearing was a little more than a year in the past. Memories were still fresh. Eatherly had been gone from the VA hospital since August 10, 1961, and was living in Galveston where I conferred with him. I therefore concentrated on the lunacy hearing. Over and over, I listened to the recording, and Mr. Bell and I sought out every person who had had a role in the hearing—the judge, opposing counsel, the jurors, some doctors, even the bailiffs.

What I report is from that research effort.

According to hospital records, Eatherly's eighth official admission was on April 13, 1959, when he was returned by Dallas

County deputies after one of his bizarre hold-ups. On December 22, 1959, he eloped. As an escapee he was picked up in Dallas a few hours later and returned to the hospital by Dallas County deputies. On October 19, 1960, he eloped again.

For two months after that elopement Eatherly, strangely, lived in Waco, in an apartment not far from the hospital. He was in almost daily touch with a former nurse he had met at the hospital and her husband. He was also in regular touch with Dr. Constantine who "kept his secret" and did not report his whereabouts and "gave him a chance to make it on the outside." But on December 19, 1960, he was drinking and in Dallas, where he again was picked up and returned to the hospital for his ninth official admission.

Meanwhile, on September 13, 1960, James E. Eatherly Jr. filed an application for indefinite commitment in the County Court of McLennan County, Texas (Waco), alleging that his brother, Claude R. Eatherly, was a "mentally ill person, mentally incompetent to the point of being incapable of caring for himself and managing his property and financial affairs, requiring hospitalization in a mental hospital for his own welfare and protection or the protection of others."

Such an application in the United States results in what is known as a "lunacy hearing" or a "sanity trial." It meant that Claude Eatherly would now come into court, represented by counsel, and face a county judge and a six-man jury. (Twelve-man juries are required usually in criminal cases; six-man juries are legal in most states in civil cases.) Eatherly would try to convince the jury that he was sane and competent, that he did not require hospitalization in a mental hospital, and that he should be allowed to go free and manage his own affairs. Opposing him and denying his claims would be the State (the County Attorney), his brothers and sisters, and the psychiatrists of the Veterans Administration.

In short, after three years the situation at Abilene would be reversed. At Abilene the psychiatrists and Eatherly's brothers had been *for* him. He had "stood mute" while the psychiatrists talked for him and freed him. Now, at Waco, the psychiatrists and his brothers would be *against* him. The psychiatrists would

240

testify against him; and Eatherly could not "stand mute" because he would have to do most of his own talking.

To persons unfamiliar with lunacy hearings, it may appear that the cards were stacked against Eatherly. How could he hope to win against the doctors and his family? Actually, the odds favored him. In such hearings in the United States the odds usually favor the "patient." Jurors tend to disregard psychiatric testimony. They look at a man on the stand and listen to him, and they decide for themselves whether he's crazy or not. They often associate with the patient; they imagine themselves in his place; and unless the evidence against the patient is overwhelming, the jury frees him. So Eatherly was not without cards for the lunacy hearing.

On the morning of the hearing, despite the weather, the courtroom was crowded by 8:30 A.M. Eatherly was ably represented. His counsel, Thomas P. Moore Jr., was narrowly defeated for Attorney General of Texas in 1956. He had been asked to represent Eatherly by the Veterans Administration. "They told me," Mr. Moore informed me, "that I must defend Eatherly with every available resource. They particularly wanted all his civil rights protected." The County Attorney was Donald O. Hall, who served in the Pacific in the Navy; and Mr. Hall was assisted by Billy Joe Webb who, as a captain in the Marine Corps 3rd Division, was in combat on Okinawa.

The jurors, in every respect, were a group of average Americans. They were:

Lawrence E. Lykins, 38, foreman. He is an Army veteran, a graduate of Baylor University, a farmer, and an employee of General Tire & Rubber Co., Waco. A stocky, square-jawed man, with penetrating blue eyes and a ruddy, outdoor complexion. His ancestry is German, and he is a "free-thinker."

Mrs. Arthur Williams, 69, a neat, courteous, matronly woman who looks like "everybody's grandmother." She and her husband have celebrated their golden wedding anniversary, and they live in Waco, at the Kate Ross Apartments, a government housing project for low-income families. Born Annie Koepf, near Bruceville, Texas, her ancestry is German. One of her sons, in the 5th Cavalry Division, was seriously wounded fighting in the Admiralty Islands.

MRS. MABEL CASSENS, 30, a slender, attractive blonde, with a doll-like face and wide blue eyes. She was born Mabel Marstaller, in North Prairie, Texas, and finished the 11th grade at Waco High School. Her ancestry is German. For twelve years she has held a responsible position at Montgomery, Ward & Co., Waco. Her husband is employed at Owens-Illinois Glass Co., Waco, and they own a substantial, ranch-style home.

CHARLIE FAJKUS (Fike-us), 54, a bespectacled, owlish-looking farmer, who cocks his head to one side and peers at you craftily as though you were trying to get the better of him in a horse trade. He has "farmed the same 160 acres near Tours, Texas, for thirty-one years, and I'm here to stay." His ancestry is German and Czechoslovak; and he is a Catholic, educated in parochial schools.

C. E. WOODLIFF, 32, a printer for the Waco *News-Tribune*. He was born in Waco and graduated from Waco High School.

KENNETH L. PELCHER, 47, a moldmaker at the Owens-Illinois glass plant in Waco. He was born in New York City and met his wife, a Waco girl, when he trained at Fort Hood, near Waco, during World War II. They settled in Waco after the war. He was overseas for three years in the European Theater with the 894th Tank Destroyer Battalion.

Eatherly arrived at the courthouse in a hospital ambulance, and he was escorted into the courtroom by three hospital attendants. He was neatly dressed, and the jurors later told me he "looked just like anybody else."

That Eatherly was "in custody" was a liability: every juror could see those three attendants sitting directly behind "the patient." So by a sudden, clever maneuver, Eatherly's counsel, Mr. Moore, converted this liability into an asset.

Without warning to them or anyone else, Mr. Moore called the custodians, one by one, to the witness stand. He established that they had "brought" Eatherly from the hospital; that he was in their custody; and that they had known him, off and on, for ten years. Mr. Moore then asked them how Eatherly acted on the twenty-minute drive from the hospital; and if, at any time in ten years, they had ever seen Eatherly "do anything crazy" or heard him "say anything crazy."

Their answers were that Eatherly had behaved "like any normal person" on the trip from the hospital, and that they had never observed him to do anything or say anything crazy. Such "lay" observation in the United States is often given more weight by jurors than the "expert opinion" of the most renowned psychiatrist.

Claude Robert Eatherly then took the stand for direct examination by Mr. Moore:

Q State your name.
A Claude Robert Eatherly.
Q How old are you?
A Forty-two.
Q When were you born?
A October 2, 1918.
Q Where were you born?
A Van Alstyne, Texas.
Q Where is that?
A Southern part of Grayson County.
Q Were you raised there?
A Yes, sir.
Q What did your father do?
A He was a farmer and rancher.
Q Is he still there?
A Yes, sir.
Q Do you have any brothers and sisters?
A Two brothers and two sisters.
Q Are you the youngest child?
A Yes, sir.

With these simple questions, bringing calm, correct answers, Mr. Moore told me he was introducing his client to the six ordinary Americans who would pass judgment on him. The attorney was showing the jurors that Eatherly was "just like they were," and that his memory was as good as theirs. The attorney also said he was "calming Eatherly down, getting him off to a good start."

Q   Where did you attend primary school?
A   Van Alstyne.
Q   Will you tell us generally what kind of grades you made?
A   Well, mostly A's and B's in primary; B's and C's in high school.
Q   Did you engage in athletics in high school?
A   Yes, sir. Football, basketball, baseball, track and tennis.
Q   After high school did you have any further education?
A   Yes, sir. North Texas State and Southwest School of Law.

Eatherly's personal tragedy seemed evident to me in almost every line of his testimony from this point. Either the cause or the effect of his mental disorder was his terrible need to exaggerate—to present himself as something other than he was. Now, for almost four years, he had been influenced by professional exaggerators. As to athletics: he had seen himself portrayed on television as a "Cotton Bowl star"; he had heard Dr. Constantine at Abilene describe him as a "military hero." Then he had met the immense exaggerations of Mr. Wellman and Mr. Anders. Not only did Eatherly not like himself as he was, but also he knew from experience that no one else of importance wanted him as he was.

Eatherly was facing six ordinary people. He wanted them to adjudge him sane. He also knew that he was facing a tape recorder, and that Mr. Anders and "important people around the world" would be listening to him. So even if he prejudiced his chances with the jury, Eatherly felt that he must try to impress the "important people."

In 1947, in fact, Eatherly had done little more than enroll at the Southwest School of Law. He knew this; without my asking him, he told me he knew it. But he had written to Mr. Anders that he had been admitted to the bar in Texas. So before his judges he had to emphasize that he had attended the Southwest School of Law.

244

Q What years were you at North Texas State?
A 1936 to 1939.
Q What did you study?
A Economics and government.
Q Did you leave there to go in the service?
A Yes, sir. I went into the Air Force as a cadet, at Dallas, Texas.
Q Did you complete your cadet training?
A Yes, sir. I was then stationed at Langley Field, Virginia, where I was selected out of a group to fly aircraft to England.
Q Were you married then?
A No, sir. I married June 3, 1943.
Q What outfit were you in then?
A Ferrying Command. Long Beach, California.
Q How long did you stay there?
A One year. Then I went overseas. To Port Darwin, Australia. I was there . . . seven months . . . no, I was in Australia thirteen months.
Q What were your duties there?
A Combat pilot. Bomber. We covered all the islands and shipping lanes coming down from Japan.
Q What year was that?
A 1943 . . . '42 and '43.

He had begun to fabricate. In the fall of 1944, training with the crew of the *Straight Flush,* he had been unable to tell his crewmen that he had held an Air Force commission since before Pearl Harbor but he had never been overseas or in combat. He had then invented an overseas combat experience, and later Mr. Wellman had given him thirty-two bloody combat missions. So now, before his judges, Eatherly felt compelled to claim an overseas combat record complete with battle fatigue.

Q Did you come back to the United States from Australia?
A Yes, sir. I was sent back on a hospital boat.
Q Had you been wounded?
A Battle fatigue. I was in a hospital in New York for two

weeks. Then I went back to duty at Davis-Monthan Field, Tucson, training combat crews.

Q Did you ever go back to combat?
A Yes, sir. I went to Tinian.
Q Before you went to Tinian, did you have any special kind of training?
A Intensive training to learn how to drop . . . to carry out a mission for the A-bomb.
Q Did you know that's what you were doing?
A We were told that it was the bomb which would end the war. Nine crews trained for sixteen months. Ten men in a crew.
Q Do you recall when you moved to Tinian?
A Yes, sir. March 28, 1945.

He departed for Tinian on June 10, 1945. His answer, placing himself on Tinian almost three months earlier, was not a simple mistake of memory but another effort to bolster his ego. In June, 1945, all the great battles of the Second World War had been fought. The war in Europe was over. The great B-29 battles over Japan ended in March, 1945. By June, 1945, a B-29 flying over Japan at 30,000 feet was so safe from attack that all turrets and guns, except the tail turret, had been removed from the 509th's bombers.

Eatherly knew this; and *it worried him*. In Galveston in 1962, discussing his testimony at the lunacy hearing, I said to him: "One of your troubles is obvious, Claude. You missed the fighting war. Before you ever went overseas the war in Europe was over, and the war in the Pacific was all but over. You never saw any combat; you flew patrols and training flights. Your flight over Hiroshima was nothing more than *another patrol flight*. When the bombing started, you were gone. So what! That was your war. You served creditably enough. Why didn't you accept your war as it was? Why, by 1944, were you claiming to be an old combat veteran with battle fatigue? Then why did you have to claim you *led* the Hiroshima raid?"

He was silent for a moment, then he said: "You know all those answers."

246

Q At Tinian what were your duties?
A Flight commander of the 509th Composite Bomb Group.
Q You were the commanding officer?
A Flight commander.
Q There is a difference in that and the commanding officer?
A The difference is in . . . you have your commanding officer and then you have your combat flight commanders that lead the flights.
Q What do you mean by leading the flights?
A Well, you have to have certain qualifications of leadership to command combat crews and to know how to command a formation.
Q Does that mean if several planes went out on a mission you were in command of them?
A Yes, sir.
Q And were you working in that capacity when Hiroshima was bombed?
A Yes, sir.
Q Was that also true of Nagasaki?
A No, sir.
Q You weren't in command that day?
A No, I flew a separate flight that day.
Q The newspapers said you were at Nagasaki, and that's where my error was.
A My mission was considered "special" that day, and that accounts for the error.

The only "commander" in the Hiroshima mission who commanded more than one crew was Colonel Tibbets. Even his command authority was restricted by a sheaf of orders which virtually specified his breathing rate. He was ordered to bomb the city of Hiroshima, with Initial Point specified, Aiming Point specified, altitude specified, airspeed specified, everything specified. *Only* if the *Enola Gay*'s bombardier could not see the Aiming Point, with natural vision, did Colonel Tibbets have the authority to proceed to the first alternate target, Kokura.

Eatherly made no flight at all on August 9, 1945, the day Nagasaki was bombed.

247

When I heard this testimony, I wondered why Eatherly in 1957 told Jim Vachule that he *led* at Nagasaki, then in 1961 had testified that he had not been at Nagasaki? Also: Eatherly knew that Mr. Wellman had both Hiroshima and Nagasaki in the film script. So why had Eatherly begun deflating his image?

I asked him this, but his answer wasn't clear. The answer seems to be that in his correspondence with people in Japan during 1960, he had dropped Nagasaki and concentrated on his "Hiroshima-guilt."

After I showed him his Air Force record in 1962, he dropped all reference to Nagasaki and promptly quit claiming that he had witnessed either the blast or the destruction at Hiroshima. So I concluded that at no time during his life was Eatherly mistaken or deluded about his roles at Hiroshima and Nagasaki. He only lied: first to support an image he himself had invented, and later to support images which others had invented.

Q   How long did you remain in service after the war?
A   I was selected to perform a duty in the Bikini bomb test, and immediately after I returned from Bikini I resigned my commission.
Q   What was your mental condition at that time? I know you hadn't been declared of unsound mind. But were you in a nervous condition at that time?
A   Possibly.
Q   Did you get a medical discharge?
A   No, sir.
Q   Did you get an honorable discharge?
A   Yes, sir.
Q   Where were you processed for discharge?
A   Biloxi, Mississippi. Keesler Field. February 25, 1947— No, January 25, 1947.
Q   Were you in the organized Reserve?
A   No, sir.

When I studied this testimony, I wondered why the County Attorney had not presented Eatherly's Air Force record to the jury. Actually the County Attorney had regarded this hearing

248

as so routine that he had not bothered to obtain either Eatherly's military record or his FBI record.

In response to questions, Eatherly then told of his marriage and gave the correct birth dates of his three children. He described his work with the Texas Company.

Q Do you recall any mental difficulties you had at that time?
A Periods of depression. But I was able to cope with it at that time.
Q What do you mean by depression?
A Sleepless nights. Anxiety.
Q Worrying?
A Yes, sir.
Q Did you talk to any psychiatrist at that time?
A No, sir.
Q Were you doing any drinking at that time?
A Some. Not heavy drinking. But some.
Q Did that give you some relief?
A Yes, sir.
Q What were your family relations at that time? Were they good or were you having trouble?
A No . . . they were good.
Q Did you buy a house?
A Yes, sir.
Q About how much were you making?
A About $550 a month.
Q Was that adequate to take care of you and your family?
A Yes, sir.
Q Then what was your anxiety about? Your family relations were good, and you had an adequate income . . . ?
A Well, at that time I . . . certain thoughts about things in my military background . . . seemed to reflect on me . . . and my anxiety was about that.
Q What was the occasion for your leaving the Texas Company?
A A better job with Ada Oil Company.
Q What was the date of your first admission to the hospital?
A 1950.

Q Who were you with then?
A Ada Oil Company.
Q Did they know about it?
A Yes, sir.
Q What was the cause of your admission to the hospital?
A I took an overdose of barbituates.
Q How many did you take?
A I think it was about thirty.
Q Was that caused by the same anxiety . . . worry . . . had you been drinking more by that time?
A Yes, sir.
Q What were your family relations by that time?
A Strained.
Q Had you separated?
A No, sir.
Q Well, when you took these pills what happened? Were you taken to a hospital? How long did you stay there?
A In the Houston hospital, two days, then I was brought to Waco.
Q Who brought you?
A My wife and my brother.
Q Is that Joe?
A No, James.
Q Where does he live?
A Midland, Texas.
Q Did he come down from Midland?
A No. He was living in Houston at that time.
Q You entered the Waco hospital as a volunteer patient? Did you know what you were doing at that time?
A Yes, sir.
Q Did you meet Dr. Constantine at that time?
A No, sir.
Q Do you recall which doctors you did meet?
A Dr. Ross was my case doctor. And I met Dr. McElroy.

This was the Dr. Ross who in 1957 disagreed with Dr. Constantine and retired from the case.

Q After you were admitted to the hospital in 1950, what treatment did you receive?

A Confinement.

Q Shock? Any medication?

A No, sir. Just confinement.

Q Did you have to be restrained?

A No, sir.

Q How long did you stay at the hospital?

A Forty-six days.

Q Did you leave against medical advice or did they tell you you could go?

A They told me I could go.

Q Did you go back to your job?

A Yes, sir.

Q Did you feel any better?

A No.

Q Did you go back to drinking?

A Yes, sir.

Q There is something in the record about bad checks. Did you pass any bad checks?

A Yes, sir. In 1953.

Q How long did you stay with Ada Oil Company after you got out of the hospital?

A About eight months.

Q Why did you leave?

A I quit.

Q Did you have a better job offered you?

A I went to work for Humble Oil Company.

Q In what capacity?

A As a trainee . . . roustabout. They put me to digging ditches. Then I went in the natural gas department. I wanted physical labor. I felt much better. I was able to sleep better. It rid me of part of my anxiety.

Q You'd get so tired you couldn't worry? How long were you with Humble?

A About fourteen months.

Q Were you still living with your wife? Same place? Were your relations with her good?

251

A   Yes, sir.
Q   When did you come to the hospital again?
A   1953.
Q   Is your memory about some of these things hazy?
A   A little bit in '53 and '54 . . . and '56.
Q   Were you in trouble . . . did you go to court before you came here to the hospital in '53?
A   Yes, sir.
Q   How long did you stay at the hospital that trip?
A   About four months.
Q   What sort of treatment did you receive?
A   Confinement.
Q   Any shock? Any medication?
A   No, sir. Just confinement.
Q   Now when you say confinement, tell the Jury what you mean. Were you locked up?
A   Well, I was locked up for a little while, then I made privilege.
Q   What does privilege mean?
A   It consists of having access to the grounds.
Q   Did you do any work, or have books to read, or anything else to keep you busy?
A   No, sir. Just confinement.
Q   Who was your doctor at that time?
A   Dr. Frank.
Q   Did the doctors release you?
A   Yes, sir.
Q   Did you have a job when you got back to Houston?
A   No, sir.
Q   Did you get one?
A   I got a job selling sewing machines. I was averaging about $150 a week. Worked about six months.
Q   Then you voluntarily came back to the hospital? You felt like you needed to come? Your wife wanted you to come?
A   Yes, sir.
Q   You do draw a pension, don't you?
A   Yes, sir. $264 a month.
Q   Did you apply for it?

A No, sir. I think the application is automatic when you go in the hospital.

I have explained this. He did apply. He applied as early as 1948 on the spermatazoa claim. He applied again at the hospital. Only on application can compensation ever be paid in such a case. But there is a measure of truth in his insistence that "application is automatic." It is not automatic, but every patient at a VA hospital is "assisted in the matter of claims for compensation."

Q How long did you stay on this third trip?
A I took insulin shock and stayed about seven or eight months.
Q Did you get better?
A Yes, sir.
Q Where did you go then?
A I went to my wife.
Q Had your wife moved in the meantime? Gone back to her people?
A Yes, sir.
Q Did you have any job?
A No, sir.
Q How long did you stay with your wife then?
A About two months. Then I went to Midland, Texas, with my brother James, and worked about six months as sales manager for Hargrove Motor Company.
Q Had you and your family separated?
A Yes, sir.
Q Now what year are we in?
A 1954.
Q Did you leave Midland to come back to the hospital?
A No, sir. I went to New Orleans.
Q Did you have any work over there? Or were you looking for work?
A No, sir.
Q Was it there that you got put in jail for passing bad checks?
A Yes, sir.
Q Do you know how many checks you had out?
A One . . . some small amount.

This "one small-amount check" was the Anders-Jungk version of Eatherly's New Orleans crimes. Apparently, they either got it from him or invented it. I have detailed the truth.

Q   I believe you got eighteen months? You served nine of them and they let you out for good behavior. Then you flew back here and voluntarily entered the hospital? How long were you there that time?

A   About two months. They put me on thorazine. Then I was released for a trial visit to my brother Joe, at Van Alstyne.

Q   What did you do at Van Alstyne?

A   I helped my brother with his oil business, and helped with the cattle on the ranch, and I stayed at Joe's part of the time and out at the ranch part of the time.

Q   I take it that didn't work out. What happened?

A   I got in some trouble and was returned to the hospital.

Q   What kind of trouble? Where?

A   Armed robbery. A grocery store. Denison, Texas.

Q   Tell us about it—all about it. Why did you do it?

A   Don't know.

Q   Was anybody with you?

A   No.

Q   Daytime or night?

A   Night.

Q   What kind of gun did you use?

A   Antique .410 shotgun.

Q   Get any money?

A   Some pennies.

Q   Were you drunk or sober?

A   I was drinking.

Q   Where did you go after the robbery?

A   I went back out to the ranch.

Q   Were you still nervous and suffering from depression and anxiety at that time? Do you think you were mentally ill?

A   At that time, yes.

Q   Did you realize that you were sick at that time?

A   I realized it. I wanted to get in jail.

Q   Why?

254

A   Well, when I was in jail I always got a certain amount of relief.

Q   Relief from what?

A   Well . . . I just wanted to be in jail.

Q   You wanted to get away from it all? Well, were you tried in Grayson County for that armed robbery?

A   No, sir. I was no-billed. I went back to the hospital and stayed about fifteen months. In '56–'57.

Q   That was your longest stay out there yet?

A   Yes, sir.

Q   What treatment did you get?

A   Thorazine.

Q   Did the psychiatrists interview you much?

A   Very seldom.

Q   Well, what do they do?

A   Well, Dr. Constantine has helped me . . . helped me to live with this problem I have . . . he has taught me how to relieve my guilt feelings. I have had some very good conversations with Dr. Constantine. . . .

Q   Do they give you any kind of work to do with your hands or your mind?

A   No, sir.

Q   Do you feel like you're getting any good out of the treatment you're receiving out there?

A   Well, up until the last year, I guess I got some good. But I've had nothing but confinement during the last year.

Q   Now after those fifteen or sixteen months did you get out again?

A   A trial visit. Back to Van Alstyne with Joe.

Q   Did you like that?

A   No, sir. I just didn't have enough to do.

Q   Well, what did you do?

A   Oh, I just helped him . . . call on farmers and filling stations.

Q   Was your living with him confining?

A   No, I could come and go when I wanted to.

Q   How long did you stay up there that time?

A   One year.

Q Did you get in trouble?

A Not up there. I came down to Dallas, to a motel, and I stayed there two days, drinking.

Q Did you do much drinking at Van Alstyne?

A None.

Q In other words you went off to Dallas on a two-day drunk. And what happened?

A I held up this grocery store.

Q What kind of gun did you use.

A .22 pistol.

Q Was it loaded?

A No, sir.

Q Did you have a car?

A Yes.

Q What time of day or night was it?

A About 10 P.M. There was one man in the store. I made him put the money in a sack and set it on the counter. I put him in the back of the store. Then I walked out. I didn't take the money. I didn't need it. I just wanted to get back in jail.

Q Did you think you were pretty sick at that time?

A Yes, sir.

Q How long before they caught you?

A Right quick . . . that night. They knew I had a gun. The man who sold me the gun told the sheriff of Grayson County, and the sheriff told Joe, and the sheriff called me at the motel and asked me if I'd give him the gun, and I told him no. So the sheriff called the Dallas police and they were on their way to pick me up at the motel when I held up the grocery store. So they were waiting for me when I got back.

Q Now what year was this?

A 1959.

Q What did they do to you?

A Nothing. Put me in jail. Then a few days later they dropped the charges and I went back to the hospital.

Q Was that your last admission to the hospital?

A Yes, sir. I eloped last October 19th.

Q Why did you leave?

A Well, I thought if they weren't going to turn me loose I'd run off and show them I could make it on the outside.

Q Did you have any trouble getting out of there?

A No, I ran off.

Q What do you mean you *ran?*

A Well, I *ran* off. I was with a group going to a theater, and I just broke and ran off.

Q Did the attendant chase you?

A Sure. I outran him.

Q Where did you go?

A I stayed here in Waco. I went to the Western Motel and got a room.

Q Did you have any money?

A Yeah, I had some.

Q Are you allowed to keep money in your pocket out there?

A You're not allowed to, but if you can get away with it you keep it.

There was a ripple of laughter in the courtroom, and Eatherly obviously began to enjoy his performance.

Q Do most of the fellows out there try to keep a few dollars hidden around?

A Yes, sir.

Q But how did you live for 60 days here in Waco? You didn't have that much money, did you?

A I had bank accounts around that I could check on.

Q Did you check on these bank accounts?

A Yes, sir.

Q Where are these accounts?

A The Bell-Mead State Bank here in Waco, and the First National Bank of Van Alstyne.

Q How much money did you have then?

A Over $2000.

Q How much do you have now?

A Over $2000.

Q Did you have any trouble cashing checks?

A No, sir.

Q Have you ever been under guardianship?

A No, sir.

Q Always looked after your own financial affairs?

A Well, in one account . . . the banker at Van Alstyne required a double signature . . . mine and Joe's . . . until I got that changed.

Q It's not that way now?

A No, sir.

Q How long did you stay at the Western Motel?

A One night. Then I rented an apartment . . . at the Sharon Apartments, 37th and Sleeper, here in Waco.

Q Did you live there the whole two months you were out of the hospital? Alone?

A Yes, sir.

Q What did you do?

A Mostly writing. For newspapers and magazines.

Q Had you ever sold anything, received money for it?

A Yes, sir.

Q Was this writing you did yourself, or with a collaborator or ghost writer?

A I've never had a ghost writer. Occasionally with a collaborator. Most of the Japanese articles I have written the money comes directly to me. The others . . . the money goes to a bank in Switzerland . . . through a friend of mine.

Q Do you have an agent in Europe?

A Yes, sir. Gunther Anders.

Q What's his business?

A He's a writer.

Q Have you written anything in collaboration with him?

A Yes, sir. I collaborated with him on a book, *The Edge of the Bridge*.

Q Did it sell? Did you get any money for it?

A Yes, sir.

Q Now I want you to describe for this Jury just what a day in your life is like at the hospital.

A Well, I'm in Building 10. That's a maximum security building. Mostly violent patients . . . very sick patients.

Q How many are in there?
A The ward that I'm on . . . about thirty patients.
Q And what kind of fellows are these?
A Very sick. They hardly know their names. They can't carry on a conversation.
Q You don't have anybody to talk to up there?
A Not unless I talk to the nurses.
Q Are any of those fellows violent?
A Yes, sir.
Q Are they able to care for themselves and keep clean?
A Very few of them are, if any.
Q Is it all one big dormitory, or are there private rooms?
A No private rooms. All one big dormitory.
Q Is it quiet or noisy?
A Noisy.
Q Are you able to write?
A No, sir.
Q Do you have access to a library?
A Well, there is one on the post, but I'm not allowed out of the ward.
Q You can't go to the shops, or to movies, or church?
A No, sir.
Q How often do you see the psychiatrist?
A Well, he comes through the ward every day about 9 A.M. He walks through and says good morning.
Q How much time does the psychiatrist spend on the ward?
A Maybe 10 minutes. I talked with three psychiatrists yesterday.
Q Well, they were getting ready for this hearing. How much time have they spent with you prior to that?
A None. Not for months.
Q You get thorazine twice a day, and is that all the treatment you get out there?
A That's all.
Q Can you sleep well out there?
A Yes, sir.
Q How many times have you talked with Dr. Constantine?

A   When I was admitted . . . when I came back . . . we talked for about 30 minutes.

Q   Did you telephone him while you were out of the hospital?

A   Yes, sir. Twice.

Q   Why did you telephone him?

A   Well, he always told me if I ran off to call him and let him know how I was getting along.

Q   Did he tell you to come back?

A   No, sir. I just wanted to tell him I was doing all right. He said that was fine.

Q   Now tell this jury why you want out of there.

A   Well, I think I'm ready now. I have some work I want to do. I want to write this book. I have an agreement to write this book on my life.

Q   Who is the agreement with?

A   Well, the publisher I haven't selected yet. But there are three writers who want to work with me . . . Margot Winthrop, David McClure, and Al Hirshberg . . . either one I want to pick.

Q   Have you heard from all these gentlemen?

A   Yes, sir.

Q   Did you contact them?

A   No, they contacted me.

Q   Are they all writers? Have they published works prior to this?

A   Yes, sir. David McClure wrote about Audie Murphy; and Al Hirshberg wrote about the baseball player who had mental trouble.

Q   Jimmy Piersall?

A   Yes.

Q   The doctors out there have seen letters from those writers to you, haven't they?

A   Yes, sir.

Q   Isn't all your mail censored out there?

A   No, sir. But I always let Dr. Constantine see letters like that.

Q   Are you mad at anybody right now?

A   (*Laughing*) No, sir.

Q   What about the hospital? They've locked you up out there

and won't let you go to church or to the library or anywhere. Do you like that?

A Well, due to my mental state in the past . . .

Q Why do you think they have treated you like that?

A Well, maybe they think that's the proper kind of treatment.

Q You admit you've been sick in the past?

A Yes, sir.

Q You realize you've been admitted out there a number of
times. Now do you think you are in better shape now than
you have ever been before when you were dismissed?

A Yes, sir. I'm in better shape now than I've been since 1950.

Q Did you have any trouble at all during the 60 days you
were living free and alone here in Waco?

A No, sir.

In response to questions, Eatherly then described how he
was returned to the hospital on December 19, 1960. He said he
ran a red light, was stopped, the officer recognized him and
knew he was a Waco escapee. So he was arrested without argument or incident and returned.

Q Now do you know why your brother James has filed this
application to keep you from leaving the hospital?

A Beyond me.

Q What is your relationship with your wife now?

A We are divorced.

Q There is something here about support. Are you supporting
your children?

A Partially. [Eatherly's ex-wife insists this is not true.]

Q Are you under any court order?

A No, sir.

Q Did you contest the divorce?

A No, sir.

Q Did you sign a waiver?

A Yes, sir. . . . She married again, and she told me I need not
pay her any more child support.

Q Does she object to you seeing the children?

A Yes, sir. I respect her wishes.

Q Do you plan to remain in Waco if you are released?
A Well, that would depend on my publisher . . . on where he'd want me to go. If I'm going to collaborate with another writer, I may have to go where he is.
Q You have the money to do that, don't you?
A Yes, sir.
Q You have the money to live whether you ever do any more work or not? Can you live on $264 a month?
A Not sufficiently. But I can make other money.
Q Do you think James has got it in for you because he signed this complaint against you?
A No, sir. I think he thinks he's doing the right thing.
Q If you were released, do you think it might be wise if you consulted a psychiatrist every now and then to see how you were getting along?
A I'd take the advice of Dr. Frank and Dr. Constantine on it.
Q If they told you you needed to go to this out-patient clinic once a week or once a month, would you do it?
A Yes, sir.
Q Do you realize that if you are released, and if you then get in trouble again, you'll probably be out there from now on?
A Yes, sir.

Eatherly was then cross-examined by County Attorney Don Hall. The cross-examination contained these exchanges:

Q Now you have testified about Building 10 and how confining it is. What other buildings have you been in out there?
A Buildings 90 and 93.
Q In those buildings did you enjoy liberal treatment? Were you allowed freedom of the grounds, to go to the movies and the library, and to come into town occasionally?
A Yes, sir.
Q And if this Jury should send you back out there, do you have any reason to think you wouldn't be allowed, with proper behavior, to reside in those buildings and enjoy liberal treatment?

A Well, I've been in there before.

Q Isn't it true that you have been placed in Building 10, and held in maximum security, only when some court ordered the hospital authorities to allow you no opportunity to elope?

A I guess so.

Q Now this money you've got in the bank . . . where did you get that money?
(Witness hesitates)
Mr. Moore has made out that you are a self-sustaining man . . . that you could live happily ever after without ever hitting a lick. . . . I want you to tell this Jury where you got that money.

A I earned it.

Q You want me to tell you how you earned it or do you want to tell the Jury yourself?

A Are you sure you know?

Q I think I know how you got some of it.

A Well, if you are sure, you go ahead and tell them.

Q After the war, you were involved in running guns down in Cuba, weren't you?

A Are you sure I got the money from there?

Q I don't know whether you did or not. I'm asking you.

A I made money while I was doing that, but it was confiscated by the government. All my equipment was confiscated by the government.

Q What kind of equipment did you have?

A I had some ships and airplanes and tanks . . . guns.

Q And you're the same man who wants to do away with nuclear weapons and write books against armaments?

A You can always change, you know.

Q All right, so you've changed. Now where else besides your gunrunning did you make money? Where else did you get this two, three, or four thousand dollars you've testified you have?

A That's not much money. I could have saved that in pennies.

Q Well, did you? Is that how you got it?

A I had some money when I left the service.

Q And this is still part of that money, is that right?

A Yes.

Q Now you have mentioned a "small check" in New Orleans and an 18-month prison sentence. The truth is you were convicted of forging checks, weren't you?

A Yes.

Q Where did you serve your time?

A In the New Orleans Parish Prison.

Q How did you manage to get out in nine months?

A Good behavior. I worked in the prison, and they counted it two days for one.

Q Now you have told this jury that confinement is good for you. You were confined nine months in a New Orleans jail. And the day you got out over there, you flew here directly to get some more confinement in the hospital. You have committed crimes, according to your testimony, deliberately to obtain confinement. What makes you think confinement won't be good for you in the future?

A I think I'm ready to get out now.

Q Now you say you began drawing compensation in 1953. How much?

A 50 percent.

Q And what are you drawing now?

A 100 percent.

Q Would they be paying you 100 percent compensation if they didn't think you were totally incapacitated?

A They do a lot of it.

Q They do?

Q Do you think a man who commits burglaries and armed robberies and forgeries is the sort of man who should be allowed to handle his own financial affairs?

A I do pretty good with it. I've accumulated a little money.

Q Gunrunning and forging and robbing and writing books?

A You do it your way and I'll do it mine.

Q That's a good answer.

Q Now you told Mr. Moore that at the time you were committing all these illegal activities, you thought you were mentally ill?

A That's what the doctors told me.

Q You don't know whether you were or not?

A I'm not a doctor.

Q Well, you're not a doctor here today, but you're telling this Jury you're sane today.

A That's my opinion, but I don't claim to be an expert.

Q You thought you were mentally ill then, but you don't think you are now?

A Well, do you know when you're sick?

Q I think I do.

A Well, I know when I'm sick.

Q Now you have stated that you have a lot of respect for these doctors, and confidence in them. Do you think that their training and experience equips them perhaps to know your mental state better than you do?

A If they had the time, I'd say yes. But except for the times I have been in court, none of them has spent any appreciable amount of time with me for the last year and a half.

Q You haven't received any treatment at all?

A Most of the time I have received absolutely nothing . . . except confinement, if you want to count that as treatment.

Q Now do you think that a trial like this, and the crimes you have committed, do you think that they may attract publicity to yourself and thereby aid you in whatever it is you want to advocate?

A I didn't bring this trial on, and I was sick when I performed those antisocial acts, and I have no reason whatsoever to seek publicity. I have had enough of it.

Q Now in preparation for this trial, did you prepare a list of questions that you wanted asked of Dr. Constantine when he testified at this trial?

A Yes, sir.

Q Then I will ask you if this is one of the questions that you

265

prepared to ask of Dr. Constantine. Here is the question: "Dr. Constantine, does a man take an unloaded gun into a grocery store, tell the cashier to fill a bag with money, then turn his back and walk out without taking any of the money, if he is not trying to prove that he is sincere in his aims to make the people remember him, so that when he publishes a book the people will want to read it and learn the true facts about nuclear warfare and the demoralizing effect it can have?" Did you write that?

A I never wrote anything like that.

Q You never wrote that? Are you sure?

A I'm sure I never wrote that. That's some of Dr. Constantine's stuff. That's something that he suggested to me. I know his wording.

THE WITNESS, addressing Dr. Constantine: "You wrote that, didn't you, Dr. Constantine?"

Q I ask you did you prepare this question: "Dr. Constantine, am I a fanatic at this time? If so, isn't it because I am a normal man in an abnormal state of affairs? Isn't it because I know from experience what can happen if we do not have total disarmament of nuclear weapons?" Did you write that?

A Yes, I wrote that one.

In preparing for the lunacy hearing, Eatherly had studied his letters from Mr. Anders, and from the letters he had written out a list of questions for the psychiatrists.

At the conclusion of the cross-examination Eatherly walked confidently from the witness stand; and most everyone in the courtroom, including Judge Mormino and the County Attorneys, believed that at the end of the day he would be free.

But waiting to devote an entire afternoon to opposing his freedom were four psychiatrists.

Nineteen

THE psychiatrist in charge of the "closed ward" in 1960–61—
Building 10 at the Waco Hospital—was Dr. T. V. Frank. He
was called as the first of four medical witnesses against Claude
Eatherly at the "lunacy hearing" of January 12, 1961. He was
examined by County Attorney Billy Joe Webb:

Q   Dr. Frank, where did you receive your college training?
A   I graduated from Georgetown University, Washington,
    D. C., in 1945.
Q   You are a recognized psychiatrist licensed to practice in the
    state of Texas?
A   I am licensed in Texas and Pennsylvania.
Q   Do you know Claude Robert Eatherly?
A   Yes. For a number of years.
Q   Is he presently on your ward?
A   Yes. He has been on my ward since he was returned from
    his latest elopement and while he has been awaiting this
    legal procedure here.

This response by Dr. Frank was the first of many attempts
by the doctors to explain to the jury why Claude Eatherly, who
was not violent, was confined "with the most violent patients
in the hospital." To free Eatherly, Mr. Moore's strategy was
to try to convict the doctors of mistreating him—of "keeping
him in there with the most violent patients where he had no
chance to get better." Mr. Moore was trying to impress on the
jurors that if they found Eatherly to be "mentally ill," they

267

would be sentencing him to "a life among those violent and hopelessly insane men."

The doctors were on the defensive because in 1959–60 they had indeed kept Eatherly in Building 10 much of the time. This fact had allowed Eatherly to write to Mr. Anders that he was being "punished as a political prisoner," and Mr. Anders and Mr. Jungk had, in turn, informed President Kennedy and the "international press" that Eatherly was the American Dreyfus being "punished by the military for repenting Hiroshima."

In my investigation I, too, kept pushing on this point. In my first face-to-face conversation with Eatherly he had told me that only after he became "famous as a pacifist" was he "thrown into the closed ward"; and he insisted to me that the doctors told him he was a political prisoner. So I searched every record I could find, and I repeatedly grilled Dr. McMahan. I examined Building 10 from basement to attic not less than three times. I studied typical case histories of men confined in Building 10. I was as willing as either Mr. Anders or Mr. Moore to convict the doctors—or the Air Force—of punishing Eatherly for his political beliefs.

I will report my conclusions as soon as I have reported all of the responses of the doctors at the lunacy hearing.

Q Dr. Frank, have you recently had occasion to examine Claude Eatherly?
A Yes, I examined him for about two hours yesterday and the day before.
Q And what is your finding?
A It is my opinion that he is suffering from a mental illness which we diagnose as schizophrenic reaction; he needs constant hospital care; and he needs to be kept in the hospital until he shows marked improvement.
Q Doctor, please state whether in your opinion Claude Eatherly is "a person the state of whose mind is inadequate to reason and does not come to judgment in the ordinary affairs of life like other rational men."
A Yes, he is such a person, in my judgment.
Q Please state whether in your opinion he is a man "whose mental illness renders him incapable of caring for himself

and managing properly his financial affairs." Is he such a person?

A Yes, in my judgment.

Here the County Attorney was reading to Dr. Frank the legal language of the "question of insanity" in the state of Texas. This was necessary for the record. Dr. Frank was then cross-examined by Mr. Moore:

Q Now, Doctor, during this two hours of interviewing Claude Eatherly yesterday and the day before, will you tell these ladies and gentlemen of the Jury just what he said that indicates to you that he is of unsound mind?

A His conversation indicated to me the primary symptoms of the disorder.

Q But what we want to know, Doctor, is *what* did *he say?*

A Well, his ideas indicate a grandiose trend, his associations are disturbed, and that indicates a thinking disturbance.

Q But, Doctor, *what did he say?*

A (*Hesitating*) Specifically, I can't state the content of what he said.

Q You mean you can't think of *one thing* he said to you?

A Yes, he shows discrepancy in the ideas he expresses . . . the ideas of how he acquires money, of what his place in society is, and what his goals are.

Q Well, where does his money come from?

A He gets some from the government. He told me that he acquired some from gunrunning.

Q Don't you know that he did not receive any money from gunrunning?

A No, I don't know that.

Q Didn't you read the write-up of this trial in the paper? Didn't you read that he flew for the Arabs?

A No, I didn't read that he had flown for the Arabs.

Q Are you assuming that the papers are wrong? That he didn't do any of those things?

A I don't know what he has done. All I know is that one time he says one thing and another time he says something else.

Q What else did he say?

269

A   He told me one time that he had received money for gunrunning and another time he said he didn't.

What startled me at every turn in this case was the lack of
positive information on the part of everyone who considered
Claude Eatherly. From 1950 the psychiatrists had tried to treat
him without knowing him . . . without knowing the devastat-
ing fact that he had been forced to resign from the Air Force
. . . without knowing the truth about his suicide attempt, or
about his gunrunning, or about his shattering disappointments,
or about the nature of his criminal acts.

Mr. Anders and Mr. Jungk had reported "around the world"
that he "flew for Israel." Two Texas reporters disclosed how
he "flew for the Arabs." Nobody bothered to determine that
he had never been issued a passport and therefore, in all prob-
ability, had never flown for either Israel or the Arabs. At his
lunacy hearing both state and defense counsel depended on
what they had read in the newspapers; and psychiatrists who
had treated him for eleven years were unable to supply facts.

Some of this confusion stemmed from there having been no
trial in two of Eatherly's criminal involvements. There was no
trial in New Orleans in 1955 to reveal facts: only Eatherly's
plea of guilty. This allowed him to claim without contradiction
that "one small check" had been involved; and it left the
psychiatrists ignorant of the whole, revealing "F. A. Baker"
mode of operation which they should have understood in order
to treat him.

Even more imperative to an understanding of Eatherly was
the truth about the gunrunning incident. There had been no
trial at Biloxi to establish facts; only pleas of guilty. This allowed Eatherly to boast to psychiatrists, and even to the jurors
at the lunacy hearing, that he had "made money" out of gunrunning. And there I found my answer to why he so stubbornly
insisted to me that he made $27,000 out of the Marsalis affair.

His "gunrunning money" was important to Eatherly as a
support for his damaged ego. At his crew reunion at Louisville
in 1958 he had comprehended the irony of the situation: he
was sitting with four former "kid sergeants" to whom he had
once loaned money, and now he had nothing and they were

270

worth several hundred thousand dollars among them. So what had he told them? That he had made "quite a bit of money" out of gunrunning, and that he had invested it "in apartment houses." At the lunacy hearing, at the cost of damaging his chances for freedom, he insisted on telling the jury that the confiscated weapons in 1947 were "his" and that he made money.

To appear sympathetic to the jury Eatherly had only to tell the truth about the Marsalis incident: that he had been only an employee, that he never "ran a gun" to anybody, that he made no money, and that the government prosecuted his employers but not him. Instead, to support his ego, he had to tell the damaging lie.

Mr. Moore continued to question Dr. Frank about Eatherly's money:

Q He told you he had received some of his money from writing, didn't he?
A Yes, he told me that.
Q Don't you know that he *has* received money from writing?
A No, I don't know that.
Q But he told you that he has received money, so you assume he is of unsound mind?
A I'm not considering that.
Q Well, Doctor, I just can't understand why you think this man is of unsound mind because he told you he got money from gunrunning or fighting for other countries or from writing.
A Mr. Moore, I certainly want the jury to understand how I feel about this.
Q We know how you feel, Doctor, but we can't understand *why* you feel that way.
A Well, I believe I have already stated that I believe he has the primary symptoms of this disorder.
Q Have you made any attempts to verify his statements as to where his money comes from?
A No.
Q If what he is telling you is true, then his statements are those of a normal man, aren't they?

271

A I have made clear, Mr. Moore, that his statements to me are conflicting, and my judgment is partially based on this.

Q All right, sir. Now you also state that his ideas about his goals or his place in society indicate to you that he is of unsound mind. Will you explain that?

A Well, again his statements are conflicting. One time he tells me that he must employ his notoriety to advance the proposition of total disarmament.

Q Well, is there anything about advocating disarmament that indicates insanity?

A No, sir. Not of itself.

Q A lot of smart people are advocating disarmament, aren't they? Has he ever told you that he thought he could carry it off by himself? There is nothing abnormal about a man advocating the cause of disarmament, is there?

A Not specifically. Only when considered with other manifestations.

Q Now about his environment, Doctor? You have him in Building 10 . . . in a ward with 30 other men. Now aren't those your sickest men? Aren't some of them helpless? Aren't some of them even dangerous?

A Yes, they are.

Q There is even some danger that this man might get hurt or even killed in that ward, isn't there?

A It's a ward which has maximum coverage of aides and attendants.

Q Of course it has. And what are all those aides and attendants in there for? To keep them from killing one another?

A Mr. Eatherly has been in that ward only since December 21st, when he was returned by police to await this hearing.

Q But such an environment is not calculated to help a man in his condition get better, is it?

A It is our maximum security ward. It is the only ward we have in which to put men who should not be allowed to elope. It is the only ward in which we can hold men in response to court orders.

Q Doctor, this man recently has lived outside, here in Waco, without any trouble at all. Does that fact have influence on your opinion as to his present mental condition?

A No influence at all. Absolutely none.

Q Well, what *could* he do to show you that he is better and ready to be discharged?

A I think he should demonstrate over a period of time that he can live at the hospital, with freedom, engage in the hospital's activities, assume more responsibilities.

Q Is he ready for a trial visit at this time?

A Not in my opinion.

Q But doesn't your testimony all boil down to this, Doctor? You think he ought to be locked up in that hospital because he has a distorted idea about his role in society and because he tells conflicting stories about where he gets his money? Isn't that what you are telling this Jury?

A No, that is an oversimplification. This man has a record of mental illness extending over many years. He has repeatedly demonstrated that he can't get along outside the hospital. He now has *no one* who is willing to assume responsibility for him outside the hospital. Therefore, it is my opinion that for both his welfare and the welfare of others he should stay in the hospital, at least for the present.

Dr. McElroy was the second State's witness. He repeated much of what he said at Abilene. In addition, his testimony included these exchanges with the County Attorney:

Q Doctor, during your military service and subsequently have you ever examined patients who were suffering from a disorder similar to Claude Eatherly's?

A Many of them.

Q Did they have the same delusions, reactions, and so forth?

A They follow the same general pattern.

Q Has Claude Eatherly, over the years, participated in the various therapies you have out there?

A Yes . . . physical therapy, occupational therapy, educational therapy . . . he went to school for a while. He is a highly intelligent man, no doubt about that. Intelligence has nothing to do with mental illness. The possibility of mental illness excludes no one.

Q What buildings has he been kept in?

A He has been in Building 90, Building 93, and Building 10. Building 90 is the Admissions Building; Building 93 is the Intensive Treatment Building . . . that's where he had his insulin. Since 1950 he has spent nearly all his time in Building 90. When he has been under court order, he has been "secured" in Building 10.

Q If this jury sees fit to continue his treatment at the hospital, what building is he likely to be kept in?

A Building 90. Claude Eatherly has the best wishes of every doctor in the hospital. We don't put anybody in Building 10 unless we have to. Our whole effort out there is directed toward giving men maximum freedom and restoring them to society . . . just as we have released Eatherly many times.

Q And if this Jury sends him back out there today, it's not going to be any life sentence, is it?

A Of course not. We'll release him the moment we think he can live successfully outside.

Q Is his present condition serious?

A Indeed it is serious. Schizophrenic reaction is one of the most common of mental disorders . . . and very serious.

Q Is he likely to harm himself or someone else if he is allowed his freedom?

A He is.

Q If he walks out of here, is he capable of handling any property he's got?

A Not in my opinion.

Q Doctor, can you tell this Jury some of the things he does or says that cause you to believe he's mentally ill?

A Without getting technical, the man has marked disorganization of thinking. He has committed bizarre acts which are very foolish indeed. . . . He gives me two reasons for these bizarre acts. One is he says he has this guilt feeling . . . he feels like he killed 100,000 Japanese. . . . Another is he says he feels like he ought to be in the limelight. . . . And he has a grandiosity trend, like he thinks he ought to be writing books to change the thinking of the world.

Q Have you ever read any of his writings?

A Yes. You repeated some of his writing to the jury . . . those questions he wanted to ask Dr. Constantine. What he writes indicates a classic case of schizophrenia. . . . You could use his writing in a textbook to help describe classic schizophrenia.

Dr. McElroy's cross-examination by Mr. Moore included these exchanges:

Q   Now, Doctor, isn't it true that except for just making your rounds you haven't interviewed Claude Eatherly since the Abilene trial? Until yesterday, that is?

A   Certainly I've talked with him. And when you say "just rounds" it's more than just walking by and saying hello. You can tell how a man is, and what his reactions are, without taking him to the office for a lengthy interview. . . .

Q   How do you tell that?

A   Well, you come out to the hospital and I'll sign you up for a course in psychiatry.

Q   Now, Doctor, you aren't helping the Jury any with a remark like that. This Jury wants to know how you come to such conclusions.

A   Well, on the basis of my training.

Q   I understand that. But you say you can tell how a man is feeling just by the way he says hello and by the way he shakes hands.

A   Certainly I can tell by the way he shakes hands.

Q   Is that the way you make a diagnosis . . . by shaking hands?

A   We don't make a diagnosis every day.

A   Mr. Moore, you keep asking about specific bits of behavior. You don't diagnose mental illness by some specific act. You must consider the man's entire behavior pattern.

Q   I know that, Doctor. And we've been told that by all you doctors. But none of you has reported any specific act that sounds unusually strange about the man.

A   You haven't listened to all this bizarre behavior of the last ten years!

Q   But, Doctor, that was in the past! Everybody knows he was sick in 1954 and 1957. Even Mr. Eatherly himself knows that.

A Everybody knows it now who is connected with him!

Q Maybe so. But every opinion you've expressed is based on something that happened several years ago.

A He still presents the same type of thinking.

Q Now, Doctor, you have stated that you don't think Claude Eatherly is capable of writing something and getting paid for it. Now I want to read you a letter from a newspaper editor in Tokyo, dated December 1, 1960. This editor says he has taken an article and printed it. So Claude Eatherly *is* capable of writing something and getting it published.

A That's a special case. He'd like to go to Tokyo as a Forgiven Hero.

Q Anything unusual about that?

A I think it's most unusual. And as for an article in a Tokyo paper, I imagine a Tokyo paper would publish most anything by any American who was on the Hiroshima mission. Eatherly has had a great deal of publicity . . . far more than is good for him and the handling of his case. But this publicity has attracted people who want to exploit him. And a lot of insane writings reach print . . . a lot of books are written in mental institutions.

Q Now, Doctor, I'm trying to find out what would indicate to you that this man is sane. If contributing articles to Tokyo newspapers doesn't indicate sanity to you, how about his spending two sane, orderly months as a free man right here in Waco as recently as last month and the month before? Doesn't that prove that he might be able to look after himself and his affairs?

A No, sir, not in that short a time. He has gone out of the hospital before when he was in better shape than he is now. For three or four months he got along all right, then something happened.

Q Doesn't the fact that he has accumulated several thousand dollars which he didn't dissipate while he was out of the hospital, doesn't that indicate to you that he may be able to handle his own affairs?

A Not necessarily. We have some very frugal men who are patients at the hospital. A man can be too frugal.

Q   Now, Doctor, you say this man suffers from delusions. Would you say that he has had any delusion within the last year?

A   His grandiose ideas are a form of delusion. The idea that he's responsible for killing 100,000 Japs is a delusion.

Q   What is a delusion?

A   A delusion is a false belief.

Q   It's no false belief on his part that he directed that bomb to Hiroshima, is it?

A   He wasn't even on the plane that dropped the bomb.

Q   I understand that. But he was the man who picked out the city, wasn't he?

A   You think he killed 100,000 people?

Q   Now, Doctor, what I think is of no interest to this Jury. But do you think that there is anything unusual about this man feeling regret, anxiety or guilt feelings about directing that bomb?

A   I think it's most unusual, considering that he is the only man in the entire 509th Composite Group to behave in this manner.

Q   Do you think he is the only one of the group?

A   As far as I know. He is the only one to have been hospitalized.

Q   Now, Doctor, why do you say that? You don't know where any of those men are. Do you just want to say anything you can think of to keep this man locked up out there with all those violent and sick men?

A   I have read such accounts. You have read them.

Q   Nothing unusual about a man having guilt feelings, is there?

A   Certainly not. Guilt feelings are very common.

Q   And yet you want to lock this man up because he feels guilty?

A   Not at all. That isn't what I have said.

Q   Then I misunderstood you.

A   You didn't understand me correctly.

The third witness for the State was Dr. John E. Talley of Waco, a private psychiatrist. He had been hired by the County to interview Eatherly and give the jury an "impartial, expert opinion." His direct examination by the County Attorney included these exchanges:

Q Please detail your education and experience, Doctor.

A After graduation I did postgraduate work at the University of Michigan and the University of California. I have been a psychiatrist since 1941. I was an Army psychiatrist with 32 months overseas. I was a psychiatrist for the 45th Infantry Division. I have been in private practice in Waco since 1946.

Q Doctor, did you conduct an examination of Claude Eatherly?

A Yes, sir. At your request I went to the VA hospital yesterday afternoon and talked to Mr. Eatherly for 45 minutes, between 4:15 and 5 P.M. I had never seen him before. . . . He and I sat down in an office alone. He was quiet, cooperative, in good contact, his memory appeared good, and very frankly I considered that I spent a pleasant hour with him. . . . I asked him how it happened that I was called out to see him, and he said that he had eloped from the hospital on October 19th. "I did it," he said, "because I thought that if I could do well for a few months I'd show them that I didn't need to be in the hospital."

Then I asked him some other questions and he began volunteering information. He began talking about writing some newspaper articles and magazine articles. He said: "I want to express my philosophy against the nuclear buildup. I have a large pacifist following among my readers. I get a lot of encouragement from them to write more."

Then he showed me the letter from Tokyo which Mr. Moore has presented, and he pulled it out of a pocket where I observed he had several other letters. He said: "I get a great deal of mail from foreign countries urging me to contribute to peace."

Then he made the further statement: "To do this aids me in solving my problem of guilt. I'm trying to relieve my guilt over killing all those people in Japan."

I asked him what medication he was on, and he answered:

278

"Nothing." I said: "Mr. Eatherly, are you sure you get no medication whatever?" And he said: "Oh, yes, I'm receiving 200 milligrams of thorazine each night at bedtime."

Q What is thorazine, Doctor?
A It's a tranquilizer used in psychiatric treatment, and 200 milligrams is a pretty heavy dose.
Q What else did you ask him, Doctor?
A I questioned him about the post office robberies, and he told me that he knocked the doors down, but he didn't enter. So I said: "Why didn't you enter? If I had knocked the door down and was going to get a federal rap anyway, I'd have got all the money I could find." He answered that he just wanted to go to jail because he thought, "Everybody with a uniform on was after me."

I repeat: there is no evidence that Eatherly ever wanted to go to jail. In 1954 in New Orleans he denied to officers that he had committed the crimes for which they had arrested him, and he pleaded with his lawyer to save him from jail. In 1957 he urged Jim Vachule to help save him from a federal penitentiary, and he wrote to his own lawyer expressing hope that the post office charges would be dismissed.

But by 1961, when he talked with Dr. Talley, Eatherly had been hearing and reading for four years that all his crimes were punishment-seeking crimes. Since society would not jail him for the crime of Hiroshima, he had to forge checks and burglarize post offices in order to get in jail. He was involved with Mr. Anders and Mr. Jungk in publishing ventures based on his seeking prison for Hiroshima. So when he told Dr. Talley that he burglarized the post offices because he wanted to get in jail, wasn't he merely keeping faith with his collaborators?

I asked myself: if Eatherly had wanted to be jailed for the post office burglaries, why did he hide his guilt for four months until the detective found him?

Dr. Talley continued his testimony:

A Mr. Eatherly told me that he had spent the last 21 months in the hospital, save for the two months he had been absent on elopement. (*Aside*) I think that's a cute term: *elopement*.

279

But the VA insists on using it. All in all, Claude Eatherly is definitely a man of higher-than-average native intelligence. He is a well-educated man, though whether he got his education in school or out of it. I don't know. But he's got it.

Q Doctor, does education have anything to do with mental illness?

A Not a thing in the world. But I found his thinking to be more or less illogical as evidenced by this. He told me that in 1947 he resigned from the Air Force . . . and this is a direct quotation . . . "because I was sick of the Air Force and what it stood for. I had just helped test the A-bomb at Bikini."

Then I asked him what employment he went into after leaving the Air Force. And he told me that at that time there were a number of countries in Central America which had Communist regimes, and revolutionaries needed arms to overthrow these regimes, so he went in with some others to provide these arms. And he said he spent from 1947 until 1950 in what is commonly referred to as gunrunning, although he did not use the term.

Now it doesn't make sense to me for a man to say that he got out of the Air Force because he was sick of "what it stands for" and then immediately start providing guns for other people so they can start killing one another.

Here again was the tragedy of lack of information. Why wasn't Dr. Talley given the Air Force record? He had been division psychiatrist for the 45th Infantry Division. Had he known the truth about how Eatherly left the Air Force, his diagnosis could have been more accurate.

Q Dr. Talley, what you are saying is that what we have heard described is a "discrepancy in thinking"?

A Yes, sir. In summary I can say that I feel that he has a schizophrenic reaction, that he definitely needs further hospitalization, perhaps more to protect him from himself than to protect others from him. I don't consider him a man who would be a threat to society as a whole. He does not appear to be by nature a violent man.

Q But, Doctor, in the act of harming himself could he not harm someone else?

A Yes, he could.

Q And what is your exact diagnosis?

A Schizophrenic reaction, chronic, undifferentiated.

Q And can you simplify that for the Jury?

A When we say schizophrenic reaction we mean that he is illogical in the way he thinks and feels, that his feelings are not in harmony with his thought content. I say chronic because I believe he has been this way, with flare-ups and periods of improvement, since 1950. Right now I think he is in one of his better periods. And by undifferentiated I mean that I was unable to find . . . for instance, any paranoid trend. He didn't indicate to me that he thought anyone was trying to persecute him.

The cross-examination of Dr. Talley by Mr. Moore included these exchanges:

Q Doctor, did you learn all that in 45 minutes!

A Yes, sir, I did. And he'll tell you he told me all of it.

Q Now, as I understand you, Doctor, you think he's crazy because he thinks he has a mission to perform . . . a destiny.

A That's correct, sir.

Q But you aren't telling us that that, in itself, is any indication of insanity. Don't a lot of men have missions and destinies, without being crazy?

A Well, frankly, I think that the extent and firmness to which he believes that goes beyond the normal. To him I think that's a messianic mission.

Q And that means he's crazy?

A I think it's the matter of extent. It's normal for most people, I think, to want to work for peace. But this man conceives of himself as a leader, with people all over the world waiting for him to lead them.

Q Do you know that he receives mail out there at the hospital from all over the world . . . from people who do want him to lead them? He receives communications from many worldwide committees?

A I wouldn't be a bit surprised.

Q He communicates with Linus Pauling, Steve Allen, Members of the Japanese Parliament. . . .

A I wouldn't be a bit surprised.

Q In other words, it's no indication of insanity just because a man wants to work for peace and disarmament?

A Not necessarily. But I think this man needs protection from the adulation and idealization and lionization of the public.

Q You think that adulation will hurt him?

A I certainly do. I think it will precipitate another flare-up of his illness. Perhaps a most serious flare-up.

Q But don't we all enjoy adulation?

A We all enjoy it. But we all don't have the abnormal need for it.

Dr. Constantine testified for an hour. He repeated much of what he said at Abilene, but he did not emphasize the guilt complex as a cause or symptom of Eatherly's disorder. "The guilt complex may have something to do with it," he said. "I've told him that he is not a killer or a robber, but he says he wants to be punished because he selected the city on which the bomb was dropped and he feels responsible for killing those people. And of course he has delusionary enemies."

The doctor surprised the jurors when he admitted that he knew where Eatherly was during the two months Eatherly was living in the apartment in Waco. He all but admitted that he had known Eatherly was going to elope. Since the doctor had also testified that Eatherly should now be hospitalized because he might hurt someone, the County Attorney asked him why he had allowed Eatherly to live away from the hospital.

"We do the best we can with these men," he replied. "In psychiatric treatment, in trying to restore men to freedom we must take calculated risks. Society must share these risks. Yes, I knew where he was. He telephoned me. But it would not have been right for me to notify the police. I would have violated his confidence, and this no psychiatrist who hopes to help a patient can do."

Mr. Moore asked Dr. Constantine: "But didn't Eatherly do pretty well while he was on the outside?"

"Not too well," the doctor replied. "He didn't talk to his children or seek to talk to them. He found him a lady friend, and he was with her when they had some sort of accident in Dallas and the police found him and returned him to the hospital. The woman claimed to be his cousin, but he's got lots of 'cousins.'"

Concluding his testimony, Dr. Constantine said: "To talk of trial visits for this man now is useless. He no longer has anyone to visit. He is sick, and someone must take care of him. Over a period of ten years he has repeatedly *visited* members of his family. But no member of his family will now assume custody of him, or welcome a visit by him. I regard myself as his friend. It is very hard for me to sit here in his presence and say these things. There is no vindictiveness in my action. If I could, I would care for him myself on the outside. If he had careful supervision on the outside, and regular treatment by a private psychiatrist, he possibly could live successfully. But if you release him now, in his present condition, and under present circumstances, you will be doing a disservice both to him and to society."

In that speech Dr. Constantine revealed that he had traveled a full circle during the thirty-seven months since he testified at Abilene. Then he had urged a jury to free Eatherly. Now he told a jury that to release Eatherly "in his present condition" would be a disservice both to him and to society.

In such trials in the United States, after all testimony is concluded, the opposing lawyers make "final arguments" to the jury. In this argument Eatherly had many advantages. Mr. Moore was abler and more experienced than were the County Attorneys; and he could point to "one little man" sitting there being opposed by those "four big doctors."

MR. MOORE: This man has been mentally ill in the past because of his unusual and horrifying military mission. But for two years now he has proved that he is no longer a danger to society or to himself. He has made great sacrifices for this country; he has suffered for the cause of America; and he is sitting right there in front of you now, needing your help, and I implore you, ladies and gentlemen, to give it to him.

Now you heard him tell you his own story. I kept him there on the stand longer than usual, because I wanted you to see for yourselves how good his mind is. You heard him recall dates from his life that neither you nor I could recall. He's got a better memory than I've got. Did he sound crazy to you? Does he look crazy? There are hundreds of people walking the streets of Waco right now who are a lot crazier than he is—and you and I know it.

I know these doctors. They are my friends. They are sincere, of course. They mean well. I have been in many courtrooms with them. But these doctors can be wrong, just like you and I can be wrong. You and I know what to think about a doctor who says he can shake hands with us and tell whether we're crazy or not. We know what to think about their "well-rounded, therapeutic treatment" which consists of a pill in the morning and a pill in the evening and a locked door the rest of the day. These doctors can make mistakes about what goes on in a human skull, and you know they can make mistakes. And now you have the opportunity to correct a mistake that they are making here.

You and I know exactly what these doctors are doing here. They are just protecting themselves and shifting responsibility to you. They have talked to Claude Eatherly two or three times in the last two years. They have shaken his hand and diagnosed him. They think there is some little possibility that he might hurt somebody on the outside. So they all come in here and they are saying to you: "Now you let him out, and if he hurts somebody then it's your fault, because we advised you not to let him out."

These doctors are not fooling you, and you know it. To them Claude Eatherly is nothing but a number. They've treated him like a number because they've got thousands of men to treat. Well, he's not a number to you. He's a man . . . a living, breathing, feeling human being. He wants to be free just like you do. And you've got the opportunity to treat him like a human being and set him free to breathe the free air of this free country he fought for and sacrificed for.

Now these big doctors sitting here, they say he has grandiose ideas because he wants to work for world peace. Now, ladies and gentlemen, I ask you—what's *grandiose* about one little man wanting to do what little he can do to work for world peace? After his horrible experience, do you think it's crazy for him to want to work to save us all from atom bombs?

Now, these big doctors, coming in here ganging up on this little man, they tell you that he manifests all sorts of disorders. But you noticed that when I asked them to tell us specifically what he said or did that was crazy, they all got tongue-tied. Well, you saw him and heard him. There he is. Did you hear him say anything crazy? Does he look crazy to you? And right here today you've seen him for a lot longer time than these doctors have seen him for two years.

Now, these doctors even tell you that this man is crazy because of the way he handles his money. They say this Court ought to appoint a guardian for him. Did you ever hear a crazier suggestion? This man has more than $2000 in the bank. I'll admit to you, ladies and gentlemen, that Claude Eatherly has more money in the bank today than I've got. I'll bet he's got more money in the bank than most of these doctors! Is that the kind of man who needs a guardian!

Finally, ladies and gentlemen, you have today a rare opportunity. You have the opportunity to set a fellow human being free. Put yourself in his place. Suppose you were sitting there, opposed by all these big doctors. And suppose he was sitting there in the jury box where you are. What would you want him to do for you? Would you want him to lock you up with a bunch of violent, insane men who might knock you in the head while you're asleep?

You'd want Claude Eatherly to set you free. The Bible says do unto others as you'd have them do unto you. I want you, ladies and gentlemen, to go into the jury room and do for him today just what you'd want him to do for you.

Under the system in the United States the lawyer for the State or the County makes the final argument to the jury. The State gets the last word.

Mr. Hall told the jury:

"Now, ladies and gentlemen, let's get some things clear. First, about this man's money. You heard him tell you where he got that money. From gunrunning. You know what gunrunning is. It's selling guns to one man so he can kill another man. The gunrunner doesn't care who gets killed just so he gets his money. Here in Texas we know about gunrunners. Gunrunners sold guns to the Commanches so they could murder our forefathers. And you know what our forefathers did to a gunrunner when they caught him? They hung him to the nearest tree. Yet you heard Claude Eatherly sit right here and boast to you that he's got money over there in the Bell-Mead bank today that he made out of selling guns to one man to kill another one with. So you know how sincere Claude Eatherly is about advocating world peace! You also heard him boast that he got money out of advocating peace. So you understand this man. Today he wants to make money out of peace just like yesterday he made money out of gunrunning until the Government stepped in and arrested him and confiscated his guns.

"You've heard Mr. Moore tell you that these doctors have treated Claude Eatherly like a prisoner. Well, have they? He's been in and out of that hospital for ten years. Most of the time he has come there voluntarily. The other times he has been sent there only after he has threatened the life or property of some citizen. And the doctors have let him out almost every time he has wanted out. You're not being asked by the State of Texas to give him a life sentence. You're being asked to send him out there for a few weeks or months until these doctors think he's well enough to go free. If you want to help Claude Eatherly today, you'll see that he gets further treatment. If you want to harm him today, you'll turn him loose.

"Finally, Mr. Moore has said a lot about responsibility. He says the doctors are shifting responsibility to you. Do you want to accept responsibility for this man going free? Hardly a week goes by that you don't pick up a paper and see where some parolee from a mental institution has mutilated a child, or committed some other serious crime. These doctors, with ten years of experience in dealing with this man, have advised you in all sincerity not to let him out until he has had further treatment. The doctors have solemnly warned you that this man may hurt somebody. Do you want to ignore their advice? Or do you want

286

to shift responsibility back to the doctors and let them decide when to let him out again?

"You can't escape your responsibility, ladies and gentlemen. If you set this man free here today, after you have been sincerely warned not to do so, and if tonight or next week he kills or injures some child, or some man or woman, then the doctors aren't responsible, and the VA is not responsible. You'll be responsible for what this man does. Do you want to accept that sort of responsibility? I don't. And I don't believe you do.

"You heard this man boast that he has been a gunrunner, that he made money out of it, and that he's still got part of the money. Time and again he has held guns on people right here in Texas. Do you want him holding a gun on you while you wonder whether the gun's empty or not?

"Right here this afternoon, ladies and gentlemen, you can do what's best for Claude Eatherly and what's best for you and your neighbors. You can make sure that Claude Eatherly gets further treatment from doctors who are his demonstrated friends. And let the doctors decide when he's ready to be free."

At the conclusion of the argument, Judge Mormino charged the jury in this manner:

"Ladies and gentlemen, this case will be submitted to you upon the following Special Issues, which when answered by you and returned into court will constitute your verdict in this case.

"You are the exclusive judges of the facts proven, of the credibility of the witnesses, and of the weight to be given to their testimony, but you are bound to receive the law in charge from the court, which is herein given you and be governed thereby.

"In connection with the following Special Issues, you are instructed that by the term 'a mentally ill person,' as used therein, is meant a person the state of whose mind is inadequate to reason and does not come to judgment upon the ordinary affairs of life like other rational men.

"A 'mentally incompetent person' means a mentally ill person whose mental illness renders him incapable of caring for himself and managing his property and financial affairs.

"A 'mental hospital' means a hospital operated for the primary purpose of providing in-patient care and treatment for the mentally ill.

287

"Special issue number one: Do you find from a preponderance of the evidence, if any, that on this 12th day of January, 1961, Claude Robert Eatherly is a mentally ill person? Answer unanimously Yes or No.

"Special issue number two: Do you find from a preponderance of the evidence, if any, that the proposed patient requires hospitalization in a mental hospital for his own welfare and protection, or the protection of others? Answer unanimously Yes or No.

"Special issue number three: Do you find from a preponderance of the evidence, if any, that the proposed patient is a mentally incompetent person? Answer unanimously Yes or No."

After half an hour the jury brought in a verdict. The foreman, Mr. Lykins, reported the jury answered Yes to Special Issue Numbers One and Two and No to Special Issue Number Three. This meant that the jury held Eatherly to be mentally ill, requiring further hospitalization, but mentally competent and not requiring a guardian.

Judge Mormino ordered Eatherly back into custody. Eatherly told reporters: "I guess I'll have to stay out there a little longer." He shook hands with each of the doctors.

"In my opinion," Judge Mormino told me, "Eatherly lost the verdict when he told those jurors he had made money out of gunrunning in 1947."

"That's ironic," I said. "He never ran a gun, and he never made a penny. In fact, during his involvement in that conspiracy he dissipated the money he had won at poker at Kwajalein [Bikini]."

Eatherly stayed at the hospital for another seven months, until August 10, 1961, when he eloped and went to Galveston where I found him in 1962.

Twenty

BEFORE I left Waco I particularly wanted the answer to one question. Had the jurors at the lunacy hearing believed Eatherly's claim that he felt guilty of "the crime of Hiroshima"? Had they liked him for claiming guilt? Or disliked him?

Here is what the jurors told me:

MRS. CASSENS, THE YOUNG WOMAN: "It was the first time I have ever been on a jury, and I tried to listen carefully to everything. I liked him. The first thing that struck me about him was that he seemed so alone. I wondered why his family was not at the hearing. I took for granted that he had had a hard time in the war. I wasn't sure that he felt guilty over Hiroshima, but he said he did. How can you dispute how a man says he feels?"

MR. FAJKUS, THE FARMER: "I started off one hundred percent for Eatherly. I'm not denying that. When the jurors were being qualified, Mr. Moore asked all of us if we thought doctors could be wrong. Well, I sure do think they can be wrong. So before he said a word I started off for Eatherly. I assumed he was telling the truth about being affected by the bomb drop. I guess the bomb got on his mind and upset him, maybe to the point where he wouldn't know what he was doing."

MR. LYKINS, THE JURY FOREMAN AND BAYLOR GRADUATE: "Three-fourths through the hearing Eatherly was a free man. We were all for him, in spite of the doctors. His appeal on his own behalf was clear and reasonable. As for his feeling guilty over Hiroshima, I don't believe he has any such feeling. A man either feels guilty of all his sins or none. A man can't just pick out one thing and go around saying he feels guilty about that. Eatherly didn't feel guilty about his gunrunning: he boasted of it . . . he seemed proud of his part in it. So how could he expect me to believe he really feels guilty over Hiroshima? I didn't believe him. But if he knows any way to save the world from war, he has my best wishes."

MR. PELCHER, THE MOLDMAKER: "I felt entirely sympathetic toward Eatherly. Whatever way he wants to feel about the bomb, that's his business. I was overseas, so I was for him. I think anybody would be sympathetic with him in his position."

MR. WOODLIFF, THE PRINTER: "Sure, I think dropping the bomb had a lot to do with Eatherly's mental problems. Nobody on the jury doubted that; nobody resented it. We were all for Eatherly."

MRS. WILLIAMS, THE GRANDMOTHER: "If it had been my decision alone, I would have turned him loose. His brothers didn't want to be bothered with him any longer; and I guess he had been a lot of bother to them. But I don't see how they could turn against him; I couldn't have. I admire him if he wants to work for peace. I'm sure his part in dropping the bomb has preyed on his mind. . . . It sure would on mine. The world would be a whole lot better off if we had never gotten the bomb. All wars are bad, but now they hurt a whole lot more people. I hope Eatherly can do something to help prevent war."

In these statements, I concluded, is part of the explanation of the "worldwide Eatherly Case."

Five of those six jurors believed that Eatherly felt guilty of Hiroshima because they wanted to believe him. Even the sixth, the college graduate who couldn't believe, said: "But if he knows any way to save the world from war, he has my best wishes."

Hiroshima is the symbol of man's predicament in the Age of Angst (anxiety); and because they, too, feel guilty, many men yearn to hear a profession of guilt.

If Eatherly's profession of guilt is a lie, then he may be the cleverest opportunist since St. Joan claimed she heard voices.

And if Dr. Oleneick Pavlovitch Constantine, peering into Ea-therly's subconscious, did not really see Hiroshima-guilt, but only for high purpose imagined he did, then the doctor may be the cleverest preacher since St. Paul looked at the massed vic-tims of Roman tyranny and shouted, "There is a greater King than Caesar!"

Mr. Wain wrote his moving poem because he wanted to be-lieve that Eatherly spurned the cash; and the program directors of the British Broadcasting Company contributed a half hour to the reading because they knew how many listeners wanted to believe. People have always wanted to believe that somewhere a good man is rejecting cash, assuming guilt, and being perse-cuted. I can understand people yearning to believe that at Hiro-shima, as on the Damascus Road, a sinner was struck down by great light and is now turned evangelist trying to save us from destruction.

Mr. Wellman's film script has thus far gone unproduced only because bankers are unimaginative. Millions of anxious ticket buyers want to see *Medal in the Dust,* and they want to believe that Major Eatherly's image looms as large over the world as Mr. Wellman wants to project it in his finale, using lights atop a fireman's tower.

The Eatherly Case outgrew a schizoid, affects-flattened Claude Eatherly because millions of human beings yearn to believe that there was and is a MAJOR EATHERLY who "carried up the bomb and let it fall," then dropped to his knees and implored: "Father, what have I done!"

But to return to facts, which only a few of us care to tolerate, I must, in an aside, correct an injustice.

When Joe Eatherly read this manuscript and learned that several jurors blamed "the family" for not being present at the lunacy hearing, he was perplexed and hurt. "Didn't they know why I wasn't there?" he asked. "I was in the courthouse, but I purposely stayed out of the courtroom. Didn't the jurors guess why?"

"No, Mr. Eatherly," I said, "they didn't know and they didn't guess. Much of a man's inhumanity to man comes from such not knowing and not guessing."

Joe and James Eatherly stayed out of the courtroom to protect Claude Eatherly. They knew that much more than "one small check" was involved in the New Orleans forgeries. If either of them had been present in the courtroom, the jury would first have expected him to testify; and if he had not voluntarily testified, he could have been summoned to the witness stand by either the judge, the County Attorney or the defense attorney.

It was to avoid risking damaging their brother that Joe and James Eatherly absented themselves from the lunacy hearing.

If the jurors believed Eatherly, why didn't they give him what he wanted: freedom? Why did they find him "mentally ill" and "requiring hospitalization"?

MR. CASSENS: "Just because I sympathized with him didn't mean I could vote to turn him loose. Dr. Constantine seemed so close to him; he obviously wanted to help him. And Dr. Constantine said the only thing that would help was psychiatric treatment. I couldn't go against that. I felt that if I let him out and he killed himself or someone else, I'd never get over it."

MR. WOODLIFF: "I didn't think the doctors were doing much for him out there. I thought they should have spent more time with him. And the whole jury felt that Eatherly should not have been pinned down like he had been. He should have been allowed freedom of the grounds. But when the showdown came, I didn't think I should go all the way against Dr. Constantine."

MRS. WILLIAMS: "I thought Dr. Constantine was sincere, but in spite of all the doctors I wanted to give Eatherly his chance on the outside. I first voted to free him; but the other five jurors thought we should listen to Dr. Constantine, so I finally went along with them."

MR. PELCHER: "I was most impressed by Dr. Constantine because he was Eatherly's friend. To the other doctors Eatherly was just a number. But Dr. Constantine said he'd take Eatherly in his own home and look after him if he could. I took Dr. Constantine's advice."

MR. FAJKUS: "Well, as I say, I started off strong for Eatherly and against the doctors. But Dr. Constantine persuaded me he was Eatherly's friend . . . he sincerely had Eatherly's best interest at heart. And Dr. Constantine looked me right in the eye and said: 'This boy is just as sick as he can be.' I couldn't go against that."

Eatherly had beaten the other three doctors. Dr. McElroy had cited his claimed guilt feelings as evidence of his disorder. The jurors liked Eatherly for feeling guilty. So Dr. McElroy had not reached the jury.

Among the doctors only Dr. Constantine could project humanity. He made the jurors feel that, like themselves, he liked Eatherly for feeling guilty. Only Dr. Constantine could make a juror feel that he was looking him straight in the eye.

". . . Dr. Constantine was Eatherly's friend . . . he sincerely had his best interest at heart . . . so how could I go against him?"

Eatherly, winning friends with humanity, more than met his match in Dr. Constantine's humanity.

Why, after adjudging Eatherly "mentally ill" and "requiring further hospitalization," had the jurors insisted on adjudging him "competent" and in no need of a guardian?

MR. LYKINS: "All six jurors were unanimous from the beginning on that point. We did not intend to find Eatherly incompetent. We didn't think he needed a guardian, and we wanted him to manage his own money because that helps a man toward reality."

MRS. WILLIAMS: "It seemed strange to me that his brother should have signed papers trying to keep him in the hospital. I don't think his brother should have done that. I sure thought a lot about that. I thought his brother might be trying to get his money. I never would have voted for that."

MR. WOODLIFF: "Since Eatherly had accumulated some money, I thought one of his brothers might be trying to take advantage of him."

MRS. CASSENS: "I wanted him to be in the hospital awhile

longer, but I didn't want to take away his privilege of handling his own affairs."

MR. FAJKUS: "No, sir, I never would have voted to give him a guardian. I thought he had a good head on his shoulders. There is nothing like handling his own business to give a man something to do and get his mind off himself."

MR. PELCHER: "As long as there is any hope left for a man, it's not right to take his property away from him. No, sir, I never would have been for that."

In the United States a man's right to handle his own property, even if he wastes it, is still precious. So Claude Eatherly's right to save or squander his "more than $2000" was never in jeopardy at the hearing.

However, in my judgment the fears expressed by several jurors that one of his brothers might have been trying to get Claude Eatherly's money were unfounded, perhaps even unjust. I was impressed by the demonstrated loyalty of Joe and James Eatherly. They are far from wealthy, yet for twenty years they gave their brother money; and for many years from their own earnings they paid his worthless and/or forged checks. Repeatedly they brought him into their homes and found jobs for him.

So to me their commitment effort was the act of loyal, well-meaning, generous but despairing brothers.

I asked the judge and the opposing attorneys for their opinions of Eatherly and their recollections of the hearing.

MR. HALL, THE COUNTY ATTORNEY: "I know very little about Eatherly. Until the day before his hearing I was unaware of his existence. I had a routine talk with the VA doctors; I engaged Dr. Talley by telephone to give the court a non-VA opinion; and I read two newspaper clippings that said Eatherly had been involved in gunrunning, that he had flown for the Arabs against Israel, and that he had served time in New Orleans for forgery. The papers also said that because Hiroshima was connected with his name, something about him or by him had been published in Tokyo. It did not occur to me to try to get his Air

294

Force record or his FBI record. I did not know that anybody, anywhere, other than his brothers, was interested in his case. I thought he was sick, a braggart, and a liar."

JUDGE MORMINO: "Expert opinion just isn't worth much in Texas courts. Sometimes it can even backfire. We have the most independent jurors on earth, and they make their own decisions. I thought the doctors were right about Eatherly. I also thought that he was going to win; and even after his damaging gunrunning testimony, I was surprised when the jury didn't free him. One factor, of course, was that the jurors knew that, with no further hearing, the doctors could free Eatherly whenever they wanted to. If they didn't free him, he could soon get another hearing. And since the doctors had freed him many times before, there was no reason to think they wouldn't soon free him again. So there was nothing final about the jury's action, purely a temporary decision. That, I think, is what caused the jurors not to set him free."

MR. MOORE, DEFENSE COUNSEL: "I talked with Eatherly three times at the hospital, and I thought I had a fair chance to free him. He was quiet, well-mannered, and well-spoken. He appeared rational, recognized his own shortcomings, and in all respects seemed as completely frank as a man could be. Since I was district attorney around here for years, I'm an old acquaintance of the doctors. I've been with them and against them many times. I know how handicapped they are with a jury. There is a language barrier between them and jurors; quite a few jurors suspect that psychiatrists are crazy; and I know how helpless the doctors are when I demand 'specific evidence of insanity.' A lunacy hearing is a mass psychology test. The jury's verdict depends ninety-nine percent on the performance of the man himself, and only one percent on the doctors. In my conversations with Eatherly I recognized that he was sick. Most mentally ill men have one subject on which they will ruin themselves. To ruin them before a jury, you only have to find the subject on which they 'talk crazy.' The subject on which Eatherly 'talks crazy' is not Hiroshima but gunrunning. The minute I mentioned it to him all his quiet good sense disappeared. He went on about all the ships and guns and tanks and airplanes he had acquired . . . how he was welding guns back on tanks . . . how he had raised an army in Cuba . . . how much money he had made. And since I suspected that most of this wasn't true—and if it was true it was even more damaging to him—I recognized that if the County Attorney concentrated on this, Eathery might ruin his chances. But the County Attorney was not well prepared, he let Eatherly off light, and when it was over I thought we might have won. Yes, I thought Eatherly was sick. But under our system it was my job to contend otherwise—to do my best to satirize and discredit the doctors and to present Eatherly as sane, likable and competent. We gave them a good fight and we almost won. In a way we did win. Six months later Eatherly was free—the doctors let him run off—and he'll remain free as long as he doesn't jeopardize someone else's person or property."

I wanted Dr. Constantine's most recent thought about Eatherly; and because of the VA edict against direct communication, I had to communicate indirectly.

"If a man says he is suffering from guilt feelings," Dr. Constantine said, "you can't say if he is or not. A lot of people suffer from guilt feelings. As soon as it was published that Eatherly was feeling guilty about Hiroshima, letters poured in from Mexico and Japan and West Germany advising him how to find relief. This is because guilt is so common. One woman in West Germany wired Eatherly flowers, and I got letters thanking me for taking care of him. Many letters described ceremonies or rituals that would relieve guilt. If a man says he feels guilty of killing a hundred thousand people, you can't disprove it. The way Eatherly acted would be typical of guilt. You just can't figure guilt feelings; they may come years and years later."

"But Dr. Constantine," he was asked, "is it possible that Eatherly feigned guilt to attract attention and perhaps profit?"

"Well," the doctor answered, "if he intended to use guilt for his advantage, why did he keep quiet about it all that time? He didn't tell anybody about guilt for eleven years after Hiroshima. He had kept quiet about it around the hospital until sometime after I took his case in 1956. Why would he do that?"

"Could someone have suggested to him, Doctor, that he felt

guilty of Hiroshima? And that he was seeking punishment for Hiroshima?"

Dr. Constantine replied: "I have no way of knowing whether or not anybody ever suggested such a course to him. I suppose he could have read some newspaper story concerning pacifism about the time he started mentioning his guilt feelings. He could have gotten a letter. Now that I think about it, and now that all this is to be brought out in the open, I wish someone would take the trouble to talk to old-timers around Van Alstyne and see what type of childhood Eatherly had; find out if he mixed well; if he played games; how he participated in sports; his relationship to each of his parents, and to his brothers and sisters; if he had friends, and so forth. No, I don't think anything useful could be gained now [1962] by questioning Eatherly himself. The man is so mixed up today he doesn't know what is real and what is not real. I don't think he could tell a story that would be factual. Imagination and reality are all the same with him."

Eatherly had told me in Galveston that his best friends in Waco were Mr. and Mrs. George F. Frels. He gave me a letter to them, asking them to talk freely with me. Mr. Frels works for an airline; he had read some of my books and as a traveler I had come to know him before either of us realized that the other knew Eatherly. Mrs. Frels worked for several years as a nurse at the VA hospital and quit in 1960 to have her third child. For five months that year she was one of the day nurses on the closed ward in Building 10 where Eatherly was a patient. And during the two months in late 1960 just prior to the lunacy hearing, when Eatherly lived in Waco as an escapee, he spent much of his time with Mr. and Mrs. Frels in their home.

I went to Mrs. Frels because I doubted that the VA doctors had told the whole truth about Eatherly at the lunacy hearing. A mental hospital with two thousand coming-and-going patients is a world in itself . . . and a vastly different world. It has public relations problems. Doctors of all sorts have always claimed the right to tell the patient what is best for him to know; and I suspected that VA psychiatrists, in talking to juries, sometimes tell "the public" what they assume is best for it to know.

297

"You are correct," Mrs. Frels said. "I attended the hearing; I heard every word of testimony; and the doctors were not telling the whole truth about Claude Eatherly. The doctors have to 'go along with the community.' They don't tell juries everything."

"How did you come to know Eatherly?" I inquired.

"I met him when he was returned to the hospital after an elopement in December, 1959. They locked him up on Building 10, and they kept him there for six and a half months. I worked there five months—from January through May. I got to know Claude at that time, and I came to know generally what treatment he was receiving."

"What was his treatment?" I asked.

"Nothing as far as I know," Mrs. Frels replied. "During the months I worked on Building 10, Claude Eatherly received no medication and no psychotherapy. There was, of course, occupational therapy and physical therapy. All the patients participate in those activities. Claude was not receiving tranquilizers then, and I didn't think he needed them. He didn't appear nervous or anxious or distressed. He ate well; he slept well; he functioned well in every way. But the doctors at the hearing testified he *was* receiving tranquilizers later that year—both before and after his elopement."

"You mean," I said, "that in early 1960 there appeared to be no medical treatment for whatever is or was wrong with Claude Eatherly?"

"Nothing more than confinement," she answered. "Do you think the psychiatrists have a magic treatment for every poor soul who checks into that hospital? Well, they don't. It seemed they locked up Claude Eatherly because they had failed; they had done all they knew to do. That's what they believe they shouldn't tell the public. During the time I worked on Building 10, they were treating him with nothing but confinement; yet at the hearing Dr. McElroy and Dr. Constantine and Dr. Frank told the jury that they had been *treating* Claude all along and that he needed to stay in the hospital for *treatment*. Confinement is recognized as a form of treatment, but that wasn't what the jurors understood the doctors to say."

"But they had to confine him, didn't they? If they didn't

confine him, wouldn't he run off and pull a gun on somebody?"

"Not necessarily," Mrs. Frels said. "Claude Eatherly has never harmed anyone—that is, unless you count that story about his trying to commit suicide, and I don't put much stock in that. If the doctors had done all they could for Eatherly, I thought he deserved one more chance to make it on the outside. Instead they kept him locked up on the maximum security building. I guess that's what drew me to him. It seemed so unfair. Building 10 is for the most disturbed patients in the hospital. But there he was—a model patient, apparently well-oriented, and he couldn't even go to church or to the canteen. That was the injustice as far as I was concerned. Elopements are fairly common at the hospital, but all the escapees aren't returned to Building 10. Claude Eatherly was. In that environment he was completely unique and out of place. He was a healthy, intelligent, thinking, feeling, articulate man locked up on a maximum security ward. I used to talk with him by the hour because he had absolutely no one to talk to and nothing to do. And I'll tell you another thing about him: he helped us care for other patients. Sometimes he could do more for them than we could."

"He received letters, didn't he?" I asked. "And wrote letters?"

"Oh, yes," she said. "He got letters telling him he was a political prisoner, that his crimes were all only efforts to obtain punishment for Hiroshima, and that the Air Force was keeping him locked up for repenting Hiroshima. He liked to believe all that. He called himself a political prisoner. And he wrote those things to other people."

"Was his mail censored, either incoming or outgoing?"

"There is no strict censorship at the hospital," Mrs. Frels replied, "but all mail is inspected. The incoming packages are checked for scissors, sharp instruments, and the like. The outgoing mail is examined for threats to people on the outside. Some of those men are always threatening to kill somebody the day they get out— And we do censor excessive obscenity. As far as I know, nothing that Claude Eatherly ever wrote or received was censored."

"Did you know that he wrote people that his mail was censored—that he had to smuggle letters out of Building 10?"

"Sure. I saw one letter in which he said that. I went over his mail at times. It's not the regular duty of the day nurses; the night nurses usually handle the mail because they have more time; but when we got caught up, we day nurses would inspect a bundle of mail. And there's nothing unusual about his saying he 'smuggled' mail out of the building. A good many patients do it. They give a letter to an attendant or a nurse, and they mail it for them. But it isn't necessary. And I never once mailed such a letter for Claude Eatherly."

"Did you regard Eatherly as sane or normal or truthful in any usual sense?"

"Yes," she said, "I thought he was a pretty normal person. But, after all, what is normal? He had false beliefs and he made up stories. So what? That's no reason for keeping a man locked up. There are thousands of people living right here in Waco who have false beliefs and make up stories. He wasn't dangerous to anybody. When they took him off Building 10 and put him back on Building 90, he of course eloped again. Can you blame him? He was a 'voluntary' patient, and as such he was entitled to end his treatment and leave the hospital at any time. So he left. He rented an apartment, but most every day for two months he visited us here for a little while. A few times, because he was so lonely, we let him spend the night here on the living room couch. We later found that Dr. Constantine knew he was in touch with us."

"What about his money?" I asked. "A lot was said at the hearing about his having several thousand dollars."

"I didn't know anything about his financial condition," she said, "but if he does have money there shouldn't be any mystery about it. He draws a pension—like most of the patients at the hospital. They purchase canteen books which they use to acquire a few things. There's a limit on the books—I think it's fifteen dollars a month. So during all that time on a closed ward he couldn't spend much. He had spent most of two years in the hospital. Money accumulates rapidly under those conditions. And here's a fact about him now: he's careful with his money. He may have once been a reckless gambler, but no more. Oh, he lives well. He had a nice apartment, and he has expensive tastes. But it wasn't unusual for him to look for bargains. A lot of times during those two months he'd go out and shop around grocery stores, just like a thrifty housewife. He'd come back and tell us where chickens and eggs were the cheapest on a particular day. He was quite capable of managing his affairs. He did it for two months that I know of, and he did it well."

When I compared that picture of Eatherly with the picture of him shooting craps at $100 a throw in 1945, I agreed with the doctors: he had indeed undergone a personality change.

"Tell me, Mrs. Frels," I said, "from all this experience with him, what do you think is wrong with him?"

"Well, I'm no psychiatrist," she said. "I'm only a nurse, a wife, a mother, and a woman. But I'll tell you what I decided is wrong with him. *Nothing!* At least nothing a psychiatrist can do anything about. He's just a man who wishes he had a more glamorous life. He wishes he were a writer . . . or that he was in show business . . . or that he was married to some rich and glamorous woman who could let him try to break the Bank at Monte Carlo."

"Do you think he has a guilt complex?"

"Nonsense! Of course a psychiatrist will tell you that we all have guilt feelings about something—and it's possible that Claude might feel some guilt. But I don't think he ever felt guilty about any war experience. He's just a man who can't endure an ordinary existence. If only you or somebody could write a big book about him, or make a big picture about him, or help him get started in show business, or if he could marry a rich woman— There is absolutely nothing wrong with Claude Eatherly that some oil wells and a million dollars wouldn't cure in a minute!"

Mr. Frels had listened quietly to my conversation with his wife, so I turned and asked for his observations.

"The stories I have read about Claude have given me some laughs," he said. "We knew he didn't drop the bomb—and he never claimed he did. But the stories said Claude hadn't had a good night's sleep in fifteen years supposedly because he felt guilty about killing all those Japanese people. I had to laugh at that."

"You mean it isn't true?"

"It's ridiculous—to my knowledge. As my wife has said, he spent the night on the couch here several times while my wife, my children and I slept in the rear bedrooms. You want to know how he sleeps? Well, as you can see, our telephone is only a few feet away from this couch. I have to be at work early—the office calls to wake me at 4 A.M. and again fifteen minutes later. When Claude slept on the couch he was no more than six feet from the phone. Yet that phone could ring several times, enough to wake me in the back bedroom, and he'd never hear it. When I'm getting ready for work I rumble like a bull in a China shop. I shave; I drop things; I bang doors; and I open and close drawers noisily. But Claude, sleeping naturally, without pills, never woke up. Also, I dropped by his apartment several times after getting off work late at night and walked in to find him asleep. He never knew I had been there."

"You had a key to his apartment?"

"I didn't need one. He didn't bother to lock the door."

"What sort of life did he lead?"

"Normal—as normal as any person who stays close to home. He read a great deal, cooked when he felt hungry, and went out when he needed to get a haircut or do his washing. I spent a lot of time with him. We watched television, played gin rummy, or just talked. Once in a while we went to get a beer or two."

"Did he drink a lot?" I asked.

"No more than other people who drink," Mr. Frels said. "I never saw him drunk. He was a lot of fun to be around, and very interesting to talk with."

"What did you talk about?"

"Most everything—from everyday topics to philosophy, religion and politics. He's a sports fan. There's no subject about which he can't talk intelligently."

"Did you ever discuss his war experiences or his feelings toward war?"

"Yes," Mr. Frels said. "We had a good time arguing. He has an excellent grasp of the relationship of the economic, ethnic and geopolitical factors involved in the cause and effect of warfare. He expressed the belief that man must rise above himself or ultimately bring about his destruction. He's opposed to war, but with me he wasn't a militant pacifist. As for his accounts of his experiences—well, I've never met an ex-soldier who didn't

302

embroider the facts. I knew when Claude was embroidering or fabricating. But I thought nothing of it. I think the writers are to blame for most of the nonsense about Claude, and they have hurt him instead of helping him."

"Make this clear about Claude Eatherly," Mr. Frels concluded. "I know him as a good-humored, easygoing person who has an interesting personality, and who is kind, generous and compassionate. I don't think there's one crazy thing about him. I hope people will leave him alone so he can live successfully on the outside."

I then asked Mrs. Frels this final question: "You have told me that Eatherly liked to think of himself as a political prisoner. Did you ever hear any of the doctors tell him that he was a political prisoner?"

"Yes," she replied carefully. "I once heard Dr. Frank tell him he was being held on Building 10 because he was a political prisoner. And Claude told me that Dr. Constantine told him that the Air Force had telephoned the hospital about him, and that the Air Force was trying to transfer him to Walter Reed Hospital in Washington so they could look after him closer and not let him out."

"Did Dr. Frank appear to be joking when he told Eatherly he was a political prisoner?"

"I don't know," she said. "But he told him. I heard him."

I went back to the hospital for a last conversation with Dr. McMahan, the administrator.

"Doctor," I said, "I'm grateful for all the help you have given me. You have been generous with your time, and you have patiently allowed me to explore this place from basement to attic. But before I leave I again want to ask you this question: from the day Eatherly got his first guilt publicity in 1957 until he left here in August, 1961, did anyone in the Air Force, at any time, attempt to influence the handling of his case?"

"The answer is an absolute no," Dr. McMahon said. "Only once have I ever had any communication from the Air Force relative to this case. I guess it was in 1959, probably after publication of one of the *Newsweek* pieces, I received a telephone call from a warrant officer in the office of General Twining.

The officer told me that General Twining had directed him to call to inquire if, to my knowledge, Eatherly's children needed any assistance. I answered that it was my understanding that Eatherly's divorced wife had married again and that the children were being well cared for. The officer then inquired about Eatherly's condition, if he was receiving adequate treatment, and if there was anything that could be done that was not being done for his welfare and interest. I assured the officer that we were doing all that we knew to do. And that is the only communication I have ever had, directly or indirectly, with the Air Force relative to this case."

I could think of no reason to challenge that statement by Dr. McMahan. Not only is the doctor an honorable man, but after the Air Force dismissed Eatherly in 1947 it had no more authority over him than it had over a citizen who was never in the Air Force. And had the Air Force wanted to "influence" Eatherly's hospitalization, the last place on earth the Air Force would have wanted him was in Washington! So only if I lost my mind could I continue to insist that the Air Force must have tried to take a hand in keeping Eatherly "in prison."

"This question then occurs to me, Doctor," I said. "Did you tell Dr. Constantine about the telephone call from General Twining's office?"

"Yes, I think I did."

"Is it possible," I asked, "that Dr. Constantine, in telling Eatherly about that call, could have conveyed the impression that the Air Force was trying to get control of him in order to shut him up?"

"No, I don't think that is possible," Dr. McMahan replied. "I'm sure that Dr. Constantine did not misrepresent the nature of the call."

"Well," I said, "whoever did the misrepresenting, it's unfortunate that Eatherly was told of it. Because it allowed him to write to pacifists overseas and tell them that General Twining was trying to get control of him."

"But don't forget," the doctor added, "the letters in which Eatherly made such charges were mailed from this hospital. His brother blames us for allowing those letters to be mailed. We not only allowed his letters to be mailed—letters in which he described many ways in which the Air Force was persecuting him—but we also allowed a German-speaking attendant in the hospital to translate letters for Eatherly so he could answer the letters and denounce the Air Force. In short, we have invited criticism and almost broken our backs leaning over backward trying to protect Eatherly's right to complain, denounce and plead guilty!"

"Only one more question then, Doctor," I said. "Mrs. Frels tells me that she heard Dr. Frank tell Eatherly that he was being held on Building 10 because he was a political prisoner. Do you believe Dr. Frank made any such statement?"

"No," Dr. McMahan replied. "A man of Dr. Frank's training and talents would never make a statement like that to a patient."

I shook hands with Dr. McMahan, told him good-bye, and left the hospital.

Twenty-One

IN the Congressional Record there are two remarkable insertions regarding Claude Eatherly. On September 12, 1961, the Honorable Frances P. Bolton, Republican Congresswoman from Ohio, addressed the House of Representatives.

MRS. BOLTON: Mr. Speaker, bombs of destruction are so much in the limelight these days that one's mind cannot but turn back to the horror of Hiroshima. Our action there is something I have never accepted.

Not too long afterward I was flying across the Atlantic, sitting in the co-pilot's seat with a young pilot. The pilot turned to me and asked if I had sons, and if they had been in the war. Then very quietly he said: "As that is so, Mrs. Bolton, may I talk to you? I must talk to someone." And then he poured his heart out: "We, a civilized Christian nation, how could we perpetrate this unspeakable horror?" He said he woke up nights with it before his eyes. I turned to him very quietly and said: "Son, I feel as you do, particularly since there was so much information indicating that the Japanese had begun to come our way, and that in a week or so they would have asked for peace."

We talked a little of the man who flew the plane that dropped the bomb. Both of us dreaded what might be the after-effects on him. Just recently I've had sent to me a story from the *National Guardian* of March 27, 1961, under a byline of Robert E. Light that answers the question of what has become of him. I hope everyone who sees this will read the tragic story of a loyal soldier who obeyed orders—orders that broke his heart, orders that haunt him day and night. These are things that should be brought to our attention as we view the immediate future. The article follows:

THE PILOT WHO LED THE WAY TO HIROSHIMA—
The Story of Claude Eatherly: CONSCIENCE OF MAN CONFINED.

"The truth is that society simply cannot accept the fact of my guilt without at the same time recognizing its own far deeper guilt" . . . Claude R. Eatherly, August 1959.

By Robert E. Light

Fourteen years ago Major Claude R. Eatherly returned to Texas a war hero. He was acclaimed as the reconnaissance plane pilot who gave the go-ahead signals for the atomic bombings of Hiroshima and Nagasaki. Today he is a patient in the psychiatric ward of the Veterans Administration hospital in Waco, Texas, adjudged insane and committed by a county court.

For a decade Eatherly was racked by the memory of the hundreds of thousands he had helped to kill. He wrote to the survivors of Hiroshima begging forgiveness. At home he rejected the hero's mantle and sought society's punishment by a series of crudely committed crimes from forgery to burglary. When he was committed to the hospital January 14, 1961, psychiatrists concluded that he was suffering from a guilt complex. The treatment presumably will be directed toward ridding him of guilt feelings.

But it is clear from Eatherly's writing that he is not insane. He seems to have come to understand what has tormented him and how best to expiate his sin. It has been suggested that the Air Force intervened to keep him confined. But there is also a move for re-examination of Eatherly by an international panel of psychiatrists—a move initiated by Austrian philosopher Dr. Gunther Anders.

Mr. Light's story, endorsed by Mrs. Bolton, continues at length in the Congressional Record; and it is the story as told by Jungk and Anders. In addition Mr. Light's story contains these passages:

Eatherly resigned his commission in 1947 and returned to Texas. He was acclaimed and publicized as a national hero. But his wife said he used to wake up at night screaming, "Bail out, bail out." His anguish increased when his wife suffered miscarriages or malformed fetuses in 1947 and 1948. Subsequent tests indicated that many of his sperm cells had become peculiarly malformed. Two daughters were eventually born to the Eatherlys, one in 1950 and the other in 1954, but both were found to have a rare blood disease similar to pernicious anemia. Blood tests at the time showed that Eatherly suffered from the same blood ailment.

If Eatherly is a Hiroshima victim, then these questions must be asked: Is he being labeled insane so that the war-makers may bear the seal of sanity? By permitting him to be confined, is society seeking to still its own conscience?

Those whose conscience is not interned might follow Dr. Anders' lead and write to President Kennedy in behalf of Eatherly's freedom.

Even earlier, on August 11, 1959, the Honorable William Proxmire, Democratic Senator from Wisconsin, addressed the United States Senate.

MR. PROXMIRE: Mr. President, on August 6 the Madison (Wisconsin) *Capital Times* wrote editorially about a letter of prayerful love from a group of Japanese citizens to the Air Force major who dropped the atomic bomb and whose resultant guilt complex has so shaken his sanity that he is now a patient in a mental institution. This editorial is remarkably revealing for what it tells of the human qualities of the plane commander, Major Claude Eatherly. I ask unanimous consent that this editorial be printed in the Record.

There being no objection, the editorial was ordered to be printed in the Record, beginning as follows:

CLAUDE EATHERLY AND HIROSHIMA
14 YEARS LATER

On August 6, 1945—14 years ago today—an American bomber based on the island of Tinian in the Marianas, made its bomb run on Hiroshima, Japan, and dropped the first atomic bomb, killing more than 100,000 men, women, and children. The commander of the plane was Major Claude Eatherly. In the years since then Major Eatherly has been haunted by the memory and driven into mental illness by an acute guilt complex. He believes the Japanese are "after him," seeking revenge for the Hiroshima holocaust.

I call these insertions remarkable because it seems unbelievable that they could appear in the Congressional Record, and go into the nation's archives without being challenged! Abroad, the Air Force was being accused of imprisoning Eatherly and making him the American Dreyfus. Yet in the Pentagon apparently no one reads the Congressional Record and bothers to correct our own Members of Congress!

In the spring of 1962 Eatherly went to Mexico City to "star" in a motion picture to be financed by Hans Deutsch, of Lausanne, Switzerland. Mr. Deutsch is a lawyer-publisher: born in Vienna in 1906; left Austria after the Anschluss for Israel; returned to Europe in 1953. The film was to be produced and written by Erwin Leiser: born in Berlin in 1923; went to Sweden in 1938; since 1958 has worked in Swedish television; and in 1961 produced a film in Switzerland called *Eichmann and the Third Reich*. Mr. Deutsch paid Eatherly's expenses, and he also brought Gunther Anders to Mexico City to meet Eatherly for the first time. Anders and Eatherly were to appear in the film together. The film was made and a great deal of footage of Anders and Eatherly was shot.

I saw Eatherly in Galveston on May 11, 1962, shortly after he had returned from Mexico City. For the first time he appeared angry at me, resentful of me. In Mexico City he had been warned that I had been hired by the Air Force to smear him. He had also been assured that his autobiography would soon be published all over the world, and that television personalities in New York, London, Paris and Tokyo wanted him for appearances.

"Everybody else is building me up," he said bitterly, "but you've been hired to tear me down. But you can't tear me down. Because I stand with the good people of the world. The good people like what I stand for. The good people don't like you. You believe in war. I'm against war. So the good people won't listen to you; they'll listen to me."

"Is that what they told you in Mexico City?" I asked.

"Sure," he said. "Nobody will read your book. They explained it to me in Mexico City. My friends all over the world are waiting to read my autobiography. They won't read what you write. And those who do . . . they won't believe you. They'll just hate you for trying to tear me down, then they'll read what I write. So you can't hurt me. The more you try to tear me down, the more the good people will build me up."

"There is some truth in that," I said. "Your friends in Mexico City were not entirely incorrect."

He seemed surprised that I should partially agree with him. So he rushed on to tell me what else he had been told in Mexico City.

"Do you know why I've got more publicity than the man who dropped the bomb on Hiroshima? You're supposed to be smart: why do you think that happened? All over the world I'm the Hiroshima pilot now and I always will be. You think you can change that? So I'm the Hiroshima pilot. A hundred years from now I'll be the only American anybody thinks of in connection with Hiroshima. Maybe they'll remember Truman, too. Eatherly and Truman. The Hero and the Villain. Isn't that right? You can't stop it. Nobody can. Anything you write will only help. The more you and the Air Force try to tear me down, the more the good people of the world will build me up."

"I've done only what I told you I'd do, Claude," I said. "And what you promised to help me do. I have tried to find the facts about you."

"What facts?" he asked. "There are just three facts about me that make any difference. I was at Hiroshima. I repented. Now I'm a pacifist and good people are interested in me all over the world. Those are the only facts that matter. Anything else you've dug up won't make a bit of difference."

He walked on in silence for a moment, then he stopped and turned to me.

"I just want to hear you say it," he said. "The Air Force

hired you to tear me down, didn't they? I know them. They want to tear me down. And your book can't make any money because people only want to read my book. So you had to be paid or you wouldn't have spent all this money and done all this work. The Air Force paid you, didn't they?"

"That's nonsense, Claude," I replied. "All your published criticism of the Air Force is nonsense. The Air Force denied you a Regular Commission because the war was over. Thousands of men like you were denied Regular Commissions. You know why the Air Force kicked you out: you pleaded guilty. From that date to now, nobody in the Air Force has ever wished you anything but well. General Tibbets spoke highly of you to me. He said you were reckless in your off-duty life, which you were, but that you were a fine pilot and had the war continued he would have trusted you to drop an A-bomb. He said he was sorry to hear of all your troubles. Everybody I talked to who ever wore an Air Force uniform and who knew you, had nothing but kind things to say."

He hesitated, then he said: "But they resent me for being a pacifist, for saying I'm sorry about Hiroshima."

"More nonsense," I said. "In the first place nobody in the Air Force believes that guilt over Hiroshima has been the cause of your mental illness. In the second place, if you have been disturbed by guilt over Hiroshima, I don't know anybody who objects to your saying so."

He reflected again, then spoke carefully: "You've told me that the 509th is having a reunion in Chicago this year. Do you think they'd . . . resent me coming? Do you think I'd be welcome . . . now that I'm a pacifist?"

"Of course you'd be welcome," I said. "They'd all like to see you again. How did your crew members act when they met you in Louisville in 1958? Did they resent you?"

"No," he said. "They seemed to like me . . . just like it used to be."

"Then go to the reunion. Tell everybody how guilty you feel. They'll all be glad to see you . . . and play poker with you again."

(He subsequently attended the reunion, at the Edgewater Beach Hotel in Chicago. He enjoyed himself as much as he had at Louisville in 1958. That wasn't surprising: all he had ever wanted out of life was to be happy-go-lucky and have a good time.)

He then asked me: "Do you believe I've felt guilty over Hiroshima?"

"You may have," I said. "Most of us feel guilty about man's inhumanity to man . . . about war . . . about all killing. But I don't believe Hiroshima-guilt caused you to forge checks and pull stunt holdups. Your mental troubles were becoming apparent long before your twenty-seventh year of life and August 6, 1945. I believe any good psychiatrist, examining you in 1948, would have predicted that you'd continue avoiding reality . . . and that you'd cause grief before you ever came to terms with your life situation. There's nothing unusual about an ex-serviceman in the United States failing to make it as a civilian and becoming schizophrenic. There are more than two hundred thousand of you. Our jails and mental wards are running over."

He looked at me from the side of his eye. "Then you aren't really trying to tear me down?"

I shook my head. "I'm only interested in the truth about you. I hope you can make it on the outside and stay out of jails and mental wards."

"You think I can stay out?"

"I think you can."

"I've got to make it this time," he said. "I've got to stay out."

The film shot in Mexico City was released in Europe in 1963 under the title *Wahle das Leben* (*Choose Life*). I asked a friend, a film critic in Zurich, Switzerland, to view the film and interview the producer. Here is his report:

> October 9, 1963: I have just seen *Wahle das Leben* and talked with the producer, Erwin Leiser. The film is a full-length feature running an hour and forty-two minutes. Some exterior scenes were shot in Mexico and Mexico City; other scenes were shot in Japan and New York City (shelters). But there are very few "live" scenes. Most of the film is documentary footage taken from United Nations archives and from various other official and private sources. The film is nothing more than

another picture about the survivors of Hiroshima, a kind of ban-the-bomb film pamphlet telling the man on the street that he has the power to ban the bomb. Teller and Oppenheimer, as well as Hideki Yukawa, voice their opinions on the bomb tests.

Eatherly does *not* appear in the film, nor is he quoted or even mentioned. It was *planned* to have Eatherly in the dominant sequence of the picture: they went to Mexico City only to rendezvous with Eatherly, and they carried with them Gunther Anders. But here is what Leiser says happened. As soon as Anders arrived in Mexico City he sequestered Eatherly from the producers. Anders guided every step Eatherly took in Mexico City and tried to make Eatherly's voice and opinions his own. The producers wanted to shoot Eatherly describing his flight over Hiroshima and his feelings while releasing the bomb. But Anders insisted that they shoot Anders interviewing Eatherly, with Anders doing most of the describing and expressing all of the opinions. Leiser shot a lot of film of Anders and Eatherly, but after he studied it he decided to leave it out. It was too much Anders and not enough Eatherly. . . .

In 1962, just prior to the Cuban crisis, the Soviet Union first began using Eatherly. In radio broadcasts to Asia, Africa, and South America, Soviet spokesmen announced that "the leader of the Hiroshima raid is now mad with guilt and is being imprisoned by embarrassed American militarists." This announcement has been repeated many times and it has become a permanent portion of the picture of the United States as presented by the Soviet Union's worldwide propaganda network.

In July, 1963, in East Berlin, a play opened: *The Trial of Richard Waverly*. The Communist press announced that this was the story of Claude Eatherly. An East Berlin magazine, *Theater der Zeit,* discussed the play, the author, and Eatherly in its issue of August 16, 1963. The author is Rolf Schneider: born in 1932; studied at Martin Luther University in Halle; writer of radio and television plays; received the Lessing Prize in 1962; *The Trial of Richard Waverly* is his third stage play. Schneider was commissioned in 1960 by the German People's Republic to write a radio play about Eatherly. His play was presented on both radio and television before being staged. The text of the play is copyrighted by Henschel Verlag, Oranienburgerstrasse 67, Berlin.

The play is Claude Eatherly's sanity trial in "Laco, Texas." Appearing against Eatherly, demanding that he be imprisoned as insane, is an Air Force general who is one of several villains. A villainess is Eatherly's former wife who describes his nightmares and reveals that she divorced him because he wanted to adopt five orphans from Hiroshima. "Think of it!" she sneers. "Five dirty, horrible Jap-kids." Another villain is Eatherly's brother who is trying to commit Eatherly so he can use Eatherly's money to avoid bankruptcy.

A noted history professor testifies. He calls the bombing of Hiroshima completely unjustified. The war was won, Japan was trying to surrender, but the militarists rushed to drop the atomic bombs trying to finish the war before Russia could join in the fighting and the conquest of the mainland.

The play's emotion-charged climax is Eatherly's testimony. Here are excerpts:

Q. You come from a wealthy family?
A. Yes, sir.

* * * * *

Q. When did you leave your home?
A. When I went to college.
Q. What happened then?
A. I started my studies at the University.
Q. You wanted to become a teacher?
A. Yes, sir.
Q. Did this profession have certain interesting aspects for you?
A. It seemed to be a worthy cause, to educate young people and teach them worthy things.

* * * * *

Q. In the year 1943 did you experience battle fatigue?
A. Yes, sir.
Q. What was the cause of this?
A. I had been in thirteen uninterrupted months of patrol flights, and my nerves were pretty bad.

The interrogator questions Waverly about the attack on Hiroshima, and Waverly relates how he dropped the bomb at 9:15 and describes his reaction to it. Waverly questions the necessity for the bombing, ". . . because we all knew Japan was on its last legs." The interrogator asks Waverly about the Nuremburg Trials, it being a canon of Communist propaganda in Germany that Hiroshima was a greater crime than Auschwitz and that at Nuremburg America should have been tried for Hiroshima just as Nazi Germany was tried for Auschwitz. Waverly says:

> I wanted to go to Nuremburg, but the people from the staff were interrogating me for days and they declared me insane.

Q. What did you do after your discharge from the Air Force?

A. Good God! A thousand things. A thousand desperate, helpless things. I was trying to live with what I had done. Before I had been a human being, like millions of others. I had thoughts and ideas. But suddenly nothing counted anymore. [He continues in this vein for a bit.]

Q. What did you do in that time?

A. I tried to explain what had happened, but everybody wanted to congratulate me. They said I was a hero. They wanted to shake hands with me, and they couldn't understand that mine were the hands of a murderer!

     *   *   *   *   *

Q. Why did you commit robbery?

A. My God, I wanted to appear before a court. I wanted to lose this terrible burden of guilt. I thought it would be better if some judge would say to me, "Richard Waverly, you are guilty of the murder of 80,000 people on Hiroshima!" I had the desperate idea I could get before a court, be tried, if I committed some other crime. But it was all useless. I know now it was not very rational.

Q. What else did you undertake?

A. I tried to help a little. I gave money to the hospital in Hiroshima. And I adopted these orphan children.

Q. You tried to commit suicide for the first time in 1950?

A. Yes, sir.

Q. For what reason?
A. President Truman ordered the H-bomb to be built.

Though not stated, the implication was clear that this announcement horrified Waverly, and he had tried to kill himself in protest.

Q. Can you tell us about [your visit to Hiroshima?]
A. (*Laboring*) I don't know whether I can do it, sir. I . . . I walked through this city for hours and hours . . . (*sobs*) . . .

Sobbing throughout, he describes the horrors he saw.

The testimony is followed by pleas for and against Eatherly, after which the jury finds him insane and commits him to a mental institution.

The last time I saw Claude Eatherly was on September 19–20, 1963.

I had spent most of eighteen months researching and writing: I had expected to do it in six months. Most of the extra months had gone into digging, checking and rechecking. In either manuscript or proof my story had been read by numerous persons: Eatherly's former wife, his brother, his crew members, all the Waco sources, the New Orleans sources, representatives of the Secretary of the Air Force, and VA authorities in both Waco and Washington. In Europe proofs had been delivered to publishers of writings about Eatherly; and I had invited publishers and authors to point out factual errors, if any. Assisted by my various publishers, I had weighed all suggestions for changes, additions and deletions. Now, with the book as accurate as human effort could make it, I had returned to Galveston to show the final proof to Dr. Thomsen and Claude Eatherly. More than a year had passed since I had seen them.

Eatherly was living in the same modest, beach-front hotel where I had found him early in 1962. His face seemed fleshier. His beauty shop associations had ended; and he had not seen Dr. Thomsen for six months.

"I don't need a psychiatrist any longer," he told me. "I don't need any more pills. I'm okay. I've always known exactly what was going on. I've now lived more than two years away from the hospital, and I'll never go back. I get along fine with the law. I live simply; I sleep a lot; I look at TV a lot; I keep up with sports; and I read some. I've got it made on the outside and I never expect any more trouble."

He said he was anxious to read my book. He thought he could read it in two days; so I left it with him and told him to call me when he had finished. Then I delivered a copy to Dr. Thomsen, and two days later I returned to talk with her.

Her interest in Eatherly had waned. He had become her patient by the coincidence that her sister's husband in Paris represents book and magazine publishers. Dr. Thomsen's visit to the Waco hospital in 1961 had been the result of a request from her relatives that she travel to Waco and try to find out something about Eatherly. When I first met her she was interested: Eatherly was a new patient and she thought she could help him. Almost certainly she did help him: Eatherly says she did. But now . . . well, she didn't see him anymore; so her interest was in what I had written about her. She suggested several changes which I made.

When Eatherly said he had completed the book, he delivered it to me, and he and I walked along the beach. He was upset. He said: "You didn't expect me to like it, did you?"

"Why not?" I asked. "You wanted me to write it."

"It'll hurt me."

"Truth never hurts a man," I said. "You've proved you can live successfully here in Galveston. The people here may like you better after they read this book."

We continued walking and he said: "You got one big lie in there. You say I wasn't paid $27,000 in New Orleans. I *was* paid $27,000. Marsalis didn't pay me but Rappleyea did."

"Then I'm protecting you," I said. "What if I reported that you were paid $27,000 in 1947 for agreeing to bomb Havana? And you admitted it? I'd really hurt you! I'd send you to Federal prison for tax fraud."

That caused him to reflect, then he said: "Your book is still going to hurt me."

"No, it won't hurt you, Claude," I said. "Remember what they told you in Mexico City? Now and forevermore you *are* the Hiroshima Pilot. You *are* the man who dropped the bomb. The Congressional Record says you are, and no Member of Congress has disputed it. You were acclaimed a hero and awarded the Distinguished Flying Cross. Then you repented. You refused your blood-money pension. On the night Truman ordered the H-bomb developed, you attempted suicide. Then you turned to crime, seeking punishment for the greater crime of Hiroshima. But the embarrassed militarists called you crazy, sent you to an asylum, and made you the American Dreyfus. That's what you *are*, Claude. I can't change it. No one can."

"But your book? Won't it change it?"

"God, no!" I said. "The readers of this book will be numbered in thousands, and many of them will believe I was hired by the militarists to smear you. But millions and millions of human beings, from our own Members of Congress down to Chinese peasants grouped around a street radio, already *know* your story. And a hundred books couldn't change it. You became what you *are* because by 1960 most of the human race wanted you to *be* the Hiroshima Pilot. So live out your life here in Galveston. Don't worry, because nothing can hurt you. You're the most secure man I know, now and forever."

As I was shaking hands with him, preparing to leave, he asked: "Will your book make money?"

"I don't see how it can," I answered. "It has cost far too much to write. And I'm not sure how many of my readers will regard the hero as sympathetic. But if I'm mistaken, if it does make money, then I'll divide the profits between you and the victims of Hiroshima. Maybe I'll let you decide what percentage should go to you and what should go to Hiroshima."

He gave me a puzzled look as I walked away.

As this book finally goes to press, in retrospect I believe it was worth writing. I believe it is worth the attention of men of reason and compassion. I believe the story of Claude Eatherly and his publicists curiously illuminates the time in which we live.

WILLIAM BRADFORD HUIE

Hartselle, Alabama
December 25, 1963

318